IGNITE A SHIFT

PRAISE FOR IGNITE A SHIFT

"*Ignite a Shift* isn't a book filled with grandiose claims of 'instant health, wealth, and romance' like so many books in the self-help space. This valuable read has proven strategies to help make significant shifts in your life that will maximize your potential."

– **TOPHER MORRISON**, BEST-SELLING AUTHOR OF *STOP CHASING PERFECTION AND SETTLE FOR EXCELLENCE*

"*Ignite a Shift* is a must-read for senior executives and leaders. Change management is critical to the success of any important strategy or plan, and Stephen [McGarvey] provides terrific insights and tools on how to create behavioral shifts to successfully navigate change management."

– **JOHN HOWLETT**, PRESIDENT, BUNZL CANADA

"Get ready to focus on the positive, let go of the negative, and leverage the amazing power of your brain so you can succeed and thrive! *Ignite a Shift* provides the tools you need to navigate the internal workings of your own brain. You'll learn how to recognize, regulate, and control your thoughts, feelings, and behaviors, which is the first step towards influencing others. *Ignite a Shift* is a unique, engaging, and necessary resource that will propel you on your journey towards self-improvement."

– **DR. BERNARD CHIASSON**, VICE PRESIDENT OF OPERATIONS AND CHIEF SCIENTIFIC OFFICER, MIRAVO HEALTHCARE

"*Ignite a Shift* is an insightful read that guides you in an intelligent reflection about your mindset."

– **BEVERLY GU**, CORPORATE SOLUTIONS, NASDAQ

STEPHEN McGARVEY

IGNITE A SHIFT

ENGAGING MINDS, GUIDING EMOTIONS AND DRIVING BEHAVIOR

AMARYLLIS BUSINESS

AMARYLLIS
BUSINESS

An imprint of Manjul Publishing House Pvt. Ltd.
• C-16, Sector 3, Noida, Uttar Pradesh 201301, India
Website: www.manjulindia.com
Registered Office:
• 10, Nishat Colony, Bhopal 462 003 – India
Distribution Centres
Ahmedabad, Bengaluru, Bhopal, Chennai, Hyderabad,
Kolkata, Mumbai, Noida, Pune

Original English language edition published by Morgan James Publishing.

This edition first published in 2024

Cover and Interior design by
Ken Cadinouche
www.kencad.com

Cover photo courtsey iStock / © pegadesign.
All cartoons designed by Robert Duncan

ISBN 978-93-5543-452-4

Printed and bound in India by Gopsons Papers Pvt. Ltd.

DEDICATION

I dedicate this book to my life and business partner Natalie Sarlo-McGarvey. We are truly opposite and inseparable sides of the same coin. I'm grateful that we committed to embarking together on this journey called life and, God willing, I look forward to having many more wonderful adventures and years to come. I love and value you very much. Thank you!

I'd also like to give a special thanks to my father, Arden, and to my late mother, Dorothy, who were always full of love and encouragement. Thank you for teaching me about God our Creator and Jesus our Redeemer.

Table of Contents

Introduction

No person is an island. Every day, we realize more and more how interconnected we all are, and how much we impact each other, both consciously and unconsciously. And each and every day, our individual success relies to some extent on our ability to persuade and influence others.

In *Ignite a Shift,* we'll embark on a journey together and explore at a deeper level the subtleties of how persuasion works, including the ways in which we influence ourselves and others.

On this journey, you will discover the importance of rapport as the foundation for persuasion and influence. We'll explore a number of communication and memory techniques and examine the often-underappreciated impact that language has on engaging and guiding others. You'll understand how to identify and harness various motivational factors that drive people's choices and behaviors. You'll also learn how to negotiate effectively. We'll consider the significance of "SMART" outcomes in the context of setting well-defined objectives, which will greatly increase the likelihood of achieving them. All of these topics—and many more—will be discussed within the context of how to move from the Current State to a Desired State.

Throughout this book, I'll present proven concepts regarding influence and introduce important distinctions and strategies to keep in mind when you are persuading others. I'll also give you the tools to apply this knowledge and, at the end of each chapter, you'll be challenged with an exercise that will provide you with the opportunity to take action to ignite a shift within your own life and in your interactions with those around you. I want to emphasize right from the beginning that my intent in sharing all of this information is to equip you to use these strategies to enrich your life and the lives of those with whom you interact. Always bear in mind that these techniques are very powerful, and it is imperative that they be used respectfully and ecologically at all times.

THE KEY TO PERSUASION

If you were to survey individuals about what it takes to be persuasive and influential, you'd get a variety of answers. Some people might say, "You need all the facts," or, "You have to know the best sales strategies," or perhaps even, "You either have to be very charismatic or very assertive—or both."

Let's look at these statements one at a time. Is having all the facts at hand enough? While it's certainly impressive, think of all the political candidates who rattle off fact after fact, then make a poor showing in the polls. As for sales techniques, we've all been annoyed by salespeople running their lines, pushing us to "buy today because the price is doubling tomorrow," or using some other "tried and true" gimmick to *attempt* to persuade us. And personality? Having a charismatic one is helpful, of course, although we all know certain very charming people who are popular and at the same time lack the ability to effectively influence others.

No, something *else* lies at the heart of persuasion and influence.

Or should I say, *several* "something elses," which we'll explore throughout this journey together.

THE BOY WHO SUCCEEDED DESPITE FAILING

First, let me tell you that the last thing I *ever* imagined or planned on doing was writing a book.

I can safely say that academic accomplishments were elusive for me and seemed to be something only others could achieve. In Grade Two, I remember being petrified of reading out loud in class; feverishly rehearsing in my head each paragraph or section numerous times before my turn came to read aloud. I was told I had a learning disability and failed the grade. My teachers were convinced that I had dyslexia. When it came to writing, it was a struggle to arrange even my simplest thoughts in a linear fashion and I had to constantly reread what I had just written before I could continue. As I progressed in school, I was always anxious during tests and exams and never managed to finish them in the allotted time. I even failed Grade Twelve math three times—twice in summer school! You get the *picture*, don't you? As I share this *story* about my past, you may even *feel* sympathetic, or you might relate to it based on your own unique challenges.

So, you can see why, if someone told me back then that I would eventually go back to school as a mature student, graduate from university, and have a career as a professional speaker—and that I would have the opportunity as part of my work to travel the world with my wife—I would never have believed them. If they had told me that I would eventually write a book, I would probably have laughed in their face.

And yet, here I am.

The thing is, I was blessed eventually to discover a subject matter that I fell in love with and that helped me better understand a lot of the things I went through in school. Most importantly, I learned that different people learn and process information in different ways.

All my life I had been taught and expected to absorb and then regurgitate knowledge; when I realized I could learn *differently*, that was when I was transformed from the child who had been terrible at reading and rarely had a book in his hand into a voracious and passionate reader. Suddenly, I wanted *more* of this new body of knowledge. It evoked a deep sense of curiosity within me, and I wanted to explore how it could help me more effectively learn. I wanted to learn to think about thinking and to understand how people process and store information.

Over time, this led to what would, by most standards, be considered a successful business and career—yet even then, I had no intention of ever writing a book because I knew the challenges it would pose for me. I knew this book project would give me painful flashbacks to school and to feeling stupid and unsuccessful—and, as you can imagine, I wanted to *avoid* those feelings at all costs. I had built my career and business on leveraging my strengths and avoiding my weaknesses to a large degree.

So, why did I decide to embrace my weaknesses and write this book?

Because of you: my clients, customers, and friends.

For years, following speaking engagements and presentations, people have told me how much they enjoyed hearing me and how much they learned. Parents have reported that it has changed the way they parent, the way they communicate with their children, and even their spouses. So many people have asked for my non-existent book that I figured I owed it to them to capture my thinking and learning and to share my story.

TAKING MY OWN ADVICE

In order to persuade someone, we need to understand where they're coming from. This means being able to identify their perspective and their thinking, including any limiting beliefs, and using those to determine our approach.

Before we start to persuade other people, though, first we need to be able to persuade ourselves. That means that as a starting point it's useful to be self-reflective about our own habitual questions, patterns of thought, and limiting beliefs.

When it came time to sit down to write this book, I had to face the skeletons in my own closet, in this case, my limiting beliefs about my capabilities based on my disempowering experiences in school. My spelling is atrocious—I spell everything phonetically—how could I write a book? I knew I needed some help. I had heard about a mysterious group of people called "ghost writers" and I thought you just talk, and they write the book for you—it sounded like a great deal! Hindsight being what it is, unfortunately nothing could have been further from the truth!

I did some research and hired a writer out of California who had a PhD; he must be very good and smart because he has a PhD, was my thinking. What came out of this process was a technically accurate manuscript that cost a fortune and was anything *but* what I wanted. It failed to be interesting for the reader and it was written in an academically solemn tone that is the opposite of my own.

Discouraged by the process, the manuscript sat on the corner of my desk in an intimidatingly thick black binder waiting for someone to complete it and bring it to life. Like with many unfinished projects, it haunted me on a regular basis.

Yet even as the manuscript sat collecting dust, I continued to receive loads of inquiries about when my book was going to be available. I realized I had to make a decision: I either had to commit to the book and take ownership for getting it done or decide to drop the project.

"I'm too busy" was getting old as an excuse, even to my own ears. It's always simply a matter of prioritizing. My embarrassment was becoming a more powerful motivating force than my looming fear of facing what the ghost had left behind. This time referrals led me to a writer at Creative Campbellville to collaborate with and… the rest is history. You are about to read a labor of love that, after numerous rewrites and seemingly endless rearranging, I am proud to share with you.

RAPPORT

Many bestselling books open with the author telling you a story about themselves and their raison d'être. You've likely listened to a speaker that opened in the same manner—giving the audience a glimpse into their personal life. This is an effective way to begin because it humanizes you and makes you more relatable. Being relatable helps you connect to other people's experiences, which is also important. People want to know that you "get" what they're thinking, feeling, and doing, that you recognize what's important to them. In other words, these authors and speakers are building **rapport** with their readers and audience members. **Rapport**, which is simply giving another person the experience of being understood—is one of the things that lies at the heart of persuasion and influence.

Why is rapport such a powerful persuasive tool? Because everyone craves understanding; it's validating. Once you give them the experience of being understood, they will be much more likely to trust you and follow your lead.

Throughout this book you'll learn many proven concepts and important ideas about persuasion and influence. And the first—and most crucial—is this:

> **Key Concept:** Rapport, or giving another person the experience of being understood, is the foundation of effective persuasion.

I'll also show you a simple process to apply this knowledge and create a shift within your own life and in your interactions with other people, whether they are your family, your colleagues, or your clients.

WARNING TO THE READER

Applying the knowledge and strategies in this book will change your life! I know this to be true because applying them has definitely changed my life as well as the lives of many of my clients, customers, and friends. I'm not suggesting that you will enjoy every page or that you will learn things at an unconscious level because I have heard from a very respected source that your unconscious knows more than you are consciously aware of.

I trust that your journey will be as exciting and fulfilling as mine. The changes that will occur are yours to discover as you think about your thinking.

Get ready to ignite a shift!

Chapter One

Are You on the Right Road?

> "Would you tell me, please, which way I ought to go from here?" Alice asked.
>
> "That depends a good deal on where you want to get to," said the Cat.
>
> "I don't much care where–" said Alice.
>
> "Then it doesn't matter which way you go," said the Cat.
>
> "–so long as I get SOMEWHERE," Alice added.
>
> "Oh, you're sure to do that," said the Cat, "if you only walk long enough."
>
> –LEWIS CARROLL, **ALICE'S ADVENTURES IN WONDERLAND**

Let's start our journey in the most logical place—at the very beginning—by exploring the human mind. In our daily lives, thoughts and various other cognitive processes impact the emotions we experience moment to moment, and these emotions ultimately drive our behaviors.

As we shift thinking, we can alter emotions which then drive a different set of behaviors. When we understand how this process works, we can create more congruent and purposeful behaviors both in ourselves and in others.

This knowledge is far from new. Throughout history there have been many examples of successful people who have understood and harnessed the power of thoughts and emotions to influence behavior. As we begin our journey together, take a moment to think of some of the amazing masterminds of generations past. Now, ask yourself, "Who was the greatest escape artist of all time?"

Did Harry Houdini come to mind?

Harry Houdini is considered by many to be the greatest magician and escape artist of his time, and although he began astounding audiences well over a hundred years ago, his name is still well-known today. Indeed, the word "Houdini" has come to mean "one who can get out of anything." Like most words though, there's more to the meaning, and like most iconic people, there's more to the story. Even for Houdini, the success he achieved was far from instant or magical. He used specific processes to achieve his goals.

In their book, *The Secret Life of Houdini: The Making of America's First Superhero*, William Kalush and Larry Sloman tell of a young boy full of ingenuity, confidence, and assertiveness, and with an interest in magic. Although a lack of funds initially prevented him from practicing magic beyond simple card and coin tricks, Harry got his hands on every book about magic that he could. His technical knowledge grew quickly, and over the course of his lifetime, he amassed what has become one of the greatest libraries of magic in existence today.

After a while, Harry's friends grew tired of hearing his explanations about how tricks were done at the magic shows they attended together, and they challenged him to go onstage himself. Harry accepted their challenge and began performing as "Ehrich Weiss" (which was his real name) or "Eric the Great."

Then, Harry found a book that changed his life: *Memoirs of Robert-Houdin, Ambassador, Author and Conjurer, written by Himself*. The French magician Jean-Eugène Robert-Houdin was obsessed with reading about magic, just like Harry. His book described marvelous stunts and tricks beyond belief. Harry was captivated. "My interest in conjuring and magic and my enthusiasm for Robert-Houdin came into existence simultaneously," Harry wrote. "From the moment that I began to study the art, he became my guide and hero… I accepted his writings as my text-book and my gospel… To my unsophisticated mind, his 'Memoirs' gave to the profession a dignity worth attaining at the cost of earnest, life-long effort."[1]

With this devout admiration for Robert-Houdin, it's clear where Harry got the inspiration for his stage name. According to Kalush and Sloman, a friend told Harry that "adding the letter 'i' to a person's name in the French language means 'like' that person. And since "'I asked nothing more of life than to become in my profession *like Robert-Houdin*,' [Houdini wrote] the transformation was complete. Ehrich Weiss was now Harry Houdini."[2]

---

1 William Kalush and Larry Sloman, *The Secret Life of Houdini: The Making of America's First Superhero* (Atria Books, 2006), p. 21.

2 Kalush and Sloman, *The Secret Life of Houdini*, p. 21.

The French magician gave Houdini more than just his name: Robert-Houdin's theories about magic also had a significant impact on the young Harry. According to Robert-Houdin, "a magician is an actor playing the part of a man who has supernatural powers. Further, that even though fundamentally what a performer says during his performance is a 'tissue of lies,' he has to believe it himself for it to be successful."[3]

With this philosophy in mind, Houdini honed his craft even further, studying acting and debate in New York in order to best persuade his audiences. While we think of Houdini mostly as an escape artist, he was much more. He was an actor, an observer of human behavior, a performer, and above all, an artist.

So now we ask: How did Houdini mystify the masses?

While Houdini's performances appeared to be either magic or technical trickery, in reality he had a deep understanding of human psychology. Equipped with knowledge and experience, he knew which tools and techniques to use in specific situations.

Best known for escaping from any handcuffs, straitjacket, jail cell, or locked box—no matter how strong or technologically advanced—Houdini seemed like a real-life superhero. Neither the number of ropes or chains wrapped around him nor the box he was locked inside were of any consequence. Even when he was dangling upside down from a rope a hundred feet in the air or locked in a safe that was tossed into the ocean, Houdini always miraculously escaped.

Like Houdini, with the right knowledge, tools, and techniques, and with the skill to deliver your messages congruently, you can become a master of your craft—persuasion. By engaging minds, guiding emotions, and driving behavior, you'll find you have the ability to ignite a shift.

As Robert-Houdin advised, the first step is to *believe* you can.

> My brain is the key that sets me free.
>
> –HARRY HOUDINI

3 Kalush and Sloman, *The Secret Life of Houdini*, p. 21.

SHIFTING FROM CURRENT STATE TO DESIRED STATE

In the 1970s, a crisis was unraveling on the Caribbean island of St. Lucia. The *Amazona versicolor*, a parrot found only on St. Lucia, was on the verge of extinction.[4] In 1975, there were fewer than a hundred of these birds left in the wild and the parrot population was decimated even further by Hurricane Allen in 1980.

Aside from hurricanes, there were more pressing threats to the parrot's survival. Like quail and duck in North America, the parrot was considered a culinary delicacy on St. Lucia. In addition to hunting them for food, islanders were also tracking, catching, and selling the birds into captivity. The parrot's survival was further threatened by deforestation, as the island's rainforests were cleared for agricultural use.

Alarmed by these declining numbers, the nation's forestry department hired a newly graduated, twenty-one-year-old conservationist named Paul Butler to help them save the parrot. Butler had good ideas—including establishing a parrot sanctuary to be funded by special, licensed rain forest tours—yet the project seemed doomed from the start and the number of parrots continued to decline.

In addition to budgetary constraints (his budget only ever amounted to a few hundred dollars), Butler realized a major part of the problem was that the parrot was for the most part irrelevant to the people of St. Lucia and the island's economy. And what's worse, the citizens' **Current State** meant they seemed to care very little for the parrot itself.

Were the people of St. Lucia capable of changing their ways to save the parrot? Of course! Yet no matter the logic or statistics Butler and his colleagues used, they failed to shift citizens' behaviors or motivate them to change. Shifting the St. Lucians to the **Desired State** continued to elude Butler.

So, how did Paul Butler get the people of St. Lucia to raise money and pass protection laws for a bird that was insignificant to them? He changed their beliefs and perceptions. He transformed the parrot's identity—and its fate—by renaming it the *St. Lucia Parrot*.

---

4 Diane Slawych, "St. Lucia's Jacquot on the rebound," *Toronto Sun* (September 17, 2012). Available online: https://torontosun.com/2012/09/17/st-lucias-jacquot-on-the-rebound

Beyond changing the parrot's name, Butler and his colleagues hired a band to write and sing songs about the parrot, persuaded ministers to preach sermons about humans' duty to protect animals, and distributed T-shirts printed with pictures of the parrot. He even enlisted a telephone company to create "St. Lucia Parrot" calling cards. Soon, the St. Lucia Parrot was on postage stamps and bumper stickers.

And it worked!

By 1979, the parrot had become the country's national bird. The people of St. Lucia had adopted the parrot as one of their own. Butler had moved an entire nation from a Current State of thinking ("this bird has little value") to a Desired State of thinking ("this bird is important"). He convinced St. Lucians that the parrot was "one of us." Rather than being just another bird, it was *their* bird: a symbol of pride, a symbol of St. Lucia, and a species worth saving.[5]

People stopped hunting, trapping, and even eating the parrots. St. Lucians supported new laws that protected the birds and their habitat. And slowly but surely, the parrot's numbers began increasing. Today, with an estimated 500 St. Lucia Parrots living on the island,[6] the *Amazona versicolor* has been removed from the endangered species list and is now considered a vulnerable species.[7]

Paul Butler thus led an entire country from a Current State to a Desired State by instilling new beliefs and thoughts that dramatically changed citizens' behaviors.

BEGIN WITH UNDERSTANDING

Before Butler could shift St. Lucia's citizens to the Desired State of caring for the St. Lucia Parrot, he first had to understand their Current State. Reading a person's Current State requires an understanding of what that person is thinking, feeling, and doing. But how easy is it to understand a person's true thoughts and feelings?

You can uncover a person's Current State by learning three things about them:

---

5 Slawych, "St. Lucia's Jacquot on the rebound." Available online: http://torontosun.com/2012/09/17/st-lucias-jacquot-on-the-rebound/wcm/f3c53793-daab-42ab-8052-dfdb14bf51b8

6 "St Lucia parrot," Durrell Wildlife Conservation Trust. Available online: http://wildlife.durrell.org/animals/birds/st-lucia-parrot/

7 "St Lucia Amazon, *Amazona versicolor*," BirdLife International (2016). Available online: https://www.iucnredlist.org/species/22686387/93109549

1. **Thoughts** are beliefs, values, and criteria that are expressed through language. *How* does the person think? Is their language more visual, auditory, or kinesthetic? What mental strategies do they use to interpret and interact with the world around them?
2. **Feelings** are the whole range of positive or negative emotional states. People can feel happy, sad, confident, hesitant, shy, eager, or any other emotion. *All* emotions, major or minor, impact a person's Current State.
3. **Behaviors** are actions. They can be small (like making eye contact) or large (like running on a treadmill). Behaviors that a person *fails* to exhibit (for example, *not* greeting you) can be just as important to notice as the ones they do exhibit.

As you gain awareness of what a person is currently thinking, including their beliefs and values, how they are feeling, and the ways in which they are behaving in the now, you'll have captured their Current State. Understanding the Current State is part of the foundation of a comprehensive strategy for mapping out an effective process of persuasion.

Next, you need to establish what it is that you want to accomplish. What is the Desired State? Clarity about the outcome you are working toward is essential.

Think back to Houdini—he went to great lengths to understand how people thought and behaved and used what he learned to influence them to feel and act the way that he wanted.

Houdini was exceptionally skilled in using both verbal *and* non-verbal communication to motivate his audience to think in different ways. To dispel some of Houdini's magic, let's look at the specific process he and others throughout history have used to engage people and guide their perceptions.

THE THINK → FEEL → DO PROCESS FOR INFLUENCE

People are *always* thinking, feeling, and doing something. In fact, there is a specific sequence that generally begins with a thought, which triggers an emotion or feeling, and leads to a behavior or action. Let's call this the ***Think → Feel → Do*** process for influence.

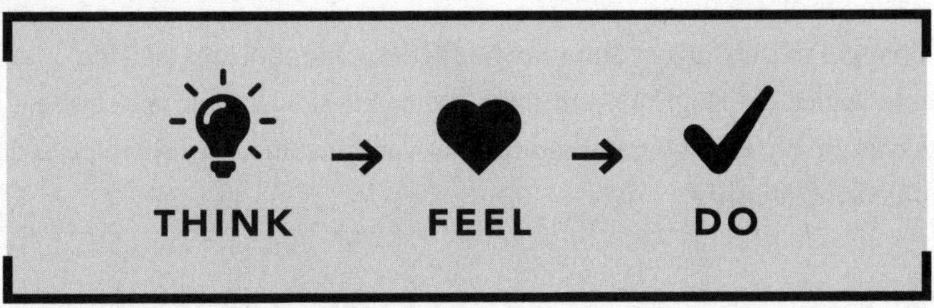

For example, the citizens of St. Lucia *thought* the parrot was inconsequential, so they *felt* apathetic toward the species, and they engaged in *behaviors* that threatened its survival.

Paul Butler initiated a change in the citizens' Current State by planting a *new thought*—that the parrot was more than just a parrot, it was the *St. Lucia Parrot*, one of their own, unique to their island, and an important part of the St. Lucian identity. This new *thinking* was the key to the Desired State. It led the people of St. Lucia to develop *feelings* of nationalism and pride regarding the parrot and caused them to change their *behavior*—to protect, rather than threaten the species.

REALITY IS A CONSTRUCT

The goal of persuasion is to change someone else's behavior. This usually begins by changing one or more of their thoughts, beliefs, and values—what we might call their "stories." Once we influence their thinking process, then their feelings and behaviors will change as well, creating a domino effect. Of course, we can use these techniques to change our own thoughts, feelings, and behaviors, too!

> **Key Concept:**
> The Current State is made up of a person's thoughts, feelings, and behaviors, which are constantly changing. You must be aware of what those current thoughts, feelings, and behaviors are to maximize your persuasive and influential impact.

Any time thoughts, emotions, and behaviors change, even minutely, our Current State is updated—which is beneficial for you because changing another's thoughts, feelings, and behavior is what persuasion is all about.

Changes in the Current State can be slight or dramatic, predictable or unpredictable, logical or illogical—and they can occur slowly or in a heartbeat. It's these continually emerging **new states** that you must focus on when persuading or influencing another.

> If there is any one secret of success, it lies in the ability to get the other person's point of view and see things from that person's angle as well as from your own.
>
> —HENRY FORD

For our purposes, a person's Current State is comprised of their beliefs, values, criteria, and other elements of their **model of the world** that function like a "mental map" for navigating life.

Your unique model of the world is like looking through a stained-glass window: the cut and colors of the glass always alter what you see. This window is your means of ordering and understanding the world: it has a powerful influence on the way you think, feel, and behave, since we each tend to treat our own personal model of the world as if it is reality.

Remember that people can have significantly different maps of the world. In the same way that looking at a map is different than walking through the landscape, remember that the map is *your* perception and understanding of the territory.

Key Concept: Your beliefs, values, and criteria, which are based on information that is filtered through your senses, help create your "model" of the world. You use this model to make sense of the external world; it is your guide to the way things operate and relate to each other, and it produces your singular version of "the truth."

AVOID ROADBLOCKS

Although you might think it's easy to know what a person is thinking, feeing, and doing, it's important to keep in mind that your own model of the world will bias your interpretation of what others think, how they feel, and what they do.

> Assumptions are the termites of relationships.
>
> –HENRY WINKLER

Dacher Keltner, professor of psychology at the University of California, Berkeley, and author of *The Power Paradox*, and his colleague Jeremy Adam Smith, found that "high-power people (say, the prime minister or the president of a company) are more likely to misinterpret nonverbal behavior." Through their research and lab work, Keltner and Smith further found that "the experience of having power makes us less accurate in reading suffering on the faces of strangers and emotions in static photos of facial expressions."[8]

---

8 Jeremy Adam Smith and Dacher Keltner, "The Psychology of Taking a Knee," *Scientific American* (September 29, 2017). Available online: https://blogs.scientificamerican.com/voices/the-psychology-of-taking-a-knee/

Why is this? According to psychologist Douglas LaBier, it could have to do with being "locked inside a self-centered world... that breeds emotional isolation, disconnection, and polarization."[9] Being unable to accurately read facial expressions was just one deficit found in people who carried positions of power. Keltner and Smith also found that "powerful people are less able to take the perspective of others; they're quicker to confuse friendliness with flirtatiousness," and they concluded that there was an "empathy deficit of people in power, one found in many kinds of studies." [10]

Being aware of another person's thoughts, feelings, and behaviors is critical to uncovering their Current State and achieving the Desired State. Your job as a persuader is to discover a deeper and fuller understanding of the other person's Current State. Relying on your curiosity and asking open-ended, well-designed questions about their thoughts and feelings will produce greater clarity about their Current State, and help you guide them to the Desired State. Remember to listen carefully to their answers while also noticing their non-verbal communication.

As you gather this valuable information about a person's Current State, continue to be aware that your own assumptions have the potential to color your understanding of someone else's thoughts, feelings, and behaviors. Engage your critical thinking skills to examine your own assumptions, preconceptions, and model of the world.

> Every man takes the limits of his own field of vision for the limits of the world.
>
> –ARTHUR SCHOPENHAUER

To persuade someone effectively, then, you need to use both your critical thinking and listening skills *and* the ***Think → Feel → Do*** process to overcome your biases and to act on evidence rather than relying on assumptions. Once

---

9 Douglas LaBier, "Are You Suffering from Empathy Deficit Disorder?" ***Psychology Today*** (April 12, 2010). Available online: https://www.psychologytoday.com/ca/blog/the-new-resilience/201004/are-you-suffering-empathy-deficit-disorder

10 Smith and Keltner, "The Psychology of Taking a Knee." Available online: https://blogs.scientificamerican.com/voices/the-psychology-of-taking-a-knee/

you do, you'll be more attuned to the information you collect about a person's Current State.

Heather Butler, a professor of psychology at California State University, Dominguez Hills, defines "critical thinking" as "a collection of cognitive skills that allow us to think rationally in a goal-orientated fashion, and a disposition to use those skills when appropriate."[11] Her research has "pitted critical thinking and intelligence against each other to see which was associated with fewer negative life events. People who were strong on either intelligence or critical thinking experienced fewer negative events, but critical thinkers did better."[12]

As we explore a Current State in order to create a Desired State, we want to **think critically** about how we elicit information. At the same time, we want to keep in mind that—as important as critical thinking is—it may still fail to defend us against **emotional framing,** a persuasion technique that we'll explore more in the pages to come. In my experience over the past twenty years, critical thinking and intelligence are at best only a slight defense against "emotional framing."

The good news is that Butler has found that, unlike intelligence, which is relatively stable over time, critical thinking is a skill that can be developed. "Improving intelligence is difficult," she says. "Intelligence is largely determined by genetics. Critical thinking, though, can improve with training and the benefits have been shown to persist over time. Anyone can improve their critical thinking skills." [13]

STEPPING INTO YOUR ROLE AS PERSUADER

As a persuader, your goal is to move a person from their Current State to a Desired State.

The Current State is based on a person's mental map and includes an individual's thoughts, emotions, and behaviors—or what they are thinking, feeling, and doing in the now. Similarly, the Desired State is what you want the individual to think, feel, and do at a specific point of time in the future. To lead them from

11 Heather A. Butler, "Why Do Smart People Do Foolish Things?" *Scientific American* (October 3, 2017). Available online: https://www.scientificamerican.com/article/why-do-smart-people-do-foolish-things/

12 Butler, "Why Do Smart People Do Foolish Things?" Available online: https://www.scientificamerican.com/article/why-do-smart-people-do-foolish-things/

13 Butler, "Why Do Smart People Do Foolish Things?" Available online: https://www.scientificamerican.com/article/why-do-smart-people-do-foolish-things/

their Current State to the Desired State, you must interrupt or shift those current thoughts, feelings, and behaviors and move them in the direction of the Desired State.

There are many techniques for leading someone to a Desired State, all of which boil down to this: engage and guide the person's thoughts. When that happens, their feelings and behavior will follow.

> **Key Concept:**
> The Current State and Desired State are both composed of thoughts, feelings, and behaviors. As a persuader, your objective is to engage and guide a person toward the desired thoughts, feelings, and behaviors.

Within my own practice, I've helped many people move from a Current State to a Desired State. Let me share one of these stories with you: Maria* was referred to me by her physician because she had taken medications for anxiety, and she didn't like the adverse side effects. She was searching for an alternative to medication to manage her symptoms.

When I sat down with Maria, I started mapping out her Current State by looking first at her state of anxiety—how her mind was working, what she was thinking that was triggering feelings of anxiety, and what behaviors the feeling of anxiety created.

I asked Maria to tell me what was happening when she felt anxious. What was she thinking about? She said mainly that her anxiety just "happened" to her. I prompted her further: Did she ask herself any questions or have certain thoughts that put her in this state? Maria reported being unaware of asking herself any questions or of having any specific thoughts—she insisted that the anxiety "just happened."

But *how* did it happen?

When I investigated further, Maria said it would start when she thought about things like what might happen to her only son, who was in his first year of university, as he drove to campus. As soon as he began to get ready to go back to school after weekends at home, her thoughts would turn to questions like, "What will happen if he gets into a car accident?" which in turn sent her brain on a search for this kind of information and kick-started her anxiety. She didn't even realize that she was asking herself this question!

Now imagine if I were to ask you that same question: "What would happen to your loved one if they were to get into a car accident on their way home?" When you hear that question, what kinds of images pop into your head? What sounds do you hear? What feelings do these internal representations create?

It's likely that you *picture* ambulances and police cars, perhaps the crash itself, blood, emergency personnel. When you *think* about the *sounds*, you're likely to *hear* glass breaking, tires squealing, the *sound* of metal on metal, sirens, and people yelling or crying.

If I then ask you, "How does that make you feel?" you would probably tell me you *feel* tense, anxious, or upset. And based on this feeling, it's likely that the next thing you might *do* is call the person you fear is in danger just to make sure they're okay.

This is exactly what Maria was doing with her son. Feeling overwhelmed by her Current State of anxiety about every bad thing that could happen, she would call him while he was driving and remind him not to speed and not to get distracted—even though in doing so, she was embedding speeding and distraction in his mind. In fact, the specific language Maria was using was increasing the likelihood of something negative happening. Calling her son while he was driving was itself a huge distraction, and her behavior increased the chances of an accident.

Now, to change this Current State and guide Maria to the Desired State, I started by asking different questions about her son:

- "What happens when he arrives at school safely?"
- "What happens when he gets the best grades he's ever received?"
- "What happens if he meets his soulmate while at school and they live happily ever after?"

Asking different questions began to change Maria's *thinking*, which changed how she *felt*, and, eventually, what she was *doing*. Maria admitted that asking these new questions made it significantly more difficult to feel anxious.

"It can't be that simple, can it?" she asked me.

It certainly can.

Maria and I ran through several other scenarios, changing the questions we asked each time. With each question, Maria's brain was sent on a new quest for a positive outcome, which changed the way she felt, and those positive feelings in turn changed her behaviors. She came to an agreement with her son that he would always call her once he arrived safely back at school, and that she would refrain from calling him while he was driving. As you can see, by guiding her thoughts through carefully chosen questions, Maria and I were able to change her Current State of anxiety to a Desired State of positive feelings about her son's future, and more positive behavior followed.

Sometimes, changing a thought is a simple matter, as simple as a word choice which can create and trigger an **emotional frame**. An emotional frame creates a cognitive bias where people unconsciously make a decision based on whether options are presented with positive or negative connotations, for example, as a loss or a gain, or as pain or pleasure.[14]

Depending on the language we use and how we use it, we can, intentionally or unintentionally, create an emotional frame that will draw attention to things that trigger a specific emotion. An emotional frame connects a positive or a negative emotion to a thing or event. This neurological connection typically occurs outside of our conscious awareness.

In a classic emotional framing experiment carried out at Harvard Medical School, physicians received statistics on lung cancer outcomes for patients who underwent surgery versus radiation. While surgery was the riskier option in the short-term, five-year survival rates clearly showed it was the preferable treatment. Half of the physician participants were given statistics on survival rates for surgery phrased as follows: "The one-month survival rate is 90%." The other half received the same information, this time in terms of mortality rates: "There is 10% mortality in the first month."[15] In other words, each group received the *same* information, although framed differently.

The results were dramatic. When framed in terms of survival rates, 84% of physicians recommended surgery over radiation. On the other hand, when

---

14 "Framing effect (psychology)," Wikipedia (modified October 5, 2020), https://en.wikipedia.org/w/index.php?title=Framing_effect_(psychology)

15 Daniel Kahneman, ***Thinking, Fast and Slow*** (Anchor Canada, 2011), p. 367.

framed in terms of mortality rates, only 50% of physicians recommended surgery—despite it being the best option for the patient.[16]

The physicians were influenced by the *emotions* evoked by the words used to frame the information they received: "mortality" is negative, and "survival" is positive. The words we choose to express an idea, to ask a question, or to tell a story, all impact our listeners. So, it's vital that we be aware of the emotional frames of our linguistic choices as we learn to be more effective persuaders.

BE ALERT, BE AWAKE, ARRIVE ALIVE!

A number of years ago, I was driving down a highway in New Zealand with my wife and business partner, Natalie, when we saw a roadside sign that read, "Tired Drivers Crash." Certainly, the intention behind the sign was to lead people to the Desired State of being safe drivers. While that's an excellent goal, just imagine that you're driving late at night, and you see that sign. Your mind zeroes in on the dominant ideas: feeling "tired" and "crashing."

Your mind is now focused on being "tired" and your body responds to anything you vividly imagine as if it's real—so there's a good chance that you'll feel even more tired.

Your mind also focuses on "crash," bringing that distracting idea to the foreground and increasing the likelihood that you'll get into a crash! Although there may be only a slight increase in your risk of feeling tired and crashing, *any* increase is dangerous. These are the opposite feelings the creators of the sign wanted to evoke!

Further down the road we saw a second sign that said, "Wake Up with Power Naps." Again, the intent was good: take a nap to avoid being tired on the road. Unfortunately, this second sign primed the driver's mind to think about taking a nap. Combined with thoughts of being tired and crashing that were instilled by the first sign, you now have a recipe for disaster.

Fortunately, there was a third sign even further down the road that said, "Be Alert, Be Awake, Arrive Alive." At last! A message that led drivers toward the Desired State. The brain zeros in on "alert," "awake," and "alive," making it

16 Kahneman, *Thinking, Fast and Slow*, p. 367.

more likely that a driver will safely arrive at their destination because the sign has guided their mind to focus on these three specific directives.

Now, let's continue with the idea of driving. Imagine that you're in your vehicle and about to go on a road trip using a GPS. What's the first thing you need to know before you get started?

Would you say… where you are going?

In fact, the first thing the GPS needs are the exact coordinates of where you are right now.

Determining a person's Current State is like turning on your GPS and waiting for the satellite to calculate their current location. Only then can you enter the coordinates of the destination. When you do, the GPS will map out your route. Leading a person to a Desired State is like entering the address of where you want them to go and driving them there: the clearer and more detailed your map is, the better you'll be at navigating the route.

Think back, for a moment, to the examples of Harry Houdini and of Paul Butler and the St. Lucia Parrot that we looked at earlier in this chapter. Both Houdini and Butler needed to engage their audience's minds and imaginations in order to guide them and trigger the emotions that would drive certain behaviors, leading them to the Desired State.

Houdini, for instance, was a master of water escapes, frequently leading his audiences to think that he had failed the escape and was in extreme danger.

His method was this: as he entered the water chamber, Houdini would ask the audience members to start holding their breath. The curtains were drawn shut and the audience would continue to hold their breath for as long as they could, until they were gasping for air. Only then would Houdini reveal that he had escaped. By causing audiences to think that he was in serious peril—or even dead—Houdini guided them into a state of suspense and fear, followed by an immense sense of relief when he reappeared free and unharmed. This emotional rollercoaster drove people to return to his performances over and over again and to tell their friends about his incredible death-defying abilities.

In the case of the parrot on the verge of extinction, Paul Butler got the people of St. Lucia to think of the bird as the *St. Lucia* Parrot and to ask themselves questions like "Who am I?" and "What kind of a situation is this?" and "What would someone like me do in this kind of a situation?" The answer Butler led them to was, "We are St. Lucians, and this bird is one of us. It's the St. Lucia Parrot and our island is the only place in the world this bird exists. It's one of our own and it's in danger of extinction. We need to take pride and do whatever it takes to protect one of our own!"

The art of persuasion hinges on our understanding of Current and Desired States. We must clearly understand what the Current State is and what we want the Desired State to be. When we have that clarity, we can engage in the activities, processes, and strategies that change people's thinking, guide them to experience different emotions, and ultimately, drive new behaviors.

> If you do not design the future, someone or something else will design it for you.
>
> –EDWARD DE BONO

Remember Maria, who came to me with anxiety about her son driving to university? In the example below, we've outlined the thoughts, feelings, and actions that were contributing to both Maria's Current and Desired State.

CURRENT STATE

THINK: (STORIES, BELIEFS, VALUES, ETC.)

What have you uncovered about the Current State, including beliefs, values, criteria, and so on?

Maria was asking herself, "What if my son gets into an accident as he drives back to university?" This question sent her imagination on a quest that resulted in her experiencing intrusive thoughts including images, sounds and feelings—her Current State:

- Maria was imagining a frightening outcome. Her mind summoned sounds of tires screeching, glass shattering, metal crunching, sirens blaring, screaming, and shouting. She conjured images of her son being placed on a stretcher, rushed to the nearest hospital and into surgery. Then she imagined his future: an education cut short, permanent physical disability, or even death.

FEEL: (EMOTIONS, STATES)

What have you uncovered about the emotions/states that are being experienced or felt?

These intrusive thoughts triggered the following emotions and states for Maria:

- Worry
- Nervousness
- Stress
- Anxiety
- Panic

DO: (ACTIONS)

What are the actions being driven by these thoughts and feelings?

In response to the thoughts and emotions she was experiencing, Maria was repeatedly calling her son as he was driving back to school and saying things like "Don't speed" and "Don't be distracted," instilling those ideas into his brain and thus putting him at greater risk of getting into an accident.

DESIRED STATE

THINK:

What do you want to think/what do you want the person to think?

As a way of engaging and redirecting Maria's imagination to a more useful storyline, I asked her questions like, "What will happen when he gets there safely?" and, "Which class does he enjoy the most?" and, "Which class do you think he'll get his highest mark in?" These questions shifted Maria's thoughts to the positive outcomes of her son attending university, including him getting good grades and graduating, securing a good job, and even the possibility of meeting his future partner on campus.

FEEL:

What emotions/states do you want yourself or the other person to experience (either by eliciting or instilling them) based on the Desired Thinking that you have described?

- Relaxation
- Calmness
- Hope
- Confidence
- Optimism
- Happiness
- Pride

DO:

What are the actions you want yourself or the other person to take based upon the Desired State you've described?

Maria agreed that each time her son returned to university, she would wait for him to call her once he arrived safely. She also arranged with her son that, if there were any delays, he would pull over and call her to update her.

OPPORTUNITY

Now, think about an area of your own life where you would benefit from modifying or updating some patterns in your thinking, emotions, and behavior. What do you want to change or improve? Visit **www.SolutionsInMind.com** to download the **Current State and Desired State Worksheets** that you see here. Use the empty worksheet to map out the scenario by identifying your thoughts, feelings, and actions as they are in the Current State. Then map out the Desired State. What would be a more useful way of thinking? How would you like to feel? If you were thinking and feeling that way, what would you likely be doing?

WORKSHEET: CURRENT STATE TO DESIRED STATE

CURRENT STATE (CS) → DESIRED STATE (DS)

Current State — THINK

(Story, Beliefs, Values, etc...)

What do you and/or others currently think?

This current thinking may include beliefs, values, criteria and so on.

Current State — FEEL

(Emotions / States)

What emotions/ states are you and/or others experiencing?

Be sure that these are emotions such as frustration, doubt, confidence, anxiety, fear, satisfaction, etc.

Engage and Guide Conversation

Desired State — THINK

(Story, Beliefs, Values, etc...)

What specifically do you *want* yourself and/or others to think?

Desired State — FEEL

(Emotions / States)

What emotion do you *want* yourself and/or others to be experiencing, based upon the Desired Thinking?

Current State — DO

(Behavior)

Given what you and/or others are currently thinking and feeling, what are you/they currently doing that you would like to influence (either reinforce if positive or discourage if negative)?

Engage and Guide Conversation

Desired State — DO

(Behavior)

If you and/or others are thinking and feeling the way that you want, what specific Behaviors do you *want* yourself/them to be doing?

Remember to express these Behaviors in SMART terms.

CURRENT STATE (CS) → DESIRED STATE (DS)

Current State — THINK

(Story, Beliefs, Values, etc...)

Current State — FEEL

(Emotions / States)

Engage and Guide Conversation

Desired State — THINK

(Story, Beliefs, Values, etc...)

Desired State — FEEL

(Emotions / States)

Current State — DO

(Behavior)

Engage and Guide Conversation

Desired State — DO

(Behavior)

Chapter Two

Perception is Real—Even When It Isn't

> Human beings constantly create or construct new mental representations, and so the content of the mind is by its nature an open, infinitely expandable category.
>
> —HOWARD GARDNER

In 1948, psychologist Bertram R. Forer asked thirty-nine students in his Introductory Psychology class to take a written personality test called the Diagnostic Interest Blank. The assessment delved into the test-taker's personal characteristics, hopes, and ambitions.[17] A week later, Forer handed each student a unique personality profile based on their answers to the survey. After reading the profile, each student rated it according to how closely they thought it fit them—in other words, how accurate it was. As a group, the students judged the profiles to be quite correct, giving them an average accuracy rating of 82.5%.

Here's the catch: all the personality profiles were *identical*, consisting of a series of generic, ambiguous statements like, "You have found it unwise to be too frank in revealing yourself to others," "While you have some personality weaknesses, you are generally able to compensate for them," and "Security is one of your major goals in life."

Like a fortune cookie or horoscope, the "personalized" profiles seemed accurate because the students' minds were focused on what they believed to be true about themselves, deleted what was false, and distorted the profile to conform to their experiences.

---

17 Bertram R. Forer, "The Fallacy of Personal Validation: A Classroom Demonstration of Gullibility," *The Journal of Abnormal Psychology* 44 (1949), pp. 118-121. Available online: http://www.scribd.com/doc/17378132/The-Fallacy-of-Personal-Validation-a-Classroom-Demonstration-of-Gullibility

What happened in this classroom is quite common. Our minds regularly delete, distort, and generalize incoming information in order to make it match our unique perception of reality. This process is called **subjective validation**. It's also known as the **Barnum Effect**, a psychological principle named after the infamous circus impresario, P.T. Barnum.

Phineas Taylor Barnum was an American showman, businessman, and politician of the nineteenth century.[18] Along with founding the Barnum & Bailey Circus, he is most famous for promotional strategies that, at the time, were often considered outlandish.

Barnum believed that circus attendance was low because it was marketed specifically to children. So, Barnum decided to use an ambiguous statement about the circus, saying that there was "something here for everyone, something for everyone of all ages" in order to appeal to adults as well. The intentional use of ambiguity in his communication influenced and shifted people's ideas about the circus. The vagueness of this statement allowed people to construct their own expectations of what the circus offered. What's most interesting and important to notice is that it worked! With this vague description, circus attendance increased as people of all ages started to attend.

The Barnum Effect, coined from Barnum's use of subjective validation to increase circus attendance, postulates that if a statement is vague enough, a person will search for a meaning that is most relevant to them—and explains why astrology, horoscopes, and fortune cookies are so popular. (Ironically, although this principle is named after Barnum, he actually wrote an exposé on spiritualists and mediums in his book *Humbugs of the World*—he was a disbeliever as well as feeling that those claiming this "sixth sense" were making a dishonest living.)[19]

I wonder what Barnum would have thought about Houdini. Houdini was well known for leveraging people's beliefs in the supernatural to create an almost superhuman image of himself, even though his beliefs about spiritualists and their lack of credibility were similar to Barnum's. Houdini's training even made it easy for him to expose spiritualists and mediums. He gained such a reputation

18 "P.T. Barnum," Wikipedia (modified September 29, 2020), https://en.wikipedia.org/wiki/P._T._Barnum

19 P.T. Barnum, ***The Humbugs of the World: An Account of Humbugs, Delusions, Impositions, Quackeries, Deceits and Deceivers Generally, in All Ages*** (1866). Available online: http://www.gutenberg.org/ebooks/26640

for debunking spiritualists that it is rumored he was called to the Russian court by Tsar Nicholas II to expose Rasputin, who was thought to have the Tsar's wife, Alexandria, "under his spell." It's believed that Houdini did not, in fact, take the Tsar up on his invitation, despite accounts by authors like C. Michael Forsyth, whose novel *Houdini vs. Rasputin* is based very loosely on history.[20]

Why were people so drawn to Barnum and Houdini? How were these great showmen so successful? Among other things, both relied heavily on subjective validation and **confirmation bias**, in which the information they provided to their audiences was ambiguous enough that each individual found their own unique and relevant meaning in it. This same skill is also part of what made the renowned psychiatrist Milton Erickson, whom we'll discuss further in Chapter Five, so successful.

Confirmation bias may bring to mind a concept sometimes known as the Pygmalion Effect or the Rosenthal Expectancy Effect. Both terms describe a phenomenon in which another person's expectations about an individual affect that individual's performance. In their book *Pygmalion in the Classroom,* Robert Rosenthal and Lenore Jacobson looked at how this phenomenon impacted students. They conducted a study that revealed a self-fulfilling prophecy in which students whose teachers had high expectations of them performed well academically and students whose teachers had low expectations of them, performed poorly. In other words, the students performed exactly the way their teachers expected them to, regardless of any innate academic abilities.[21]

As persuaders, we have the opportunity to consider how we, like the teachers in this study, are communicating based on our expectations of others and how our expectations may cause other people to react and behave accordingly. When we change our expectations, we can help others tap into their full potential.

Key Concept:
The mind is constantly altering information to make it relevant to our beliefs, previous experiences, and expectations.

20 Michael C. Forsyth, ***Houdini vs. Rasputin*** (Freedom's Hammer, 2018).
21 "Pygmalion effect." Wikipedia (modified August 14, 2020), https://en.wikipedia.org/wiki/Pygmalion_effect

Whether you believe in fortune cookies or horoscopes, that you're great or horrible at math, or that you've got a team that's capable or incapable, the mind is constantly altering information to make it align with what you already believe and expect—and that knowledge is a critical element of persuasiveness.

REVERSE PSYCHOLOGY

In his book *Sleight of Mouth,* Robert Dilts tells the story of a castle under siege in the Middle Ages.[22] Enemy troops had surrounded the castle to prevent the people inside from getting any food, weapons, or other supplies from the outside. Because castle walls were designed to withstand attacks (and cannons had yet to be invented), the enemy just camped out and waited for those inside to run out of food and surrender.

> Perception is real even when it is not reality.
>
> –EDWARD DE BONO

When the castle dwellers were just about out of supplies, they made a final show of defiance by pelting their besiegers with their remaining food. When the enemy saw bread, cabbages, potatoes, and the like cascading over the castle walls, they formed a surprising belief:

If these people can afford to throw food at us, they must have plenty of it!

Discouraged and "knowing" they could never conquer a castle that was so well-provisioned, the invaders gave up and slunk away into the night.

The invaders' belief ("The enemy has so much food, it's impossible to win!") was based solely on the fact that food was flung over the castle wall. The belief was powerful and perfectly reasonable—and yet entirely incorrect. It prompted the invaders to back off just when they were about to succeed. Beliefs are "judgments and evaluations about ourselves, others, and the world around us."[23] Beliefs are created by your mind, based on your experiences and the information you've gathered. Once formed, these beliefs become the rules

---

22 Robert Dilts, *Sleight of Mouth* (Meta Publications, 1999), p. 80.

23 Dilts, *Sleight of Mouth*, p. 110.

that tell you what is good and bad, as well as what is possible and impossible for you to do, think, or be. Your beliefs then become part of *your* reality—your model of the world—and of course, each of us has our own unique reality.

> **Key Concept:**
> The mind filters information to create and support beliefs, values, and criteria. These in turn form the basis of your model of the world, shaping the way you understand the world, and determining what's truly important to you. Understanding how the mind filters information is key to being persuasive.

Once a belief has been planted, the mind filters incoming information and either accepts the data that supports the belief or alters the information by distorting it so that it supports the belief. In this way the mind **deletes, distorts, and generalizes** millions of pieces of incoming information every day.

Our minds tend to seek subjective validation and search for evidence to support our existing beliefs. These beliefs are like seeds that, when planted and watered, will grow roots. Rather than being intractable or permanent, these beliefs can be altered because they are actually processes rather than things. It's up to us to engage and guide the imagination in different directions in order to shift biases and update or change a person's process of believing.

THE PARADOX OF WHY

Consider for a moment how often we ask the question "Why?" without understanding its impact. Most of us use this question haphazardly; in fact, "Why?" is the most overused and detrimental question in the wrong context—and the most underused and advantageous question in the right context. Let's unravel this paradox.

When we ask "Why?" we grow roots and deepen beliefs—and this is the reason the question must be used thoughtfully and strategically. For example, let's say you want to engage in an extreme sport like kite surfing but you're afraid. If I ask you, "*Why* are you afraid?" the question serves to reinforce your fear, encouraging your mind to consider all the reasons *why* you're afraid. When used in this way, "Why?" deepens your rooted beliefs and existing fears. When we ask, "Why?" in the wrong context, as in this example, we deepen the story, beliefs, and values already ingrained in the other person's mind.

Instead, what we want to do is shift that person's thinking toward the Desired State. To do this, look for opportunities to ask questions that deepen roots and grow a story that supports the Desired State. For example, to move you toward the Desired State of experiencing kite surfing, I might ask, "What would make you confident to kite surf?" or "How would it feel to successfully kite surf?" Once I get your mind shifting toward the Desired State, that's the perfect opportunity to ask a follow-up "Why?" question in order to deepen and grow those roots or beliefs and move your mind further in the desirable direction. These questions and others like them grow the Desired State of confidence, rather than reinforce the Current State of fear. Makes sense, doesn't it?

Here's another example: imagine a child says that they're feeling upset. Instead of asking them, "Why do you feel upset?" which only reinforces their current negative emotional state, you could instead clarify by saying, "Help me understand what you mean by that," and then lay the groundwork for the Desired State by asking "How would you like to feel instead?" or "What could you think about that will make you feel calm and happy?" Remember to then follow-up with questions such as, "Why do these thoughts make you feel calm and happy?" These questions will engage and redirect the child's imagination, resulting in a more desirable state and feelings of calmness and happiness.

As you can see in this example, when used in the right context the question, "Why?" reinforces or deepens the Desired State. Think of the question "Why?" as if it's a watering can that, when used, has the effect of growing roots. The key is to use "Why?" in the right context, at the right time, and in the right way. When we do, it's a very powerful question, one that can help grow desirable roots as we engage and guide ourselves and others toward the Desired State.

ARE YOUR BELIEFS LIMITING OR EMPOWERING?

Back in the 1970s, Russian weightlifter Vasily Alekseyev won tournament after tournament and kept setting new world records for overhead weightlifting. He seemed unstoppable—until he finally encountered a barrier that prevented him from lifting the weights. That barrier was 500 pounds.

Although Alekseyev had lifted very close to 500 pounds several times, try as he might, he repeatedly failed to break the 500-pound barrier. He *knew* it was impossible, and this limiting belief was based on plenty of real-life experience—his repeated failure to lift 500 pounds.

Alekseyev's trainer had an idea. He had a set of weights made that looked exactly like the set that Alekseyev knew he *could* lift. The weights were stamped to indicate that they weighed an amount that the champion could lift, although in reality they weighed 500 pounds. Then the coach asked the famous lifter to hoist the weight—which Alekseyev did! Having overcome this mental barrier, Alekseyev went on to become the first man to cleanly lift 500 pounds in competition.[24]

The difference to his success lay in Alekseyev's brain rather than his muscles. Holding the empowering belief that lifting under 500 pounds was possible, he accomplished the lift even though the load was heavier. This little trick by his coach proved that the weight limit in this instance was all in Alekseyev's mind.

Rather than thinking of beliefs as being either true or false, it's useful to think of them as either **empowering** (helping you move closer to your goals) or **limiting** (standing in your way).

> Beliefs create the actual fact.
>
> —WILLIAM JAMES

Let's look at another example.

Roger Gilbert Bannister was born in London, England, in 1929. Bannister was highly educated, eventually taking a degree in medicine at the University of Oxford. He was also an athlete, and during his time in medical school he was keenly interested in a lesson about the capabilities of the human form. Bannister's professors taught him and the other would-be physicians in his class

24 "Vasily Alekseyev," Wikipedia (modified June 15, 2020), https://en.wikipedia.org/wiki/Vasily_Alekseyev

that there were limits to what the human body was capable of. It was impossible, they said, for a human to run a mile in four minutes or less; the human form would simply break down under such force. This was an undisputed medical belief. No one had ever run that fast because humans simply *couldn't*. This belief sparked questions for Bannister. Was it a limiting belief about the human body that was holding runners back? Or was the medical community correct and a person could die simply in the attempt itself?[25]

Bannister set out to answer these questions and in 1954, when he was twenty-five years old, he ran a mile in three minutes and 59.4 seconds, breaking the supposed "four-minute barrier."[26]

> Doctors and scientists said that breaking the four-minute mile was impossible, that one would die in the attempt. Thus, when I got up from the track after collapsing at the finish line, I guessed I was dead.
>
> –ROGER BANNISTER

The following year, *Sports Illustrated* named Bannister its first Sportsman of the Year, and as word of his accomplishment travelled, many other athletes around the world also began to break the four-minute mile barrier.[27] Since Bannister's accomplishment, the four-minute mile has become the standard for most male middle distance runners. In fact, the mile record has since been lowered by almost 17 seconds![28]

> The man who can drive himself further once the effort gets painful is the man who will win.
>
> –ROGER BANNISTER

---

25 "Roger Bannister," Wikipedia (modified August 20, 2020), https://en.wikipedia.org/wiki/Roger_Bannister
26 "Roger Bannister," Wikipedia, https://en.wikipedia.org/wiki/Roger_Bannister
27 "Roger Bannister," Wikipedia, https://en.wikipedia.org/wiki/Roger_Bannister
28 "Four-minute mile," Wikipedia (modified October 4, 2020), https://en.wikipedia.org/wiki/Four-minute_mile

While Bannister's athletic accomplishments were formidable, what made him a true game changer was his shattering of a medical belief that had been holding humanity back from doing something we were very capable of doing. The four-minute mile was supposed to be unbreakable, and yet Bannister thought—and proved—otherwise.

The story of the four-minute mile begs the question: What other limiting beliefs might be holding us back?

THE DRIVING FORCES BEHIND BEHAVIOR

As you engage in understanding a person's beliefs and potentially in modifying or changing their process of believing, you are likely to simultaneously uncover their values: what they value and why they value it. The processes of believing something and valuing something are closely connected, and usually even interconnected.

> Everything begins with belief. What we believe is the most powerful option of all.
>
> —NORMAN COUSINS

We value intangible things such as love, success, achievement, creativity, or freedom; physical things like jewelry, a nice house, or the latest tech gadget; things that bring instant gratification like eating chocolate or getting a massage; and things that pay off in the future, such as education or hard work.

Bear in mind that throughout this book, when I say "beliefs," what I'm actually talking about is the *process of believing*, the act of making judgements and evaluations about yourself, others, and the world around you. When I discuss values, I'm referring to the *process of valuing* something. This is an important distinction because, as you may remember, what we value is intertwined with what we believe. For example, I *value* honesty and *believe* I should always tell the truth because honest people are truthful. Or I *value* a good education and *believe* it will help me get ahead in life because it will allow me to secure a good job.

We often mistakenly think that honesty and education are actual "things," treating them like abstract nouns, when they're actually processes: the process of being honest or the process of educating myself or someone else. In this way, both "beliefs" and "values" are actually processes. We'll discuss this more in a moment when we look at nominalization.

WHAT ARE YOUR CRITERIA?

> **Key Concept:** Beliefs are formed as you judge and evaluate yourself, others, and the world around you. The processes of believing something and valuing something are closely connected, and usually even interconnected.

When we think of a value as a process, it becomes a verb, an action word that describes the process of *valuing*, *finding* value, or *assigning* value. This subtle difference matters because while a *thing* is fixed, a *process* is changeable. We can often learn what someone values by where they're willing to invest their time, money, or other resources.

If we want to change the process of how we value something, we can change the criteria connected to the fulfillment of the value. We can also do this by changing the hierarchy or ordering of those criteria. **Criteria** are standards, rules, or principles, used to determine whether you've upheld a value. Of course, criteria will vary from person to person and situation to situation. As well, individuals can value similar things and yet have different criteria for what they value, meaning that they will approach and uphold that value in different ways.

As an example, consider two people who both value "adventure." One person's criteria for the fulfillment of adventure may include hiking in a new area, while the other person's may include an adrenaline rush from white water rafting or skydiving. Fulfillment of the value "adventure" will therefore be different for each person because, while they both place value on the same thing, their criteria for it are very different.

Music is another example where values often coincide while criteria may differ. Many of us value "good music." I might prefer classical music because my criteria for "good music" is that it is timeless and has an intricate composition.

On the other hand, someone else who values "good music" may prefer the genre of rock music because their criteria for "good music" is that it has energizing beats and powerful lyrics. We each have different criteria for why we believe our music choice is "good" and neither of us is right nor wrong. We both value good music; our criteria are simply different.

The best way to know if a value has been fulfilled is by understanding its fulfillment criteria. In addition to knowing that someone *values* safety, you must also understand their *criteria* for safety. Consider "safety" in the context of driving: for you, the criteria might be having a vehicle that has won top safety awards. For someone else, the criteria might have less to do with the vehicle and more to do with the driver paying attention to the road, instead of their phone.

Key Concept: Uncovering a person's beliefs, values, and criteria is an important part of the persuasion process. Knowing how to align your offering with another person's beliefs, values, and criteria is equally important. Doing so will make your offering relevant to the person you are influencing and create an overall experience that's emotionally fulfilling.

WORKING THROUGH NOMINALIZATION

We discussed above that most of us tend to refer to beliefs and values as "things" when instead they are processes. The term for this is "nominalization." **Nominalization** is when a **verb** (a process word) is transformed into an **abstract noun** (a non-material thing). This transformation is like taking a snapshot of a moving object, ultimately converting a dynamic process (a verb) into a static thing (a noun). When we nominalize process words, we turn them into nouns and freeze them in an instant of time.

A great example that we use every day is the word "communication." If a manager says, "The communication in this company is poor," they are treating communication as if it's a "static thing," when communication is actually a process that can be changed. In this example, it's more effective to *de*nominalize the verb and instead ask, "How can we communicate more effectively?" This also keeps us solution-focused and redirects our attention in a productive way toward a positive Desired State.

As you can see, when a verb is nominalized by transforming it into an abstract noun, it becomes stagnant. In turning that stagnant noun back into a process or action by denominalizing it, we facilitate empowerment as you and the person you're speaking with become aware of the processes associated with the word. This subtle shift in language also holds us accountable for how we are contributing to the process. For example, there is an inherent accountability and empowerment in the phrase, "How can we communicate more effectively?" that's lacking in the phrase, "The communication in this company is poor."[29]

THE WHEELBARROW TEST

The "Wheelbarrow Test" is a simple way to determine if you're dealing with a nominalization (that is, if you've distorted a process by turning it into an abstract noun). In most cases, if you can put the noun into a wheelbarrow, it's a true or concrete noun, something that is material in the world. If it's impossible to put the noun into a wheelbarrow, it's likely a nominalization. Keep in mind that this test holds true regardless of the size of the noun. A transport truck or even a planet like Earth could fit into a wheelbarrow if it were large enough!

> **Key Concept:** Listen for nominalizations in people's language (including your own) and, when you hear them, remember that your goal is to denominalize them by turning the abstract noun back into a process. You can utilize the power of denominalization to encourage change, accountability and empowerment in yourself and others.[30]

Let's look at a couple of examples. When someone says, "I don't have enough time," they're treating "time" as though it's a physical *thing* that can be put in a wheelbarrow. Go ahead and *try* to put time in a wheelbarrow and you'll discover that what you *can* put in a wheelbarrow is a clock or a watch, which are true nouns. As Einstein

29 Richard Bandler and John Grinder, *The Structure of Magic: A Book About Language and Therapy*, volume 1 (Science and Behavior Books, 1979), p. 74.

30 Bandler and Grinder, *The Structure of Magic*, p. 74.

famously said, "Time has no independent existence apart from the order of events by which we measure it." Time is a *process* by which we organize the events in our daily lives, rather than a material thing that you can or can't have. So, if someone says, "I don't have enough *time*," what they're really saying is, "This isn't a priority for me at the moment."

These kinds of nominalizations are disempowering in that they leave us with an external locus of control (which we'll discuss in a later chapter). Instead, we want to create an empowering sense of ownership and accountability in ourselves and other people through denominalizing abstract nouns by turning them back into verbs.

LANGUAGE INFLUENCES VALUES

While nominalizations may seem like pretty minor things, in language nuances like these are extremely important because the language we use influences our perceptions, beliefs, and values. And remember, rather than thinking of values as tangible things (abstract nouns), it's important to keep in mind that what we are referring to is actually the *process* of how we value something and the reasons *why* we find it of value. These processes are also directional, meaning that we want to move *toward* or *away from* them.

We call the values that we want to move in the direction of **toward values** and those we want to avoid **away from values**. For example, one person might say, "I want to make lots of money and be very wealthy," which is a value they are moving *toward*, while another person may say, "I don't want to be poor," where poverty is a value they want to move *away from*.

It's important to note that toward values and away from values are different than "means values" and "ends values." A **means value** is simply one that helps you achieve or move toward an end goal or **ends value**.

Let's look at the example of money again. If I ask the audience in one of my seminars whether money is a means value or an ends value, most people say it's a means value, because they only want money to buy a new car, a better house, or a special vacation. Money is the *means* to acquiring those things. On the other hand, for someone who likes looking at or counting piles of money (like Scrooge McDuck!), money might be an ends value. If, however, that person likes having lots of money because saving money gives them a sense of security and confidence, then money is actually still a means value that will bring them closer to their ends values of feeling secure and confident.

Since the language people use reveals their values, you can adjust your own language when you're speaking with someone in order to connect more closely with their motivations and with how they think. Through the process of learning more about another person, you'll discover which of their values are toward and which are away from, and you can use that knowledge to leverage those values and become more persuasive.

For example, let's say you're a financial advisor and you know that your client has a toward value of "making lots of money." Rather than recommending a mutual fund that's safe and will offer low growth (which will fail to match the client's toward value), you could recommend a mutual fund that's a little riskier and is more likely to offer moderate-to-significant growth. Conversely, if you have a client with the away from value of "avoiding risk," you would recommend the more conservative fund, even if it meant the client would earn less money.

In 2013, researchers at the Motivation Science Center at Columbia University quantified this concept in a study of toward and away from values. They looked at people's motivational focus, and whether individuals saw opportunities as a way to advance (they called this a *promotion focus,* what we would call a toward value), or as a way to escape getting hurt and avoid change (they called this a *prevention focus*, what we would call an away from value).[31]

In the study, the researchers asked undergraduates to complete a questionnaire about their values in exchange for five dollars. Unbeknownst to the participants, this allowed the investigators to know whether they were motivated by a promotion focus (toward value) or a prevention focus (away from value). When they were finished, each participant was told that, in addition to the five dollars, they could choose a gift—either a logo-embossed Columbia mug or a disposable Bic pen. Some participants were asked to make their choice by thinking about what they would *gain* by choosing the mug and what they would

31 Heidi Grant, "How to Get Customers to Value Your Product More," ***Harvard Business Review*** (May 1, 2013). Available online: https://hbr.org/2013/05/how-to-get-customers-to-value-you

gain by choosing the pen. In contrast, other participants were asked to consider what they would *lose* by not choosing the mug and what they would *lose* by not choosing the pen. Seems like an obvious choice, right? The participants thought so too, and everyone chose the mug.

After the undergraduates decided on their gift, the researchers asked them, "What do you think is the price of the mug?" Findings showed that the participants perceived the mug to be more expensive when the language the researchers had used in asking them to make their choice matched that participant's value. "Toward value" individuals perceived gains as having more worth, while "away from value" individuals perceived the avoidance of loss as having more worth.

The critical takeaway from this research is that when the language matched a person's value, that person's perception of the cost of the mug *always* increased.[32] This study demonstrated that when we align our offering with someone's toward or away from values, the worth they attribute to that offering increases, which in turn enhances our persuasiveness. To align your offering with a person's values, you must first understand the intricacies of their values and their beliefs, then consider how to frame and position your offering accordingly.

Key Concept:
Remember that beliefs and values are a part of a person's model of the world and are the "Why?" behind what drives their behavior. What you have to offer will either be in alignment with their current model or will conflict with it, depending on how you frame it.

WHEN VALUES COLLIDE

The things you believe and the things you value are determined by various sources—parents, peers, authority figures, society, and so on. As you move through life, what you believe and what you value will be continually shaped and refined based on your personal relationships, life events, evolving emotional intelligence, travel, work experiences, and exposure to different people, ideas, and situations.

---

32 Grant, "How to Get Customers to Value Your Product More." Available online: https://hbr.org/2013/05/how-to-get-customers-to-value-you

The result of this is that everybody possesses their own unique blend of toward values and away from values—and sometimes, these values conflict. When this happens in the context of goal setting, a person may feel paralyzed or stuck because their values are working against each other.

Remember!
Remember our earlier discussion of criteria? Each value has a set of criteria for its fulfillment. When we talk about values that are potentially conflicting, it's also worth considering whether there is conflict within the criteria for each value.

I had a client once, let's call him Andreas, who came to see me because he went up in an airplane to skydive several times, and each time he failed to have the courage to jump. Andreas was looking for personal coaching, thinking that what he needed was simply more confidence to jump out of the airplane. What we discovered, though, was that Andreas had a conflict in his values and criteria. Andreas valued safety and he also valued adventure. We worked together to help him reorder and realign his criteria, so that Andreas was able to get himself up in the airplane and actually jump. To do this, I ensured that his criteria for *safety* and *adventure* were in alignment by focusing on the safety measures that were put in place by the company offering the skydiving adventure. Initially, Andreas had conflicting criteria that put him in a state of paralysis. Once he was able to see that the two criteria were complementary, Andreas succeeded in accomplishing his goal.

You've likely experienced a values conflict at some point yourself. Some of the more common ones include:

- **Success versus failure**: you want to be successful, and you're terrified of failure, so you do nothing at all.
- **Intimacy versus avoidance of emotional pain**: you want a romantic relationship because you value intimacy and, at the same time, you're afraid of getting hurt.
- **Responsibility versus freedom**: you want a full-time, high-powered job as well as the ability to take days off and have fun whenever you feel like it.

- **Feedback versus criticism**: you like the feedback of your team and are simultaneously uncomfortable with criticism.
- **Fame versus privacy**: you want the glory of being famous or well-known, yet you value your privacy and detest the thought of being regularly torn apart by the media.

When you encounter a values conflict, look carefully at what you value, and at your criteria and belief systems. Your values serve as an internal navigation system, so when you're cognizant of what you value and why you value it, you can make better and more congruent choices in your life. In doing so, you will be drawn toward people, ideas, and situations that support and assist you as you achieve your goals. If you happen to identify a values conflict, examine your criteria and work to realign them with your values.

As we've been discussing, part of understanding another person's model of the world is first identifying their beliefs and values, including their criteria. This understanding will give you insight into how that person thinks, feels, and behaves as well as what is most likely to motivate and persuade them. Taken together, this knowledge and understanding can guide you as you design an effective and persuasive approach to influence them in the most meaningful way.

How do you do this?

It would be nice if you could simply walk up to a person and say, "I'd like to know what your model of the world looks like. What are your beliefs, values, and criteria, and how do you make sense of the world?" Obviously, if you tried that you might get some strange looks! There's another way to discover a person's model of the world, though, and that involves simply engaging them in a conversation.

In order to learn about a person's beliefs, values, and criteria in a conversation, you need to ask insightful and strategic questions and listen carefully to the responses. Your goal is to remain in a state of curiosity and to learn everything you can about how they think, store information, and process the world. Then you'll be equipped to interact in a way that is most meaningful to them, providing them with the experience of being listened to and understood.

Remember the example about money as a means or an ends value? Think about one thing you value and why it is of value to you. Asking yourself "Why?" is important here because it creates leverage; when the "Why?" is compelling enough, it can empower us to navigate obstacles creatively and resourcefully. Is the value for the thing itself (an ends value)? Or is it a means value, something you value because it will lead you to something else?

Think of your children, friends, family, and coworkers. Choose one person in your life whom you'd like to persuade. What kinds of questions could you ask to uncover their values and the fulfilment criteria they have in place? What have you discovered that is important to them and why?

Chapter Three

Can You Trust Your Mind?

> Brains aren't designed to get results; they go in directions. If you know how the brain works, you can set your own direction. If you don't, then someone else will.
>
> —RICHARD BANDLER

Think back for a moment to your childhood and go way back to Bear Country. Do you remember Mama Bear, Papa Bear, Sister Bear, and Brother Bear? Now ask yourself: Were they the *Berenstain* Bears or the *Berenstein* Bears? Because although no one has been able to turn up any photos or copies of a book in which the name was spelled Berenstein, the number of people who are *certain* this is the correct spelling (not Berenstain) is staggering.[33]

What about Bugs Bunny, Daffy Duck, Tweety Bird, and Sylvester? Were they a part of Looney *Tunes* or Looney *Toons*? The correct title is Looney *Tunes*, and yet curiously enough an astonishing number of people remember it spelled "Toons."[34] However strong their memories, it is entirely possible that thousands of people have simply mixed up the spelling of the Berenstain Bears and Looney Tunes. You'll find many such individuals on a dedicated subreddit called r/MandelaEffect, where people with false memories can share their experiences.

A more curious example, though, is the confusion around the 1990s movie *Shazaam*—a film about a genie (played by comedian David Adkins, better known as Sinbad) who helps two young children with a lonely dad. While it seems a likely movie plot from the '90s, the strange thing about this film is that *its existence is a complete fabrication*—even though thousands upon thousands of

---

33 Amelia Tait, "The movie that doesn't exist and the Redditors who think it does," ***NewStatesman*** (December 21, 2016). Available online: https://www.newstatesman.com/science-tech/internet/2016/12/movie-doesn-t-exist-and-redditors-who-think-it-does

34 Fiona Broome, "Looney Tunes or Looney Toons," ***Mandela Effect*** (January 20, 2016). Available online: http://mandelaeffect.com/looney-tunes-or-looney-toons/

people who haven't met each other have vivid, shared memories of the movie and can recount the same specific details about it.

Are people confusing this movie with *Kazaam*, a 1996 film in which a genie, played by Shaquille O'Neal, helps a boy reconnect with his father? Redditors who believe there was a movie titled *Shazaam* are skeptical of the *Kazaam* confusion as an explanation. They're *certain* this movie exists although evidence of it is entirely absent.[35]

What's going on in people's memories here?

In 1957, American linguist and philosopher Noam Chomsky published *Syntactic Structures*, a seminal book on transformational grammar, which later became a cornerstone of linguistics. **Transformational grammar** focuses on how people modify the information that they gather in order to communicate better—in other words, how they delete, distort, and generalize information.

This innate tendency of the human mind impacts the way we process existing memories, beliefs, and expectations. If, for example, you "know" that people have a low opinion of you, your mind will interpret all kinds of non-offensive words and actions as being slights or slams, thus "proving" that people look down on you.

Henry Roediger, a professor at the Washington University Memory Lab, shares his view on the *Shazaam* phenomenon: "Lots of people remember detailed, but utterly false, memories. In fact, we all have them."[36] Roediger explains that one person's memory influences another person's, and so false memories can spread this way, like a virus. He calls this phenomenon *memory conformity* and believes it is the cause of the collective false memories about the non-existent movie *Shazaam*.[37] These innocent and inconsequential examples show how prevalent collective false memories are and they give us a good reason to pause before accepting collective memories as truth.

As individuals, we're also prone to false memories. Elizabeth Loftus, a professor of psychology and law at the University of California, explores the

---

35 Tait, "The movie that doesn't exist and the Redditors who think it does." Available online: https://www.newstatesman.com/science-tech/internet/2016/12/movie-doesn-t-exist-and-redditors-who-think-it-does

36 Tait, "The movie that doesn't exist and the Redditors who think it does." Available online: https://www.newstatesman.com/science-tech/internet/2016/12/movie-doesn-t-exist-and-redditors-who-think-it-does

37 Tait, "The movie that doesn't exist and the Redditors who think it does." Available online: https://www.newstatesman.com/science-tech/internet/2016/12/movie-doesn-t-exist-and-redditors-who-think-it-does

unreliability of our memories in her TED Talk, "How Reliable is Your Memory?"[38] Loftus shares the story of Steve Titus: one evening in October 1980, Titus was driving with his fiancée when he was pulled over by police. A woman had been assaulted in the area, and her assailant matched Titus's description and drove the same make and model car. Titus vehemently denied accusations that he had assaulted the woman, insisting he was innocent.

When the woman was first shown a photo of Titus in a lineup, she said that he *could* be the assailant, yet during the trial she told the jury that she was *certain* it was Titus who had assaulted her. Titus was convicted of the crime on the strength of her memory, and—although his conviction was eventually overturned—the stress of the experience and the negative impact on his life caused him to suffer a fatal stress-induced heart attack in his mid-thirties.

According to Loftus, stories of false memories leading to convictions are more common than we'd like to think. Over 300 individuals in the United States who were wrongly convicted of crimes have been exonerated due to new DNA evidence. Of these 300 people, three-quarters were convicted due to faulty eyewitness memories. In Canada, it's believed that faulty eyewitness memories are a contributing cause in approximately 70% of the convictions that have been overturned because of DNA testing.[39]

Why is this? How can so many eyewitnesses be wrong?

Loftus says that "many people believe memories work like a recording device, you just record the information, then you call it up and play it back when you want to answer questions or identify images."[40] In fact, this is false. Decades of work in psychology have proven that memories are both constructive and reconstructive. "Memory works a little more like a Wikipedia page," Loftus says." You can go in there and change it, but so can other people."

Are our memories pliable? Well, let's consider hypnosis, a state in which the power of the imagination is amplified. Just as a facilitator can use questions to cleanly elicit historical memories, they can also use **presuppositions** (ideas

---

38 Elizabeth Loftus, "How reliable is your memory?" ***TED Radio Hour*** Podcast/***NPR*** (October 13, 2017). Available online: https://www.npr.org/2017/10/13/557424726/elizabeth-loftus-how-can-our-memories-be-manipulated

39 "Causes of Wrongful Convictions," ***Innocence Canada***. Available online: https://www.innocencecanada.com/causes-of-wrongful-convictions/

40 Loftus, "How reliable is your memory?" Available online: https://www.npr.org/2017/10/13/557424726/elizabeth-loftus-how-can-our-memories-be-manipulated

or statements taken for granted and accepted as true) to intentionally, or even unintentionally, install false memories. While memory recall under hypnosis has been done successfully, there are also examples of people who have created false memories, which is why it's important to understand the power of presuppositions.

Memory creation, whether "eyewitness" or under hypnosis, is often a result of presuppositions that are intentionally or unintentionally used in our language. For example, if someone believes in past lives, then using *presupposing language* under hypnosis can encourage the mind to imagine something that never happened.

Be cautious of using presuppositions in everyday language, as well. For example, think about the difference between "How fast was the car going when it crashed into the other car?" and "What speed was the car doing when it bumped into the other car?" You're likely to get a wide range of answers based on the presuppositions found in the questions. In the first example, "fast" and "crashed" are the two primer words that presuppose higher speeds. In the second example—"What speed was the car doing when it bumped into the other car?"—"speed" is more neutral and "bumped" presupposes a low-speed impact.

As you can see, the mind is easily influenced by others—and by itself. In addition to being open to presuppositions, our minds regularly delete information and create distortions and generalizations by changing things and "filling in the blanks" when information is lacking.

Go ahead and read the following paragraph quickly:

> Aoccdrnig to rscheearch at an Elingsh uinervtisy, it deosn't mttaer in waht oredr the ltteers in a wrod are, olny taht the frist and lsat ltteres are at the rghit pcleas. The rset can be a toatl mses and you can sitll raed it wouthit a porbelm. Tihs is bcusease we do not raed ervey lteter by ilstef, but the wrod as a wlohe.[41]

41 Yoram (Jerry) R. Wind and Colin Cook, *The Power of Impossible Thinking: Transform the Business of Your Life and the Life of Your Business* (Wharton School Press, 2004), p. 9.

Did you notice that when you read quickly, even though the words are misspelled, the paragraph is easy to decipher? When information is missing or confusing, the mind generalizes based on past experiences, in this case, based on your experience about how certain letters combine to make an expected word.

It's critical to evaluate what exactly our mind is doing in these circumstances. Are we presupposing, filling in blanks, deleting certain things, distorting others, generalizing, or imagining something that was close to what happened but which, in fact, never happened at all?

SHIFTING FROM THE UNCONSCIOUS MIND TO THE CONSCIOUS MIND

Does the mind *really* distort information? Absolutely. It deletes information, too. In the following sections we'll take a closer look at how the mind filters: that is, how it deletes, distorts, and generalizes information.

First, here's a little test: You've probably seen a lot of movies over the last decade. Name them all.

If that's too tough, name half, a quarter, or even a tenth of them.

Unless you have a photographic memory, you'll probably have difficulty with this task. It is likely, though, that you can quite easily name and vividly recall scenes from a favorite movie you saw one, five, ten, or even thirty years ago. This is an example of your deleting mind at work.

While the human mind is able to process a seemingly infinite amount of information at the subconscious level, it appears to be limited to processing between five and nine (seven, plus or minus two) chunks of information at the conscious level at any given moment in time.[42] Throughout this book, we'll use the terms subconscious mind and unconscious mind interchangeably.

---

42 George A. Miller, "The Magical Number Seven, Plus or Minus Two: Some Limits on Our Capacity for Processing Information," *Psychological Review* 101:2 (1994), pp. 343-352.

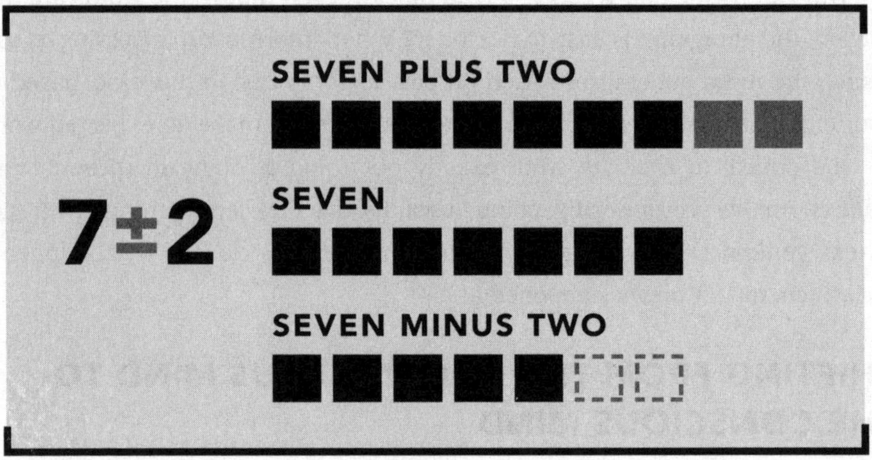

The unconscious mind stores all your experiences and memories like a virtual filing cabinet and can make you aware of them by moving them from storage (your unconscious) into your conscious thoughts based on relevance. The conscious mind would be overwhelmed if it attempted to juggle all the information available to it at the unconscious level. The information that you focus on at a conscious level depends on the context you're in and what's most relevant to you at that point in time. Other people can also guide your conscious mind to focus on things that were previously outside of your awareness. For example, until I mention your feet inside your shoes, you're probably unaware of how your feet feel right now. Notice where your attention goes, though, when I mention your feet. Whether you're wearing shoes or not, your feet have now popped into your conscious awareness, haven't they? In addition, have you ever wondered whether you are right or left toe dominant? Notice, did you wiggle your toes as part of even contemplating that question? Which toe did you test—it was likely your big toe, wasn't it?

Although you might expect this focus to be strictly objective, the unconscious mind is very selective and subjective. The subconscious mind alters much of the information it receives to conform to our existing beliefs, values, ideas, previous experiences, and expectations, before passing the information on to the conscious mind. In other words, every sight, sound, smell, and other sensation entering the unconscious mind is "checked" to see how it can be filtered into our existing perception of reality.

A moment ago, I gave you a suggestion that led you to be consciously aware of your feet. What if someone made a suggestion that was contrary to your best interest, though? Thankfully, the human mind has a built-in protective mechanism known as the **critical faculty**. The critical faculty acts as the gatekeeper of the unconscious mind: its role is to determine what suggestions may bypass the conscious mind to enter the unconscious. Information is continuously moving back and forth from the unconscious to the conscious, or from the conscious to the unconscious. Your critical faculty is the filter that determines which suggestions and information are acceptable and allowed through to the unconscious mind or are rejected and blocked from the unconscious. External suggestions you receive can easily bypass your conscious mind and move into the unconscious, so long as they are in alignment with your morals, beliefs, ethics, and standards.

For example, if someone were to give you a suggestion that violated your morals, beliefs, ethics, or standards (like, say, robbing a bank), your critical faculty would block that suggestion, enabling you to critically evaluate it and accept or reject it based on your purposeful evaluation. The information or suggestions that are accepted based on this evaluation would move to the unconscious mind, being allowed through by your critical faculty. In this way, the critical faculty acts like a defense mechanism, or guard, for your unconscious mind. The **Reticular Activating System** (RAS), on the other hand, is the attention center of the brain. The RAS is a primitive part of the brain that determines what you pay attention to in the outside world based on what's relevant to you in your inside world.

These concepts are quite simple when you understand the nature of the conscious and the unconscious mind: information continuously flows back and forth between the two depending on relevance, and the conscious mind holds a limited amount of information (7 ± 2 chunks) at any moment in time.

Isn't it amazing that your mind does all of this almost instantaneously? We are indeed wonderfully and marvelously designed!

THE POWER OF RELEVANCE

Now think again about what you consider to be important, what you value… your mind filters for things that relate to those values. When an idea or a piece of information is or becomes relevant to you, your mind will then scan the environment around you for any and all pertinent or related information. For example, imagine that you were going to buy a new car. What make and model would it be? You're more likely to start noticing that make and model of car in different colors on the road now because it's become relevant to you, even though those cars were there before.

When I speak of the filtering mind, Natalie often thinks of an experience she had when she first learned the Danish word "*hygge*," which refers to a mindset that helps people embrace the dark, winter months by celebrating being cozy, comfortable, and content, often through restorative time spent indoors. As soon as Natalie learned this word, she began seeing it in advertisements and stores as brands like Chapters/Indigo and Lululemon sold *hygge*-related products. Natalie also began to hear people saying things like, "that's so *hygge*." Was Natalie ahead of the trend? It's more likely that once the word *hygge* became relevant to her, her mind started filtering differently, and she noticed the word, even though it was there all along.

As you can see, new data is constantly being combined with existing information that is already stored in your mind. It is filtered from your unconscious through to the conscious mind to continually strengthen your beliefs, values, and ideas—your own understanding, which is your model of the world. This process is the reason that everyone views and understands the world in a unique way.

> **Key Concept:**
> The mind is much more than an impartial observer. It's constantly filtering information by deleting, distorting, and generalizing based on a number of factors including a person's existing beliefs and values, previous experiences, and expectations.

SPOT THE GORILLA

What's interesting is that the mind deletes more than just the minutiae of our everyday existence. It can delete important—even startling—information and prevent it from reaching the conscious mind though you may be staring right at it.

Consider where motorcycle accidents occur. Do you think more accidents happen where there are *more* motorcycles or where there are *fewer* motorcycles?

In fact, there are more motorcycle accidents in areas where there are fewer motorcycles simply because motorcycles are less expected there. When your mind deletes something that is actually there it's known as a **negative hallucination**; in other words, the brain can cause your eyes to fail to see something that is, in fact, right there. The phenomenon is sometimes also called "inattentional blindness" or "perceptual blindness," yet I find these terms to be limiting, as they refer to only one sense—vision. I find "negative hallucination" to be more accurate, as this phenomenon can involve one, some, or all of the senses.

Negative hallucination was brilliantly illustrated by a pair of Harvard researchers, Daniel Simons and Christopher Chabris, in the late 1990s. They recruited six students to play basketball, dividing them into two teams of three. One group wore white shirts, the other black shirts. Each team was given a basketball and instructed to pass it only to their teammates, while dribbling and weaving through the other team and jockeying for position. The researchers then videotaped this exercise, which lasted less than a minute.[43]

The video was then shown to numerous other students who were asked to count the number of times the players in the white shirts passed the ball to each other. The viewers had to pay close attention, as the teams were in constant motion.

While many of the students correctly counted the number of passes made by the team in the white shirts, *half* of them failed to notice that a gorilla walked straight through the group of basketball players in the middle of the game, stopping center stage to thump its chest before moving off screen!

It was, in fact, a student dressed up as a life-sized gorilla, covered with dark hair from head to toe and, under normal circumstances, impossible to overlook. Yet half the viewers missed it entirely. When they viewed the video a second

---

43 Daniel J. Simons and Christopher F. Chabris, "Gorillas in Our Midst: Sustained Inattentional Blindness for Dynamic Events," *Perception* 28 (1999), pp. 1059-1074.

time—just watching rather than counting passes—most were astonished that they had missed "seeing" the gorilla the first time.

The truth was their eyes *had* seen the gorilla, yet their minds had essentially "erased" it, another example of a negative hallucination. Indeed, each person's mind was functioning exactly as it should: it focused on the task at hand and deleted all its conscious memory of what it considered to be irrelevant information.

In this case, the unconscious mind was operating under guidance from the conscious mind about what was important in the moment, and it decided that the appearance of the gorilla was secondary to the number of passes by the white-shirt team. So, the unconscious mind prevented the gorilla from moving to the conscious mind, thus creating a negative hallucination.[44]

In this context, a negative hallucination is when the mind takes something that is there and deletes it (by contrast, a positive hallucination is when you vividly imagine that something exists when in actuality it is absent, and you respond to that imagination as though it's real). In the case of the gorilla, the mind created a negative hallucination because of the specific instructions that were given in the experiment.

> **TIP**
>
> Have you noticed analogue marking in this book? Pay attention to the analogue marking moving forward!

In the original Harvard experiment, 50% of the participants saw the gorilla and 50% missed it entirely. I decided to replicate the experiment, with changes to one thing—the way the instructions were delivered. As a persuader, I wondered how easy it would be to increase the number of viewers who deleted the gorilla by refining the way I delivered the instructions in my presentations. By leveraging **analogue marking** (which is a way of telling a person's unconscious mind, "This is important, so pay attention!"), I was able to significantly increase the number of people who deleted the gorilla.

---

44 Daniel Simons, "Selective Attention Test," YouTube (uploaded March 10, 2010). Available online: http://www.youtube.com/watch?v=vJG698U2Mvo

Here are the instructions that I used—pay attention to the analogue marking:

> This is an experiment that was done at Harvard University by Dr. Daniel Simons and his team. It's a counting experiment where men typically fare differently than women. There are two teams with three people on each team. Three of the players are wearing black shirts and three are wearing white shirts. Each team is passing a basketball between themselves. It's important to ***ignore the black team*** and ***go ahead and focus on the white team***. As you ***focus on the white team,*** your task is to ***count the number of passes that the white-shirted players make between each other.*** There are two types of passes: bounce passes and direct passes. You want to ignore the dribbles and just go ahead and ***count the number of bounce passes, direct passes, and total passes that the white-shirted players make between each other***. The ball is right here (as I point to it on the screen). Ignore the first catch and count from there. Ready?

By changing the instructions in this way, I changed the emphasis and actively guided participants as to what to focus on, engaging their filters at an unconscious level. These instructions dramatically increase the likelihood of the mind deleting anything black and filtering in everything that is white instead, resulting in 95–98% of participants deleting the gorilla.

> **Key Concept:** Although we believe that we think things through carefully and objectively, the truth is that most of our thoughts, feelings, and behaviors are based on deleted, distorted, and generalized information.

Aren't hallucinations, either positive or negative, fascinating phenomena? I heard a story once about a positive hallucination that Dave Elman, a noted hypnotist and radio host, experienced. Elman conducted a thought experiment on himself where he used his vivid imagination to create a pet polar bear. He imagined that the polar bear followed him around all the time and eventually, because his imagination was so vivid, he tricked his mind into thinking the bear was real. When Elman stopped the experiment, he became delusional, feeling very concerned about the absent polar bear. This concern, although delusional, was understandable when you consider that the polar bear had become a part of Elman's reality.

In addition to deleting and distorting incoming information based on what it deems important in the moment, the mind creates **generalizations** to construct a larger or more detailed story based on a few pieces of information—which may have already been distorted. Most of us are familiar with generalizations, and often these generalizations lead us to make assumptions, or to pigeonhole people and situations. For example, we may believe a group of teenagers are "up to no good," or that a senior behind the wheel is a "slow driver."

> An average human looks without seeing, listens without hearing, touches without feeling, eats without tasting, moves without physical awareness, inhales without awareness of odor or fragrance, and talks without thinking.
>
> –LEONARDO DA VINCI

Take a moment to consider some of the details you've observed today and record them as in the examples in the chart below. For each example you have identified, consider what's priming your mind to filter these details. Record the existing beliefs, values, experiences, or expectations that are at work. Then, consider the connection between your Current State and how your mind is filtering information.

What's priming your mind to filter this detail? Think about existing beliefs, values, experiences, or expectations	What's Your Current State?	What Have You Observed?
A neighbor recently told you they are adopting a dog.	You're experiencing a state of curiosity as you wonder what the new dog will be like.	You noticed a different neighbor walking their dog this morning.
You injured your knee playing soccer last week and are waiting for test results to come back to see if you'll need to have surgery.	You're feeling nervous about the test results and anxious about the unknown—will you be able to run like you used to?	You noticed a lot of people jogging this morning.

Chapter Four

Igniting Motivation

> The world is a very puzzling place. If you're not willing to be puzzled, you just become a replica of someone else's mind.
>
> –NOAM CHOMSKY

So far, we've discussed the different ways in which our minds delete, distort, and generalize information. Yet in order to move toward the Desired State, we must also understand the ways in which we are motivated.

Brothers Chip and Dan Heath have written and spoken extensively about how motivation works and how leaders use motivation to effectively solve problems. In 2017, Dan Heath shared a story about Microsoft's Scott Guthrie in his YouTube video *Tripping Over the Truth*.[45] Back in 2011, Guthrie had been tasked with leading the company's cloud-computing service, Azure. According to Heath, when Guthrie and his team interviewed customers about Azure, they consistently received the same feedback: "It's great technology but it's really hard to use." In the video, Heath then pauses his story to ask the audience an important question: "If you're Guthrie, how do you get your people to take that seriously? How do you avoid explaining to them, and get them to trip over this truth?"

How do you think Guthrie did it?

Rather than explaining the usability issues to the company's developers who might be apathetic and think the problems were with the users themselves rather than with the program or their code, Guthrie took the developers off-site and asked them to "build an app with Azure, the same way that customers have to." The developers struggled. "Some of them couldn't even figure out

45 Dan Heath. *Tripping over the Truth*. YouTube (uploaded October 5, 2017). Available online: https://www.youtube.com/watch?v=KZ_N77OquQA

how to log in," Heath says, adding that Guthrie later told a reporter, "It was a complete disaster." Although the challenge itself was a disaster, the experience was extremely motivational for Guthrie's team. Struggling first-hand in the same way customers did, helped the developers clearly "see what the problem was, and they all committed to overhauling Azure to make it more customer friendly," Heath says.

Like the developers in this story, we all have moments where we're unconvinced and therefore unmotivated to do what needs to be done. At these times, it's useful to reflect upon what motivates both us and others to create, act, change, or otherwise do what's necessary.

When we think about the factors that motivate us, we can generally divide them into two categories: motivational traits and working traits. For our purposes, we'll focus on **motivational traits**, also called motivational factors or triggers. Included in these motivational factors are:

- Internal and External
- Toward and Away From
- Options and Procedures
- Sameness and Difference

To identify a person's motivational factors, pay attention to their language patterns, which give clues as to their underlying motivations. When we understand the factors that motivate people at a deeper level, we can then adjust our language, which ultimately enhances our ability to influence them. In this chapter we'll explore some of these motivational factors, identify how we can recognize them, and discuss how to adjust our communication based on this awareness.

First, a word of advice regarding nominalizations, which we discussed in Chapter Two. In our day-to-day language we often treat "motivation" as an abstract noun—a static thing that is relatively fixed. When we instead use "motivation" as a verb, recognizing that it is a process that is easily changed, then we're priming our brain for success.

Second, keep in mind that as individuals, each of us is motivated in our own unique ways depending on the context. While it's important to recognize that some people may lean toward one motivational factor over another, in different contexts they are likely to be influenced by different motivational triggers. Hence, it's useful to avoid thinking about motivational factors as something that people "have." Rather than nominalizing the idea of motivation, think of the concept as a verb. Ask yourself, "In what ways am I thinking that generate a state of motivation or trigger a state of procrastination?" Always remember that the ways in which we are motivated are likely to vary depending on many different factors.

WHY THIS MOTIVATION, NOW?

We've already said that motivational tendencies are context dependent. In addition, many of the factors that motivate a person are typically working outside of conscious awareness. How, then, can we know what motivates an individual at any given time? As we've been emphasizing throughout, pay attention to their language and ask questions in order to better understand what actually motivates them.

A person's language patterns can give us essential clues about their underlying motivation. If we miss the significance of these details in their communication, or fail to adjust our language to match theirs, the opportunity to trigger their motivation eludes us like the invisible gorilla in Daniel Simons's experiment. For this reason, when we desire to motivate someone, it's important to consciously adjust our language patterns to match what's relevant and motivating to them.[46]

Key Concept: Each of us experiences different motivational triggers in different contexts, and these factors themselves are neither positive nor negative. Each is equally useful depending on the situation.

INTERNAL AND EXTERNAL MOTIVATIONAL FACTORS

We know that, as human beings, we are influenced by various factors that motivate us. The first factor we're going to consider is **internal motivation** versus **external motivation**. And as we just discussed, *how* we are motivated can

46 Dan Mariani and Natalie Sarlo-McGarvey, "The Power of Unconscious Communication," *Canadian Pharmaceutical Marketing* (December 2004), p. 30.

change at any given time depending on our Current State, which includes factors like our environmental context, our experiences to date, and our expectations.

When your source of motivation is internal, you tend to react or make choices based on what *you* already know, think, feel, or believe. You rely on your own internal standards, values, criteria, beliefs, and so on, to make decisions. While you might investigate expert opinions or check other trusted sources of information, such as your friends or family, ultimately it is you who decides what that information means and how you will apply it. In other words, when you are internally motivated, you decide whether you'll act based on an expert's opinion or whether that opinion is just another piece of advice or data to mix in with the rest.

If you are someone who is driven by an internal source of motivation, you'll often resist being told what to do. Indeed, if someone tells you to do something, you may take that instruction as just another piece of information, rather than as an instruction. Overall, you decide for yourself how you will respond to the information you receive.

Alternatively, if you are externally motivated, you tend to react or make decisions based on other peoples' opinions, outside direction, or external sources of feedback. You may be eager to get information and opinions from others—whether friends, experts, or celebrity endorsers—and you tend to treat the information and opinions almost as an instruction. In fact, when you are motivated by external sources, you often look forward to being guided and wish someone would help you decide because you may feel uncomfortable making the decision on you own.

For example, celebrity athlete Michael Jordan has endorsed many brands like Hanes and Nike over the years. Even if you personally put little stock in his opinions, it's likely that you heard about or knew of someone who rushed out to buy his latest Air Jordan sneakers the second they hit the shelves. Like kids who believe they'll shoot hoops like MJ just by wearing his endorsed shoes, if you are externally motivated, you are driven by someone else's opinion or endorsement of something.

Remember those Microsoft software developers? It's likely that initially they were internal with regard to their work, believing that Azure was straightforward to use. Once they were put in the position of an end user, they went more external as they recognized the need to incorporate customer feedback after struggling themselves. This led the developers to identify creative ways to enhance the functionality of their code, resulting in a more user-friendly program.

Understanding whether you or another person is influenced by internal or external sources of motivation in any given context is an important part of the process of persuasion. Suppose you're selling a home water purifier to a person who is motivated by external sources when purchasing items for the home. You might tell them what other clients think about the purifier, refer to its positive ratings, and point to quotes from authorities. You could say things like: "Studies show…"; "Research indicates…"; "Nine out of ten customers surveyed recommend…"; "Most people in your situation decide to…"; or "In my professional opinion you would benefit from…"

This approach would backfire, though, with a person who is internally motivated. A better approach with this person would be to say things such as, "Test it yourself and see what you think," "You're the only one who can decide," or "You can see for yourself."

TIP Beware of Assumptions! **Ask Questions Instead.**

Remember that what motivates us in any given situation is either internal or based on external sources. The simplest way to determine if a person is guided by internal or external sources of motivation is to ask a question such as "How would you know that this product is right for you?" or "How do you know you did a good job on that project?" If the person replies, "I'll just know," or gives you criteria specific to them, you can tell that their motivation is internal. On the other hand, if the person says, "My friend suggested it" or "I received positive feedback from my boss," you can assume that in this instance their source of motivation is external.

Beware of making assumptions based on your observations alone, though! If you see a customer holding a copy of a "Consumer Guide" article rating water purifiers, or a printout of "Yelp" reviews, you know that they're considering external opinions as part of their research. This may mean *either* that their source of motivation at that moment is external *or* that a person who is internally motivated is collecting relevant information as part of their research before deciding for themselves.

The point here is that even if you think you know, still ask questions! The specific language people use to answer you will give strong clues to help you identify how they're thinking.

TOWARD AND AWAY FROM MOTIVATIONAL FACTORS

Do you follow traffic laws while driving because doing so makes everyone safer, or because you want to avoid getting a ticket? Are you driven by what you can gain, attain, achieve, or get? Or is what gets you moving a desire to avoid, eliminate, prevent, or get away from certain people, problems, and/or situations?

In other words, are you generally motivated by *toward* or *away from* situations and circumstances?

When you're motivated by a **toward orientation** or **motivation**, you want to attain something or achieve an objective and you focus on goals, outcomes, and rewards—things you move toward. You're more likely to pay a bill early if you get a discount for doing so, rather than out of fear of being penalized if you're late. Having a toward motivation, you recognize opportunities rather than identifying pitfalls or problems. Sometimes, you may come across as being unrealistic or blind to potential problems because you are so focused on what you want. In extreme cases, you may run into trouble because you fail to consider the things that might go wrong or should be avoided.

In contrast, if you're driven by an **away from motivation** you tend to focus on what needs to be avoided or eliminated, and you're concerned with the threat of consequences or punishment. Generally, you're more likely to pay a bill early to avoid being penalized. Having an away from motivation, you are better at recognizing potential problems than identifying opportunities, and you're motivated to solve problems and to fix what's going wrong. For example, you may search for a new job only when your current position is unbearable. While you are likely adept at problem-solving, you may at times focus too much on the current problem, losing sight of the overall objective or goal. You may also sometimes come across as being negative or pessimistic.

Traditional Eastern medicine is a great example of a toward orientation: people go to the doctor to discover how to stay healthy. They go even when they are feeling great, so they can learn to do more things to maintain their health. Compare this with Western medicine, which has an away from orientation. Rather than going to a Western physician when they are healthy, people often wait until they are sick, then have the doctor treat their illness.

In an article Natalie co-wrote for *Canadian Pharmaceutical Marketing*, she reported that in work situations, 40% of the population has a more toward motivation, 40% has a more away from motivation, and the remaining 20% experience a combination of the two.[47] It's worth noting that people with these different motivational traits have the potential to complement or clash with each other in the workplace. Success comes through appreciating each other's differences and leveraging them toward a common goal.

You can determine which of these two factors motivates a person by asking neutral questions. For example, you might ask an acquaintance, "I hear you're going on vacation—where to?" If they respond, "I'm going to the Bahamas to lie on the beach, soak up the sun, and relax for a while," they're experiencing a toward motivation. If they say, "I asked my travel agent to help me escape the cold, and they recommended Croatia as a great destination to get away from the frigid temperatures," they're experiencing an away from motivation.

OPTIONS AND PROCEDURES MOTIVATIONAL FACTORS

People who are **options-oriented** are motivated by choice and generally focus on possibilities, variations, and alternative ways of accomplishing things. If you're motivated by options, you probably enjoy designing, developing, and creating. While you're good at coming up with ideas and setting projects in motion, you may sometimes struggle with executing the procedures required to keep those projects going. When required to follow procedure, you likely prefer to change and adjust it as you go. Rather than seeing a right or a wrong way

47 Mariani and Sarlo-McGarvey, "The Power of Unconscious Communication," pp. 29-30.

of doing things, you consider a number of possible ways.[48] You may also be inclined to chase one exciting option after another, tempted to move on to other things before you finish what you've started. Basically, you like to break the rules once in a while.

In contrast, if you are motivated by **procedures**, you typically believe there is "a right way" to do something. You have a keen interest in the "how," yet may overlook "why" something is being done. In other words, you tend to focus on the process rather than the bigger picture. You are likely compelled to finish what has been started and may at times resist options so strongly that you miss a better plan, choice, or outcome. Health-care professionals may be particularly motivated by processes.

In the same article for *Canadian Pharmaceutical Marketing* mentioned above, Natalie and her co-author reported that in the work environment, 40 % of the population is more options-oriented, 40 % is more procedures-oriented and the remaining 20 % tend to be a combination of both.[49]

You can determine this motivational style (in yourself or others) by asking the following question: "Why did you choose your current work situation?" Individuals who tend to be motivated by processes will unconsciously delete the "Why?" in the question and replace it with "How?" If you answer the question by telling a story or describing an event from start to finish, you are probably more motivated by procedures within the work environment.

I once counselled a family where the father was strongly procedures-oriented, while the teenage son was strongly options-oriented. The son understood this as soon as I explained it to them, while the father kept denying it. "No, no, no," he scoffed. "This is nonsense."

A few weeks later father and son were having difficulty communicating, and the father called me. He got my answering machine and began leaving a detailed message: "This is Frank. The first thing I would like to discuss is the difficulty my son, Aaron, and I are having communicating. The second thing I want to discuss is this issue of the school dance, which is in one month. The third thing I want to discuss is…" He didn't finish. My answering machine cut him off!

---

48 Mariani and Sarlo-McGarvey, "The Power of Unconscious Communication," pp. 29-30.

49 Dan Mariani and Natalie Sarlo-McGarvey, "You Can Influence Thoughts and Behaviour," *Canadian Pharmaceutical Marketing* (2004), p. 29.

So, Frank called back, started his message again from the beginning, and got cut off again at the same place.

It happened again a third time!

Then, when I hit the button to play Frank's fourth message, I was surprised to hear him begin by laughing: "Now I get it," he said. "I really am procedurally oriented, repeating the exact same message over and over even though I know your machine won't take it!"

By now you know that adjusting your language to help shift others toward the desired result is a highly effective persuasive technique. For example, someone motivated by procedures will likely be more engaged and respond more favorably when you say things such as, "There are a number of steps we can follow as we map out this process," or ask, "What's the first step we need to take?" and, "What's our plan from there?"

Individuals motivated by options, however, will be engaged when hearing communication such as, "Our choices are limitless, let's brainstorm the various possibilities," and questions like, "How many ways can we approach this?" and, "Is there a better way?"

Suppose your child is having some difficulty in school. If they're motivated by options with respect to school, it would be advantageous to engage them with language such as, "How many different ways do you think there are to improve your studying?" and "Would you prefer to study after school with Mr. Singh or at the enrichment center?"

If, on the other hand, your child is motivated by procedures, they would be more engaged when hearing, "What do you think the best plan is to improve your grades?" and "Where should we start?"

SAMENESS AND DIFFERENCE MOTIVATIONAL FACTORS

Next, let's look at **sameness** versus **difference** as motivational factors and how we can search for these traits in everyday situations. One of the best ways to determine if people are motivated to choose things that are more similar or more different is to take three or four different coins, spread them out on a table and ask them to comment on the *relationship* between the coins. Make specific note of the language in the answers you receive. We'll return to this example in just a moment.

In general, if you are motivated by **sameness**, you'll typically find value in continuity and comfort in maintaining consistency with respect to things like foods, clothes, friends, music, and other aspects of life. You may tend to resist change, which you feel is stressful and disruptive. Once you've settled into a project, you're happy to see it through as is, without feeling the need to change the plan just for the sake of it.

By contrast, if you are motivated by **differences**, you likely thrive on change and enjoy the process of creating. If things stay the same for too long, you'll find ways to shake them up just for the sake of change. You'll only follow the rules and procedures for a limited time before you begin searching for a different way of doing things. Your "nightmare" job would be one that requires you to do the same thing all day, every day.

Everyday scenarios can help you understand a person's sameness versus difference motivational preference. Remember those coins? Imagine putting them on a table and asking someone, "What's the relationship between these coins?" This is where you'll need to watch and listen very closely to the first thing their minds go to. What will they notice first?

Someone motivated by sameness might point out that they're all currency, they're all coins, all of them are silver, they're round, or they're all on the table, and so on. Their language emphasizes how the coins are similar and you would have to prod them to identify and talk about the differences.

A person motivated by differences might say things like, "This coin is smaller than the others," "They all have different dates," "They are worth different amounts," "Some are heads up and some are heads down," or otherwise focus on what *separates* one coin from the others.

I demonstrated this in a recent three-day communication excellence accreditation program that Natalie and I conducted for a small group of trainers from a multi-national corporation. I arranged three coins of different sizes and metals in front of a participant, placing one of the coins on a book while putting the other two coins on the desk, all at various distances from each other. Before I was able to even ask what the relationship between them was, the participant immediately moved the coin that was on the book down to the desk and lined up all three coins in a row. Can you guess his motivational tendency?

Let's look at another example: historically the nature of an administrative assistant's role tended to attract sameness-oriented individuals. Interestingly, when marketers first introduced desktop computers to this group, they failed to take that into account and described the computers as, "new, different, and revolutionary." As expected, the administrative assistants resisted using the computers, instead preferring their familiar typewriters. When the marketers changed their approach and presented computers as "essentially the same as typewriters with the added benefit of making your job much faster and easier," the administrative assistants finally warmed up to using them.

Thus, if you're persuading a person who is motivated by sameness, point out commonalities. Use words like "similar," "identical," and "consistent." When persuading a person who is motivated by differences, it's beneficial to emphasize differences, using words and phrases like "new," "innovative," "unlike anything you've seen before," and "one of a kind."

SHIFTING MOTIVES

On April 23, 1985, the Coca-Cola Company announced that, for the first time in 99 years, it was changing the formula of its popular soft drink. The reformulated Coca-Cola—which became known as "New Coke"—was a big risk, one that the company felt was needed to re-energize its brand.

The move backfired. More than that, it's known as one of the biggest marketing failures of all time.

The Coca-Cola Company received thousands of calls and consumer complaints. In fact, by June of 1985, the company was receiving 1,500 calls a day on its consumer hotline (compared to just 400 calls a day before the launch of New Coke). The public outrage went even further. Protest groups were formed including the "Society for the Preservation of the Real Thing" and the "Old Cola Drinkers of America." People began to buy up all the "old" Coke they could, hoarding the soft drink in their basements.

It took no time at all for the company to recognize their failure and, in July of 1985, they announced that the "old" Coke formula (now referred to as Coca-Cola Classic) would return to shelves.[50]

What happened?

Nothing was wrong with the new Coke formula, per se. In fact, "New" Coke sold successfully when offered alongside Coca-Cola Classic. Instead, the problem came from *how* the company marketed the new product. The Coca-Cola Company had neglected to consider their consumers' motivational factors and, in doing so, completely misread both their consumers *and* the market. Coca-Cola's marketers failed to take into account that many of their loyal consumers were motivated by sameness and, as such, would be unlikely to give a new, different Coke formula a chance. In fact, when the original Coca-Cola they had to come to love was removed from the shelves and replaced with something new, loyal Coke consumers took offense and reacted so strongly that they complained, hoarded what was left of the original formula, and took to the streets to protest.

It's easy to talk about motivational factors as if they are "either/or," as if you are either 100% sameness-oriented or 100% difference-oriented, with nothing in between. In reality, motivational factors lie along a spectrum, so you might be *very* motivated by sameness, shuddering at the thought of any whiff of change to your beloved soft drink; moderately motivated by sameness and open to ordering a Root Beer instead of a Coca-Cola Classic now and then; mostly motivated by difference and eager to try any new soft drink that hits the shelves—or anywhere between.

That's because, as we've discussed, what motivates us is typically context-specific and content-free depending on the situation. In other words, what motivates us may change as the context or topic changes, and in most cases, we're affected by a combination of different motivational factors at any given time.

---

50 "The Story of One of the Most Memorable Marketing Blunders Ever." Available online: https://www.coca-colacompany.com/news/the-story-of-one-of-the-most-memorable-marketing-blunders-ever

FLOWERS OR A PHONE CALL: WHAT SAYS "LOVE" TO YOU?

One of the couples I have counselled was struggling with relating to each other. When I asked the husband how he knew his wife loved him, he replied, "I just know. She wouldn't have married me if she didn't love me. And I know she still does."

On the other hand, the wife noticed that her husband never bought her flowers anymore, never said he loved her, and never seemed to respond when she said she loved him.

The mismatch was obvious: the husband thought the wife should "just know" he loved her, which is internal, while she was more external-focused and thought it was important to demonstrate love. I explained this to the couple, and their new awareness helped them communicate more effectively. He now understood the importance of saying "I love you," buying flowers, and otherwise giving his wife external reassurances of his love, while she understood that giving reassurances of love was less important to him.

Identifying a person's motivational factors in a specific context is just the tip of the iceberg. You can combine knowledge of motivation with your knowledge of a person's preferred processing system. In the case of that couple, if the wife was more visually oriented, she would greatly appreciate looking at the beautiful flowers, while if the husband were more auditory, he might appreciate hearing "I love you," and spending time talking with his wife at the end of the day. In my own life, my wife, Natalie, whose primary representational system is visual, thinks I'm not listening to her if I'm not looking at her. Pay attention to the clues!

CATCHING THE CLUES

What motivates us is content-free and context-specific, and it's often identifiable even before we communicate verbally to others. Think back to the example of the coins, when I placed two different coins on a desk in front of a participant and another coin on his instruction manual, all at different angles and spaces away from each other. Before I had the opportunity to ask him anything, he took the coin on the manual and put it together with the coins on the desk, arranging them all in a row. This is a great example of someone giving us clues as to what their preferences are for sorting before they even say anything.

As with the individual who sorted the coins, most of us are unaware of the role our preferred motivational traits play in our lives, even when that role is life changing. My own father is a prime example. The language he uses to describe the reasons our family left Ireland clearly reveals some of his motivational traits. Back in 1969, my uncle immigrated to Canada from Ireland to work as a tool and die maker. In 1970, when I was just four years old, the rest of my family joined him, including my grandparents, my parents, my siblings, and me.

Our family and many others left because of the Northern Ireland Conflict known as "The Troubles," which began in 1968 and lasted for thirty years (ending with the Good Friday Agreement in 1998). During this time, the Republic of Ireland and Northern Ireland were the site of a violent and bloody internal struggle between groups like the Irish Republican Army (IRA) and the Ulster Defence Regiment (UDR) as they fought over complex and intertwined issues including political (British) rule and religious beliefs.[51] The conflict crippled the country as Catholics and Protestants, nationalists and British loyalists targeted each other. During these thirty years, bombings were commonplace and a great many families were affected, families like mine.

> And the battle's just begun
> There's many lost, but tell me who has won
> The trench is dug within our hearts
> And mothers, children, brothers, sisters torn apart...
>
> –U2, **"SUNDAY, BLOODY SUNDAY"**

You may recognize these lyrics. That's because the horrors of the conflict have been retold to the rest of the world by well-known Irish musicians like U2, a Dublin band famous for their 1983 song "Sunday, Bloody Sunday," about the

51 John Dorney, "The Northern Ireland Conflict 1968-1998–An Overview," *The Irish Story* (February 9, 2015). Available online: https://www.theirishstory.com/2015/02/09/the-northern-ireland-conflict-1968-1998-an-overview/

massacre on Sunday, January 30, 1972, in which the British Army shot and killed thirteen unarmed demonstrators.[52]

Throughout the decades-long conflict, artists like U2 used their lyrics to protest the fighting. As we saw with Paul Butler and the St. Lucia Parrot, national and revolutionary songs are powerful persuasive tools, and we'll talk more about the power of music in the next chapter. While the world watched the conflict unfold, both Australia and Canada offered to accept Irish immigrants. My family considered both countries and when my grandfather offered to pay our way to Canada, it was settled. We waited until just a few months after my sister's birth so that our entire family would be Irish citizens and, in May of 1970, we said goodbye to Belfast as we set sail on the *Empress of Canada*, arriving in Montreal eight days later.

If you ask my father why our family came to Canada, he'll tell you it was to get away from the troubles in Ireland, a reason that's perfectly sensible and understandable.

Did you catch the clue?

What motivational factor do you think was at play for my father?

Rather than saying we came looking for a better life in Canada (a *toward* motivational factor), when my father tells the story of immigrating to Canada, he says we left Ireland *to get away from* the troubles there (an *away from* motivational factor).

Language is a subtle indicator of a person's motivational tendencies. As we've learned in this chapter, there are many other subtleties to pay attention to. As persuaders, identifying what motivates a person in any given context teaches us a great deal about their Current State, how they think and feel, and why they do what they do. This knowledge combines to help us move them toward the Desired State.

---

52 John Dorney, "Today in Irish History, Bloody Sunday in Derry, 30 January 1972," ***The Irish Story*** (January 29, 2012). Available online: https://www.theirishstory.com/2012/01/29/today-in-irish-history-january-30-1972-bloody-sunday-in-derry/

Remember the example with the coins we talked about earlier in this chapter? You can determine somebody's sameness or difference motivational orientation by carrying out that same experiment with them. Lay the coins on a table and ask the person, "How would you describe the relationship between these things?" Listen carefully to their language to help you determine if they are primarily sorting by sameness or by difference. Have fun!

Chapter Five

Diving into Your Unconscious

> The effectiveness of communication is not defined by the communication, but by the response.
>
> –MILTON ERICKSON

If you're a craft beer drinker, then you probably prefer some types of beer over others. Your preference for a stout, a radler, or an IPA is just dictated by your taste buds. Right?

Maybe not.

Maybe your beer really tastes like the thoughts you're thinking, the clothes you're wearing, the people you're with, or the ambiance of the environment. Or maybe your beer tastes like the music you're listening to? In other words, the taste of your beer may vary according to several factors, many of which you're unaware of because they're operating at a subconscious level.

A study by Professor Adrian North at Heriot-Watt University, Edinburgh, explored this phenomenon using wine. Over the course of several years, Professor North invited 250 students to sip either Montes Alpha 2006 Cabernet Sauvignon or Chardonnay and then rate the wine.[53] Unknowingly, they did more than simply sip wine. There was music playing in the background which had previously been categorized by other volunteers as either "subtle and refined" (Tchaikovsky's "The Waltz of the Flowers" from the *Nutcracker Suite*), "powerful and heavy" (Carl Orff's "Carmina Burana"), "zingy and refreshing" (Nouvelle Vague's "Just Can't Get Enough"), or "mellow and soft" (Michael Brook's "Slow Breakdown").

---

53 "Music makes wine taste better," ***The Telegraph*** (November 11, 2011). Available online: http://www.telegraph.co.uk/news/8862520/Music-makes-wine-taste-better.html

One group of students quaffed their Cabernet Sauvignon to Tchaikovsky, another to Orff, a third to Nouvelle Vague, a fourth to Brook, and a fifth to no music at all; this was repeated with the five groups drinking the Chardonnay. The participants were unaware of the music ratings—indeed, many paid no attention to the background music at all.

At the end of the wine tasting, the students were asked to rate the wine they had sampled using the same adjectives that had previously been used to describe the kinds of music: subtle and refined; powerful and heavy; zingy and refreshing; or mellow and soft. The students consistently selected the rating that matched the music they had heard while drinking! The music had clearly influenced the taste of the wine at a subconscious level.

Savvy marketers use this knowledge all the time to sell messages and products subliminally, playing French or Italian music in a liquor store to increase the sales of French or Italian wines, for example. We tend to think we're aware of what drives our thoughts, feelings, and actions, yet the reality is that a lot of the "driving" takes place in our subconscious and we only become aware of it—if at all—when we stop and examine our behavior.

> Consumer decision making and buying behavior are driven more by unconscious thoughts and feelings than by conscious ones. These unconscious forces include ever-changing memories, images, sensations, and stories that interact.
>
> –GERALD ZALTMAN, **HOW CUSTOMERS THINK**

Advertisers and marketers are very familiar with this concept. It explains why certain colors are used on websites, certain types of music play in the background in stores or elevators, and shops smell certain ways. These sensory experiences have a **priming effect** at an unconscious level, and they often influence our behaviors without our realizing it. When asked, most people are completely unaware of having been primed or having seen the colors, heard the music, or smelled the aromas that influenced them at such an unconscious level. It's outside of our awareness. Think back, for instance, to the Harvard study we looked at in Chapter One, where physicians' treatment choices were influenced by language. This study examined how, outside of our conscious awareness, language impacts emotions and in turn drives specific behaviors and choices.

The influence of external stimuli on our minds affects more than just our senses, though. Neuroscientist Greg Gage has demonstrated that it is even possible to control *another person's* body with *your* mind. Neuroscientists like Gage are particularly interested in the electrical messages sent between the brain and the body and the subsequent "motor action potentials" (a term used to describe the electrical study of muscle function).

> **Key Concept:** Sights, sounds, and other sensory inputs absorbed at a subconscious level can change conscious thoughts, feelings, and behaviors.

In his TED Talk, aptly titled "How to Control Someone Else's Arm with Your Brain," Gage tells the audience that there are "eighty billion neurons inside your brain right now. They're sending electrical messages back and forth, and chemical messages. But some of your neurons right here in your motor cortex are going to send messages down when you move your arm."[54] Using electrodes and a computer, Gage hooks up two audience volunteers, Sam and Miguel, sending the electrical pulses from Sam's brain directly to the ulnar nerve in Miguel's arm. By copying the brain signals that go out to the hand to tell it to move, as Sam moves her own arm, Miguel's arm moves too![55]

As cool as this is to see, the point is that most of what our brain accomplishes is done subconsciously or as a reflexive action.

IS OUR FILTERING MIND THE ROOT OF AMBIGUITY?

Most of what we consciously think about is based on deleted, distorted, or generalized information. This is problematic because it's this filtered information that we use to communicate with each other. As a result, our communication

---

54 Greg Gage, "How to Control Someone Else's Arm with Your Brain," *TED* (April 28, 2015). Available online: https://youtu.be/rSQNi5sAwuc

55 Gage, "How to Control Someone Else's Arm with Your Brain." Available online: https://youtu.be/rSQNi5sAwuc

is inherently ambiguous since it is based on summarized, incomplete, and distorted information. To complicate things further, we communicate with each other using words that are nothing more than labels for experiences; even though we may use the same label as the people we are speaking with, that label can mean different things to different people.

Remember the example we mentioned about adventure? When we talk about *adventure* or when we label something as *adventurous*, it's likely that you and I have different ideas about what that adventure is. If I say my idea of "adventure" is trying a new international cuisine and you say yours is taking a local Scout group on a camping trip, then even though we start off using the same label, the meaning we each attach to that label is very different.

> I know that you believe you understand what you think I said, but I'm not sure you realize that what you heard is not what I meant.
>
> –ROBERT MCCLOSKEY (ATTRIBUTED)

We can also apply this concept to our values. Although we may both agree that *honesty* is an important value, your definition of honesty and my definition of honesty, and the criteria we each associate with honesty, can be very different. This is where conflicts can occur between people: we assume that just because we're using the same label, the rules, criteria, and fulfillment of the criteria are the same for both of us. We think we're on the same page until we find out (often through conflict) that we are, in fact, thinking quite differently.

THE PERSUASIVE POWER OF GOING META

During the 1970s, linguist John Grinder and mathematician Richard Bandler studied prominent therapists to learn what made them so successful with clients. One of the therapists they observed was Virginia Satir, a well-known marriage and family counsellor. Satir intuitively used **strategic questioning** to clarify her clients' statements and thoughts by getting them to fill in missing information, which in turn, increased their understanding. Using her work, and that of others, Grinder and Bandler developed the **Meta Model of Language**, often called simply the Meta Model. The Meta Model is a linguistic model that ultimately uses clarifying language to seek greater understanding by identifying a deeper level of meaning within the communication.

> We get together on the basis of our similarities; we grow on the basis of our differences.
>
> –VIRGINIA SATIR

Part of what makes us more persuasive is our ability to recognize what's been deleted, distorted, and generalized in our own and in other people's communication. Using the Meta Model, we can clarify these deletions, distortions, and generalizations by asking questions like "Why?" "How?" and "Who?" The idea behind these questions is to recover missing information which serves to expand the limits of the other person's thinking and uncover the meaning they've attached to a situation or event.

Here's how it works.

You've likely heard someone say, "This is a better way to do it." This phrase is an example of a **comparative deletion**, a language pattern where a comparison omits the thing to which it is being compared. Words like "good," "better," "best," "worst," "more," "less," "most," and "least" can frequently signal comparative deletion in action.

Using the Meta Model, we can respond to the statement, "This is a better way to do it," by asking "Better than what?" or "Better how?" or "Compared to what?" The answers to these questions allow us to recover missing information, thus clarifying the deletion.

Next, let's look at an example of how the Meta Model clarifies **distortions**. Have you ever been in a situation where someone claims to know how you're feeling? It's annoying, isn't it? We call this language pattern **mind reading**: claiming to know the thoughts or feelings (the internal state) of another person without specifying the process by which you acquired or came to know this information. For example, someone might claim, "He's not happy with my work." Using the Meta Model, you could respond to this statement with questions that recover the source of the missing information, questions like, "How, *specifically*, do you know he is not happy with your work?" You may also clarify who "he" is in order to reduce ambiguity.

Finally, let's look at universal quantifiers as an example of how the Meta Model **clarifies generalizations. Universal quantifiers** are a set of words that contain universal generalizations or a lack of clarity around what is being referenced. Common universal quantifiers include "all," "every," "never," "everyone," "no one," and so on. Let's say, for example, you're talking to a friend about her boss, and your friend says, "She *never* listens to me." Using the Meta Model, you would respond to this universal quantifier by asking questions like "Really, never? Think back, surely there must have been at least one time that she listened to you?" or "What would happen if she did listen to you?" or "How would you know that she is listening to you?" These questions can help your friend recover counter examples and put things into a more useful perspective by clarifying her evidence criteria for listening and by acknowledging that there are times when her boss is, in fact, listening to her. In doing so, she will shift to a more resourceful model of the world.

It's important to note that there are a variety of different language patterns to look out for when recognizing deletions, distortions, and generalizations. Comparative deletions, mind reading, and universal quantifiers are just a few examples. Visit our website at www.SolutionsInMind.com for a complete list.

> I believe the greatest gift I can conceive of having from anyone is to be seen by them, heard by them, to be understood and touched by them. The greatest gift I can give is to see, hear, understand, and to touch another person. When this is done, I feel contact has been made.
>
> –VIRGINIA SATIR

Ultimately, the human mind is constantly deleting, distorting, and generalizing information, which is why so many interactions are ambiguous—and as we already know, ambiguity can lead to communication breakdown. This breakdown can even be a problem between people who know each other well. That's why it's essential to remain curious as you recognize deletions, distortions, generalizations, and other forms of ambiguous communication, and to use the Meta Model to constantly clarify and expand the other person's thinking. Also keep in mind that it's important to be aware of when you yourself may be deleting, distorting, and generalizing as you communicate with others.

THE PERSUASIVE POWER OF AMBIGUITY

As we've just seen, Grinder and Bandler explored therapist Virginia Satir's language and questioning patterns and examined what it was that made her so successful, building the Meta Model based on her work and interactions with her clients. In researching exceptional therapists, Grinder and Bandler also studied Milton Erickson, a world-renowned psychiatrist specializing in hypnosis. Like Satir, Erickson was known for achieving remarkable results, albeit in a different (and sometimes more controversial) way.

> Until you are willing to be confused about what you already know, what you know will never grow bigger, better, or more useful.
>
> –MILTON ERICKSON

Their research led Grinder and Bandler to the realization that Satir's and Erickson's methods were essentially opposite sides of the same coin. As they had done with Satir, Grinder and Bandler developed the **Milton Model** after studying Erickson's language patterns during his interactions with patients.

Let's look more closely at the Milton Model, which leverages ambiguity to engage the client's unconscious resources. As Sidney Rosen explains in his book, *My Voice Will Go with You*, Milton Erickson used storytelling techniques and "teaching tales" to influence the unconscious mind with positive input and with ambiguous questions and statements.[56] "In the telling of stories, Erickson adds new data, evokes new feelings, and prescribes new experiences," Rosen writes. "A single remembered phrase from one of Erickson's stories may change the feeling of an entire day," he continues. Rosen recounts a specific instance: "This happened to me while I was walking beside a meadow. Suddenly the sentence 'Did you know that every blade of grass is a different shade of green?' popped into my head and I looked at the grass more closely. Indeed, it was true! For the rest of the day, I walked around with my eyes more open than usual."[57] In the same way, it's my intention that by exposing you to the persuasive techniques in this book, you will learn to engage your eyes, ears, and other senses more fully and actively on a daily basis.

> Patients are patients because they are out of rapport with their own unconscious... Patients are people who have had too much programming–so much outside programming that they have lost touch with their inner selves.
>
> –MILTON ERICKSON

As Rosen experienced, the Milton Model uses ambiguous statements and questions—like the question about the color of the grass—to prime the mind. Other ambiguous examples include:

- "There are things that you'd still like to accomplish in your life."
- "We all have things about ourselves that we like, and other things that we'd like to improve..."
- "You've found significant enough value in this book to read it to this point."

Does this strategy remind you of another master persuader? P.T. Barnum, perhaps? Like the Barnum Effect, the idea is to let the receiver fill in the missing

56 Sidney Rosen, *My Voice Will Go With You–The Teaching Tales of Milton H. Erickson, M.D.* (W.W. Norton, 1982).

57 Rosen, *My Voice Will Go With You*, pp. 29-30.

information in a way that best matches their model of the world and is most meaningful to them. Enabling them to fill in the gaps increases their sense of being understood and makes them more receptive to what you are offering.

If you want to be more persuasive, you can intentionally use communication that's ambiguous so that your audience will attach their own meaning to it, thereby making your communication more relevant to each individual. Barack Obama did this brilliantly with "Yes, We Can" during his 2008 primary campaign. The slogan "Yes, We Can" is intentionally ambiguous so that the audience fills in the context with what's most meaningful to them. Yes, we can do *what*? The audience members answer the "what" based on what's most relevant and important to each of them. As American musician will.i.am exemplified in his song and viral music video, "Yes We Can," which he released during the campaign, the power of "Yes, We Can" is in the ambiguity of the statement.[58]

> That's the whole point of good propaganda. You want to create a slogan that nobody's going to be against, and everybody's going to be for. Nobody knows what it means, because it doesn't mean anything.
>
> –NOAM CHOMSKY

Using the Milton Model, we can leverage ambiguity by using deletions, distortions, and generalizations in our everyday language.

Remember our earlier example of comparative deletions? You may recall that a comparative deletion is a language pattern in which a comparison is made that omits to what, when, or whom something is being compared. We can use the Milton Model to **leverage ambiguity by using comparative deletions** in our own language. For example, we may say, "This is a decision that is relatively easy to make." Notice the intentional ambiguity of "relatively easy"? "Easy" in relation to what? We're leaving it up to the individual's mind to fill in the most meaningful and relevant comparison. With the phrase "It's *more or less* the

58 will.i.am, "Yes We Can Obama Song," YouTube (February 2, 2008). Available online: https://youtu.be/2fZHou18Cdk

right thing," the comparison is once again missing, and we've left it up to the listener's unconscious mind to select the most suitable comparison. Similarly, the phrase, "This is a safe car and provides exceptional value!" uses ambiguous language to encourage the person we're communicating with to attach their own meaning to the comparison. "Safe" in comparison to what and "exceptional value" as compared to what? The listener fills in what they are comparing "safe" and "exceptional value" to, based on what's of relevance to them. Comparative deletions also tend to bypass conscious resistance because it takes considerable amounts of conscious effort to evaluate and understand the actual comparisons. The brain is lazy by nature at a conscious level and would rather take the easy route by simply accepting the comparative deletion.

Next, let's look at an example of how the Milton Model **leverages ambiguity by *generating* distortions and deletions with mind reading.** You may recall that **mind reading** is when we claim to know the thoughts or feelings of another person. For example, I might say to you, "It seems that you are learning a lot and that you really value the learnings." The ambiguity around "learning a lot" and "really value" leaves it up to the listener's unconscious mind to determine what the learnings are and how specifically they are valued. If I say to you, "I realize that you are reading this book for a reason," notice that the "reason" is intentionally left out so that your unconscious mind can determine the reasons that are most relevant for you. If I were to say, "I know how important this is to you," your unconscious mind is once again left to fill in the level of importance.

Finally, let's look at an example of how the Milton Model **leverages the ambiguity of generalizations like universal quantifiers**, which you may remember are a set of words that contain a universal generalization or a lack of referential index. For example, I could say, "Nobody can resist experiencing it." The listener is therefore left to conclude that if "nobody" can resist, then they should probably experience it as well. The effect is similar with the statement, "Everyone knows it to be true." The listener is led to conclude that, "If *everyone* knows it's true, then I should probably accept it as truth too." In the statement, "Every word read leads to the integration of new learnings," the reader is led to think, "Wow, *every* word? I must be learning a lot from reading this book!" All these examples use generalizations that contain a tremendous amount of ambiguity in order to leverage social proof.[59] Did your parents ever ask you, "If your friend jumped off a cliff, would you jump off too?" This common saying refers to **the Law of Social Proof**, a term coined by Robert Cialdini in his 1984 book, *Influence*, to describe the social psychological phenomenon where people copy the actions of others. Simply put, social proof suggests that if *everyone* is doing it, then it *must* be the right thing to do. Thus, we get thoughts like, "If nobody is buying it, then I probably shouldn't buy it either," and "If everyone thinks the restaurant is amazing, then it must be great," and so on.

Remember that with the Meta Model we seek to *clarify* ambiguity. In contrast, with the Milton Model, we discover that ambiguity can be *leveraged* to help others tap into and utilize their own unconscious resources. Keep in mind that the Meta and Milton models are different sides of the same coin, either clarifying or leveraging ambiguity depending on the outcome you're after.

OPPOSITE SIDES OF THE SAME COIN: THE META AND MILTON MODELS

In this chapter we've barely scraped the surface of many valuable concepts and learned that the Meta Model and the Milton Model are opposite sides of the same coin. Each uses language strategically, yet differently, for specific purposes. As persuaders, it is critical for us to understand and use both models in order to gain a deeper understanding of a person's Current State and to shift them toward the Desired State.

59 Robert B. Cialdini, *Influence: The Psychology of Persuasion*, Revised Edition (HarperCollins, 2007).

The Meta Model	The Milton Model
Recognizes deletions, distortions, and generalizations and uses questions in order to delve into more specifics.	Leverages ambiguity to move to higher levels of abstractness and vagueness.
Moves from high-level ambiguous language that represents the experience to deeper level details of the experience itself.	Focuses on higher level ambiguous language that represents various experiences, learnings, etc.
Focuses on bringing deeper structures into conscious awareness.	Leverages unconscious resources and builds rapport between the person's conscious mind and unconscious mind.

It's also important to remember that the ethical choice is our responsibility. While some people may use deletions, distortions, and generalizations for self-serving or underhanded purposes, it's our duty to use them ethically and ecologically. We'll talk more about ethical and ecological choices in Chapter Eleven.

Occasionally, when Milton Erickson's peers would accuse him of being manipulative, he apparently responded by reminding them that life is one big manipulation. He believed his job was to manipulate his clients in order for them to have a deeper rapport with their unconscious minds. Erickson was even known to say that if a baby couldn't manipulate its parents, it would likely die! He repeatedly emphasized the point that it was the *intention* behind the manipulation that was of the utmost importance. As you begin to utilize the Meta and Milton models in your interactions with others, always be aware of your positive intention in guiding them toward greater awareness and in leading them to a Desired State which will enhance their lives.

Observe where you can use the Meta Model in your everyday conversations to clarify missing information by identifying deletions, distortions, and generalizations. Uncover the deeper experiences behind the surface language of these conversations to improve how you communicate with and relate to those around you.

In terms of the Milton Model, be aware of how and where both you and others use ambiguous language, either intentionally or unintentionally. Remember that the Meta Model is the opposite side of the same coin, empowering you to counteract ambiguity with clarifying questions.

Chapter Six

The Experience of Being Understood

Law enforcement agents, officers, and hostage negotiators—from the CIA to CSIS, from the FBI to the RCMP—have jobs that rely heavily on them being persuasive, often in situations involving extreme time limits, high stakes, and other stressful parameters. But most of us rarely see any of these professionals in action. Only in television shows and films do we get a glimpse of some of the tensions and stakes of persuading someone in risky, life-in-the-balance situations.

Thankfully, our own persuasion techniques are usually practiced in safer and more relaxed circumstances. In fact, master influencers weave persuasion techniques into their daily lives, at work, at home, and at play. Still, one can't help wondering how persuasion is done—and done well. The truth is that while it may come naturally for some, most agents and master negotiators—like you—have been *taught* how to be persuasive.

Remember the French magician Jean Eugène Robert-Houdin in Chapter One? There is evidence that he worked as an envoy in Algeria to quell an uprising.[60] And he's just one of many master persuaders who have aided government agencies in their training by sharing persuasive techniques. In another example, illusionist Joseph Dunninger advised the U.S. Armed Forces on camouflage techniques during WWII.[61] And Kalush and Sloman, authors of *The Secret Life of Houdini*, argue that Houdini himself worked as a spy for the British.[62] It's worth noting that some academics, like historian Thomas Boghardt of the International Spy Museum in Washington, D.C., argue there is little evidence to support the claim that Houdini was an international spy.[63] This ambiguity means that almost

---

60 Gary Shapiro, "Houdini Was a Covert Agent, New Book Claims," ***The New York Sun*** (August 28, 2006). Available online: https://www.nysun.com/foreign/houdini-was-a-covert-agent-new-book-claims/38654/

61 Shapiro, "Houdini Was a Covert Agent, New Book Claims." Available online: https://www.nysun.com/foreign/houdini-was-a-covert-agent-new-book-claims/38654/

62 William Kalush and Larry Sloman, ***The Secret Life of Houdini: The Making of America's First Superhero*** (Atria Books, 2006), p. 21.

63 Shapiro, "Houdini Was a Covert Agent, New Book Claims." Available online: https://www.nysun.com/foreign/houdini-was-a-covert-agent-new-book-claims/38654/

a hundred years after his death, Houdini still continues to elicit wonder and mystery in his admirers!

A range of professionals in diverse occupations—from magicians to personnel in government agencies and law enforcement—put years of practice into mastering persuasive techniques like effective questioning. This is because questioning is critical to understanding another person's model of the world and is useful in engaging and guiding their mind toward a Desired State.

> There's so much space between "yes" and "no," it's as big as the Grand Canyon.
>
> —CHRIS VOSS

My practical application of the **Law of Requisite Variety** postulates that the person who has the most mental, emotional, and behavioral flexibility will ultimately have control over a system or situation.[64] Effective crisis negotiators, like Chris Voss, a former FBI Chief International Hostage and Kidnapping Negotiator, are perfect examples of this theory in action: they use their mental, emotional, and behavioral flexibility to manage the outcome of their interactions. We can compare this to Houdini's behavioral and mental flexibility in how he approached different situations, constantly thinking outside the box to creatively solve problems.

THE PREREQUISITE TO PERSUASION

In the introduction to this book, I shared an interaction I had in a corporate training session in which I asked participants what they think it takes to be persuasive and influential. As you now know, it takes much more than simply being charming, charismatic, or knowledgeable!

One thing lies at the heart of persuasion and influence—and that something is *rapport*.

---

64 The Law of Requisite Variety was formulated by Ross Ashby in his book *An Introduction to Cybernetics* (Chapman & Hall, 1956).

Masterful persuaders first build **rapport** with the person they are persuading and ask questions in order to gain a deeper understanding of that person's model of the world including their beliefs and values. Then, as progress is made toward the Desired State, the persuader knows how to connect what they are offering to something of relevance to the person, something that is meaningful to them. Of all the concepts and techniques that we'll explore in this book, rapport is the most important because it is the foundation for influence.

To learn about the person you're persuading, you must first establish **rapport**, which simply means giving another person the experience of being understood in order to trigger emotional fulfillment. As you continue to learn about building and maintaining rapport effectively in this chapter, remember: the best way to get someone to care about something they don't yet care about is to connect it to something they *do* care about. We'll learn more about making, breaking, and reinforcing these connections in Chapter Ten.

> **Key Concept:**
> Rapport is the key to persuasion. By establishing rapport and providing another person with the experience of being understood, we trigger emotional fulfillment within them. Once you've established rapport, the individual will be much more likely to communicate freely with you and follow your lead to the Desired State.

Why is rapport so critical to persuasion? Because everyone craves the feeling of being understood; it validates our model of the world and gives us a sense of connection. By understanding how a person thinks and reflecting that understanding back to them, you provide them with the experience of being understood and they will be much more likely to trust you and follow your lead.

Rapport is also the *pacing* of experience. It provides a communication loop whereby you become, for another individual, an unconscious, accurate source of feedback about what they are experiencing. Former crisis negotiator Chris Voss says that "hostage negotiators have actually designed an approach that takes emotions fully into account and uses them to influence situations, which is the reality of the way all negotiations go."[65] You too can learn to leverage emotions, build rapport, and persuade others.

It all begins with establishing rapport with those you want to persuade. So, how do you do that?

Rapport is critical in many areas of life, whether it's relating to a waiter in a restaurant, your boss, your doctor, your therapist, or your team coach. In his book, *Persuasion and Healing,* psychiatrist Jerome Frank isolated the aspects of a successful therapeutic relationship. Frank found that three factors in particular influenced the outcome of therapy:

- The client's expectations
- The client's trust in the therapist
- The personal attributes of the therapist, specifically their ability to:
    - Show keen interest in the client
    - Be a concerned listener
    - Speak the "same language" as the client
    - Give the client the sense that they are being understood.[66]

So, whatever your role—whether you're a hostage negotiator, a therapist, or a parent—it's important to establish rapport *before* you begin to use persuasion techniques—and rapport *always* starts with providing the other person with the experience of being understood.

UNDERSTANDING EACH OTHER

There are a variety of ways to show you understand while continuing to maintain your own viewpoint. There's a fine line between empathy and agreement, between understanding a person's world view and adopting it yourself. There is also a fine line between the elicitation of what someone is truly thinking as you interact with them versus the instillation of ideas, beliefs, and biases as you move them toward the Desired State.

---

65 Chris Voss, interviewed by Eric Barker, "Hostage Negotiation Techniques That Will Get You What You Want," ***Bakadesuyo*** (June 2013). Available online: https://www.bakadesuyo.com/2013/06/hostage-negotiation/

66 Quoted in *Magic of NLP Demystified: A Pragmatic Guide to Communication & Change* by Byron Lewis & Frank Pucelik (Metamorphous Press, 1990) pp. 13-14.

When hostage negotiators build rapport with a suspect, are they in agreement with the suspect and their position? Or is their goal simply to build rapport and empathize for the purpose of ensuring a positive outcome? Probably the latter. Hostage negotiators are experts at gaining trust by showing they understand the suspect, while steering very clear of actually agreeing with the suspect's viewpoint or developing feelings for them.

How do they do this?

The negotiators show the hostage taker that they "get" them by matching and mirroring the hostage taker's physiology, tone and rate of speech, and language patterns. *Demonstrating understanding* (rather than simply saying, "I understand") is critical to building rapport, because it's a key element in any trusting relationship. As you can see here, you can establish rapport in the absence of liking or caring about the other person.

Matching and mirroring another person's linguistic style can help you build rapport, and research by Maxim Sytch and Yong H. Kim shows that it can advance your career, too. The two researchers examined patent infringement cases, studying how lawyers influence judges. The study, which was published in *Administrative Science Quarterly*, showed that those lawyers whose linguistic styles best matched the judges' were able to win approximately 28% more cases. The successful lawyers "had a better sense of whether their judges would be moved by data or by emotional appeals, whether they would respond better to confidence or to arguments that left room for ambiguity, and how much they valued personal disclosure." Sytch and Kim found that the lawyers who knew the approach that would resonate with each judge and tailored their communication style accordingly had a huge advantage.[67]

THINKING ABOUT YOUR THINKING

Rapport can be established almost instantly as you enter into another person's model of the world—and it can be broken just as quickly as it can be built. If broken unintentionally, if, say, we push too hard, rapport can be easily re-established. We can think of it as being elastic. Our objective is always to intentionally

---

67 Maxim Sytch and Yong H. Kim, "Want to Win Someone Over? Talk Like They Do," ***Harvard Business Review*** (December 8, 2020). Available online: https://hbr.org/2020/12/want-to-win-someone-over-talk-like-they-do

establish and maintain rapport as the first step in our journey to becoming experts in persuasion.

When building rapport, it's also important to remember that communication consists of so much more than just what is said out loud. Yes, you must pay attention to your spoken language, that is, what you say, and how you say it. Remember Milton Erickson in the last chapter? He had specific things he paid attention to in building rapport with his patients.

Words, tonality, and physiology (body language) are crucial in building rapport, and these elements can be broken down into the following seven building blocks of rapport:

1. Postures, gestures
2. Facial expressions, blinking
3. Breathing
4. Voice—tone, tempo, pitch, volume
5. Word cues—visual, auditory, kinesthetic, etc.
6. Eye patterns
7. Key words and the language of motivation

You might notice that many of these building blocks, such as postures and gestures, are physical. Similarly, tempo and pitch relate to tonality, while visual, auditory, and kinesthetic word cues and key words align with spoken language. All of these building blocks can be categorized as either linguistic, tonal, or physiological.

As effective persuaders, we can gain understanding about another person by listening to that person's speech (their language, tone, inflections, and so on), which is critical to successfully building rapport and giving them the experience of being understood. Yet while words and tonality are important, physiology makes up the bulk of the impact of our communication.

In her 2012 talk at TED Global, "Your Body Language Shapes Who You Are," social psychologist Amy Cuddy tells the audience, "We make sweeping judgments and inferences from body language. And those judgments can predict really meaningful life outcomes, like who we hire or promote, [or] who we ask out on a date."[68]

Cuddy, who specializes in nonverbal expressions of power and dominance, has found that body language is a predictor of more than just our internal thoughts and feelings—it predicts our life outcomes. She goes on to explain that her research has found that "our nonverbal [cues] govern how we think and feel about ourselves."[69] In other words, our body language influences how we think as well as how we feel.

Recall, now, the ***Think* ➔ *Feel* ➔ *Do*** process we discussed earlier. In that process, our thinking impacts our emotions, which drives our behavior. So far, we've looked at the ***Think* ➔ *Feel* ➔ *Do*** process as a linear progression with a starting point and a finishing point. It's important, though, to realize that this process works in both directions. This means that a shift in our physiology can act as a catalyst to change our emotional state, which in turn causes us to think differently. For example, if you're feeling lethargic or upset, a physical shift can help change your state, which is likely to change your focus.

Let me share an example. Back in the days before cell phones, I had a client who paged me three times in one morning. When I called her back, she answered the phone crying. She was crying so much that I could barely understand her, let alone figure out what was wrong. "What are you doing right now?" I asked. "I'm sitting on the couch," she replied. "Stand up," I said. "Now bend your right arm like a chicken wing and start flapping it." She started to laugh. "You're crazy," she said. "You might think I'm crazy," I told her, "But you're laughing now instead of crying."

Getting my client to stand up and do something ridiculous was enough of a **pattern interrupt** to change her emotional state, which I knew was likely to help shift her thoughts. The purpose of a pattern interrupt is to shift someone's physiology, state, or internal representation. If you interrupt someone's physiology dramatically enough, it will directly shift their state (emotion) and/or their internal representation (thinking).

---

68 Amy Cuddy, "Your body language may shape who you are," TED (June 2012). Available online: https://www.ted.com/talks/amy_cuddy_your_body_language_shapes_who_you_are/

69 Cuddy, "Your body language may shape who you are." Available online: https://www.ted.com/talks/amy_cuddy_your_body_language_shapes_who_you_are/

BE AUTHENTIC

Coming from a place of **authenticity** is critical when building rapport. If you're curious about what's important to someone—and *why* it's important and relevant to them—that in itself is being authentic.

Think about the last time you felt someone was being sincere—or insincere. What aspect of their words, tone, or body language affected you the most? How did you feel about that person after the interaction?

> Authenticity is when you say and do the things you actually believe.
>
> –SIMON SINEK

Your own success in building rapport hinges on whether you are consistently perceived as being genuine and transparent. When you are, you can more easily gain other people's trust. Remember, rapport on a consistent basis generates trust. Ultimately, rapport—and the trust you earn through building it—are critical to persuasiveness.

US, WE, AND THEY

A Yale University study posed a question to nine- and fourteen-month-old infants by using hand puppets that looked like bunny rabbits.[70] Well, not so much a "question" as a scenario. The goal was to test the degree to which infants preferred people—or in this case, puppets—that were either similar or dissimilar to them.

The researchers began by determining whether each youngster preferred eating graham crackers or green beans. The children then watched as the puppets, identical except for the color of their shirts, either showed a preference for graham crackers over beans, or liked green beans and disliked crackers.

---

70 J. Kiley Hamlin, Nehan Mahajan, Zoe Liberman, and Karen Wynn, "Not Like Me = Bad: Infants Prefer Those Who Harm Dissimilar Others," *Psychological Science* 2013 24(4): 589-94. Available online: https://www.ncbi.nlm.nih.gov/pmc/articles/PMC4374623/

Then the infants, one at a time, were shown both hand puppets and asked which one they liked best. The babies who preferred crackers tended to reach for the cracker-loving puppet, while those who preferred beans reached for the bean-loving puppet. This was expected: babies, like adults, prefer people who are like them, even if in very trivial ways.

Then the researchers went a step further.

The infants were shown little skits in which a puppet who was playing with a ball dropped it. In one skit, a "nice puppet" came to the first puppet's aid, returning the lost ball. In the second version of the skit, a "mean puppet" grabbed the lost ball and kept it.

If the puppet who dropped the ball was neutral—that is, had not shown a preference for either graham crackers or green beans—the babies liked the "nice puppet" who returned the ball more than they did the "mean puppet." And if the ball-dropping puppet shared their taste in food, they also preferred the "nice puppet" over the "mean puppet." This showed that, as expected, babies prefer nice people over mean people.

The surprise came when the researchers measured the babies' reactions when the puppet who dropped the ball *had a different taste in food from themselves*. In this case, the babies preferred the "mean puppet" instead. This study (and other similar research) makes it quite clear: liking and trusting people who are more like us is a hard-wired feature of human beings.

> All the people like us are We, and everyone else is They.
>
> —RUDYARD KIPLING

So, how do you show other people that you are like them? By **pacing** them: pacing their movements, words, thought patterns, and more (think back to the seven building blocks of rapport discussed earlier in this chapter).

Pacing is an important process because it helps us develop rapport. When you pace another person, you become their "reflection"—physically, mentally, and emotionally. When done correctly, the person will unconsciously see themselves reflected in you. This reflection will provide a sense of similarity and help give them the feeling of being understood, and ultimately, will trigger emotional fulfillment.

THE MIND'S REACTION TO PACING

Laughter is something that most of us pace naturally. When someone else laughs, we tend to follow suit, which is why sitcoms often use a "laugh track" to encourage laughter from the studio audience.

While many people have long suspected that laughter is contagious, it's only relatively recently that neuroscientists have proven it. Christopher Bergland has reported that social laughter releases endorphins in specific areas of our brain, which produce "pleasurable and calming effects [that] might signal safety and promote feelings of togetherness."[71] Bergland goes on to say that "human laughter engages brain areas that facilitate social reciprocity and emotional resonance, consistent with its established role in promoting affiliation and social cohesion."[72]

In other words, in addition to being contagious, laughter also promotes feelings of togetherness. When we pace someone's laughter, for instance, our brains release a chemical response that helps us feel safe and part of a cohesive unit. When we pace another person's speech, body language, feelings, or thoughts, their subconscious tells them that we are like them and that we understand them.

These subconscious feelings of understanding trigger feelings of emotional fulfillment, also referred to as emotional satisfaction. "People may think that their behavior is purely rational, but it rarely is," explain the authors of "Managing Your Human Sigma," John Fleming, Curt Coffman, and James Harter. "Twenty years of research in two very different fields—neuroscience and behavioral economics—has established quite clearly that people base their decisions on a complicated mixture of emotion and reason."[73] This has certainly been my own experience! Think back to the Harvard study that examined emotional framing that we looked at in Chapter One. What drove the physicians' behavior was

---

71 Christopher Bergland, "The Neuroscience of Contagious Laughter," *Psychology Today* (September 29, 2017). Available online: https://www.psychologytoday.com/blog/the-athletes-way/201709/the-neuroscience-contagious-laughter

72 Bergland, "The Neuroscience of Contagious Laughter." Available online: https://www.psychologytoday.com/blog/the-athletes-way/201709/the-neuroscience-contagious-laughter

73 John H. Fleming, Curt Coffman, and James K. Harter, "Managing Your Human Sigma," *Harvard Business Review* (July 2005). Available online: https://hbr.org/2005/07/manage-your-human-sigma

outside of their conscious awareness and based on the emotion triggered by the framing language. It's my belief that decisions are generally based on emotion and justified with logic.

We know that our thoughts and emotions play a key role in our behavior—and so do marketers. Companies invest heavily in marketing aimed at building rapport between consumers and brands. Extensive research in the fields of organizational and consumer behavior shows that rapport can be built between employees and a company and between consumers and a company in the same way that it can be established between individuals. In fact, Fleming, Coffman, and Harter's research showed that people with a strong emotional connection to a company demonstrated differences in brain activity and that "the increased activity was concentrated in parts of the brain related to emotion, emotional-cognitive processing, and memory."[74]

MIRROR, MIRROR ON THE WALL...

Remember the building blocks of rapport including verbal patterns, vocal tone, and physiology? When we pace these building blocks, we enter into someone else's model of the world. Building rapport is pretty straightforward, then: as you match and/or mirror these building blocks, reflecting back to a person what they are actually experiencing at an unconscious level, you demonstrate that you understand them. Matching and mirroring others is part of how we pace their current reality in order to give them that experience of being understood, and it's how we begin to build rapport.

Let's take a quick look at the difference between matching and mirroring using examples of body language.

74 Fleming, Coffman, and Harter, "Managing Your Human Sigma." Available online: https://hbr.org/2005/07/manage-your-human-sigma

Matching is when you copy the other person exactly (e.g., if they cross their right leg, you cross your right leg).

Mirroring involves copying the other person as if you are a mirror image of them (e.g., if they lift their right hand, you lift your left hand).

These two methods are equally effective. It is important to be subtle when practicing these techniques, though—the goal is to do this outside of the other person's conscious awareness. If a person thinks we're mimicking them, then it can damage rapport. Instead, we want to pace their current experience and reflect their Current State with the goal of building or strengthening rapport. Some people mistakenly think that an established relationship is required to influence and persuade. Remember that there is a clear difference between a "relationship" and rapport. While we are inclined to view relationships as a noun (or a nominalization, as we discussed in Chapter Two), relating is actually an ongoing process—how we relate to someone and how they relate to us over time. Rapport, by contrast, can be established immediately and is elastic. If we happen to stretch the dynamic beyond what's useful and break rapport, we can re-establish it fairly quickly and easily.

Overall, pacing is simple and easy to do. You can pace something simple like a gesture or a combination of things that might include verbal patterns, styles of thinking, and strategies. Whichever approach you take, your goal will always be the same: to reflect the person's Current State back to them enough to give them the experience of being understood.

> **Remember!**
> Recall that in Chapter Two we discussed how the mind filters information–including images, thoughts, and feelings–to help us make sense of the world and to communicate with others.

Let's add on to that by noting that our speech literally reflects how our mind is processing. For instance, if our minds are accessing pictures, we tend to use more visual words. In listening to someone's language, we can also detect their mental strategies (the equivalent of mental recipes) in that moment in time. This in turn gives us additional information to add to our toolbox which may be used to engage and guide them toward a Desired State.

Each of us has a primary way of thinking that comes easily to us—naturally, unconsciously—and this way of thinking is typically either visual, auditory, or kinesthetic. Some people think more in pictures, some more in internal dialogue, and others through experiences. Although everyone uses all three representational systems at different times, we each have one that acts as our preferred, or primary, representational system.

To discover a person's preferred way of thinking, tune into their word choices and watch their eye patterns (we'll discuss this further in Chapter Seven), both of which will offer revealing clues.

A **visual thinker** may use phrases like:

- "I *see* your point."
- "*Show* me what that would look like."

An **auditory thinker** tends to use phrases like:

- "I'm *listening*."
- "Let me *tell* you about this in detail."

A **kinesthetic thinker** may use phrases like:

- "Let me *get a handle on* this before we *move forward*."
- "I am *comfortable* proceeding with your plan."

If you're unsure of a person's preferred representational system, you can also use unspecified or non-specific language in your questions. This type of language allows your communication to match any preferred representational system. When you use unspecified language, a visual person will interpret your language as visual, an auditory person will interpret the same language as auditory, and a kinesthetic person will interpret what you're saying as kinesthetic. Using unspecified language allows the person you're communicating with to interpret your language in accordance with their preferred representational system and will help you to learn how they think.

As soon as you've identified an individual's primary representational system, you can match your language to it. If the person is visual, you might say something like, "Do you *see* the *big picture* here?" If they're more auditory, you could say, "It *sounds* like you'd like to..." And if they're kinesthetic, you might say, "I get the *feeling* that you..."

A fascinating fact about us as human beings is that our bodies react to anything that we vividly imagine as though it is real. By using a vocabulary that fully engages all the senses, we can create a sensory-rich experience in a person's imagination. When the experience is sensory-rich, a person's body will respond as though what they are imagining is real, triggering the accompanying emotional reactions.

After one of my corporate seminars, a woman named Indira came up to me and said that she disagreed with my assertion that people process thoughts in visual, auditory, and kinesthetic ways and that you can identify their style of processing based upon the language that they use. She also believed that matching your style of communication to someone else's would be ineffective in terms of building rapport.

When I found out that Indira had a husband and two teenage daughters, I asked her to pay close attention to her family that night and listen carefully to the kind of language they used. She agreed to do so.

The next morning, she returned to our seminar room with a big smile on her face. Here's the story she shared with me:

> I really didn't believe all that stuff, but last night my oldest daughter, Lily, wanted to talk to me about which dance class she should take. And as happens a lot—and I've never known why—things got out of hand. Lily started saying, "Mom, you're not listening to me! You're not hearing what I'm saying!"
>
> I was trying to be a good mother and help her make a sound decision, so I replied, "You're not looking at this the right way. You're not seeing the big picture."
>
> Lily was practically in tears, I was frustrated; we got nowhere. This happens so many times between Lily and me. Yet my other daughter, Sarita, and I have a much easier time communicating.
>
> Then it suddenly hit me: Lily primarily uses auditory words while I use visual ones! That's our pattern. She says, "You're not *listening* to me," and I respond with, "You're not *seeing* the big picture."
>
> It's like we're speaking different languages. Sarita, on the other hand, uses mostly visual words just like I do. So, I apologized to Lily and asked her to tell me about the dance class again. This time I used lots of auditory words: hear, listen, sounds, loud, and clear. It was like night and day! We had the best talk we've ever had, and I felt like we both remained calm.

Instead of clashing with Lily's preferred representational system, Indira paced it. And it made all the difference!

EMPATHY VERSUS AGREEMENT

While you were probably taught that people should be empathetic, there is a fine line between **empathizing** with someone by demonstrating that you understand their feelings, and unintentionally **agreeing** with them. Many people think they're empathizing when what they're actually doing is inadvertently agreeing. For example, if you're dealing with a customer who is frustrated, that customer is likely looking for satisfaction and/or resolution. It may be tempting to confirm that they have a right to be upset, and to reassure them that things will be okay or urge them to calm down. This is actually more likely to exacerbate the problem! A more effective approach would be to *pace* their current situation by acknowledging their feelings and saying something like, "I appreciate your initial frustration based on the experience that you had." Notice that this response moves the negative experience to the past and, while demonstrating that you understand the customer may have been justified in how they felt, you're already beginning to shift them toward satisfaction or resolution. Even with your tone of voice, you can pace the customer by staying slightly below both the volume level at which they're speaking and the degree of frustration that they are displaying, thus guiding them toward a calmer state.

> **Key Concept:** Remember there's a fine line between empathy and agreement. Many people think they're empathizing with someone when they're actually unconsciously and inadvertently agreeing with them. Our objective is to empathize with them while maintaining rapport and then, gradually, to shift them toward the Desired State.

> Empathy is mastering what the other side is going to think and articulating it in order to diffuse or pre-empt.
>
> –CHRIS VOSS

A note of caution, though! Overdoing the pacing of *negative* ideas or feelings, or entering into them yourself, may unintentionally reinforce them and create bigger problems.

YES, IT'S SIMPLE, AND YES, IT WORKS

You may be asking yourself, does establishing rapport by pacing another person's words, verbal tone, gestures, and all the rest really work? Absolutely! Pacing, when done properly and subtly, can significantly boost your persuasive power.

How much pacing do you need to do? Is it a more-or-less constant technique that you apply to everybody, all the time? Or do you just engage in it initially? The answer is simple: pace the current experience as you establish rapport and then start leading toward your Desired State. Notice if the person is willing to follow you. If they follow you, then you know that you've paced enough. If they fail to follow, then you need to pace some more, deepen your rapport with them, and then lead again. Pace only as long as necessary for them to begin to follow as you begin to lead.

We've already discussed Amy Cuddy's research into body language or physiology. She found that people really struggled to mirror someone else's posture that was different from their own because it felt fake. "When I tell people about this, that our bodies change our minds and our minds can change our behavior, and our behavior can change our outcomes, they say to me, 'It feels fake.' Right? So, I said, 'Fake it till you make it.'"[75]

While I agree that there is some validity to Cuddy's suggestion to "fake it till you make it," she seems to be saying that changing your physiology or your body's position influences your thoughts and feelings—in that order. I agree that changes can happen that way, and I would add that this shift happens in *both* directions, as we discussed earlier in this chapter.

Your physiology can influence your thoughts and feelings, and your thoughts and feelings can also influence your body. I believe **future pacing**, in which you imagine performing something successfully in your mind, is a more effective technique than Cuddy's because "faking it" leaves us open to errors and the

---

75 Cuddy, "Your body language may shape who you are." Available online: https://www.ted.com/talks/amy_cuddy_your_body_language_shapes_who_you_are/

mixed emotions that follow. People often think of future pacing as visualization; it is that—and so much more. When we mentally rehearse, we can associate into that future performance as we imagine a successful outcome, and we wire that feeling of success into our nervous system before we ever execute the behavior.

Any behavior that you want to do, including matching and mirroring, can be practiced in your mind. Imagine that the next time you meet someone, you're able to comfortably match and mirror their behavior. Doing so programs that future success into your nervous system, like a rehearsal or a dry run. There are artists who practice this way—pianists envision themselves hitting the keys on their piano, in the correct sequence and rhythm while using just the right amount of pressure and emphasis with each note. Athletes, like figure skaters and gymnasts, are known to do this too, practicing the sequence of moves in their mind. They envision the performance using sensory-rich stimuli: *hearing* the sound of the crowd as it reacts to each technical maneuver, *feeling* sweat drip down the back of their neck, vividly *imagining* how their body responds to each movement as if they were successfully executing the movements in real life.

Remember, with the ***Think → Feel → Do*** process, our *thinking* impacts our *emotions*, which then together influence our *behavior*. This process flows in two directions: we can also shift our behavior, thereby impacting our emotions and influencing our thinking. Cuddy found that when people "fake it" (by changing their body position even though it feels unnatural), they eventually get more comfortable and master it.[76] For us, the message is clear: practice pacing in your mind as well as in real-life until it feels natural and becomes your default behavior. Eventually, it will be something you do automatically to build rapport.

Once you've successfully paced someone and established rapport, it's time to forge ahead and get to the heart of the matter: leading them to the Desired State. And that's where things get even more exciting!

How fast can we lead? Keep reading to find out!

---

76 Cuddy, "Your body language may shape who you are." Available online: https://www.ted.com/talks/amy_cuddy_your_body_language_shapes_who_you_are/

Remember the seven building blocks of rapport:

1. Postures, gestures
2. Facial expressions, blinking
3. Breathing
4. Voice—tone, tempo, pitch, volume
5. Word cues—visual, auditory, kinesthetic, etc.
6. Eye patterns
7. Key words and the language of motivation

Let's focus on a couple of these building blocks for this exercise. Think of a person in your professional or personal life whom you'd like to persuade. This person could be a manager, a co-worker, a client, a spouse, or a child.

As you interact with this person, begin by practicing pacing their experience. For example, if their arms are crossed, you cross your arms in a similar fashion. Once you have paced them, then go ahead and begin to lead them in a direction (e.g., uncross your arms, lean forward, stand up) and notice whether they follow you in that direction (do they uncross their arms, lean forward, and stand up as well?). Interesting sidebar: I once had a skeptical client in a corporate seminar who decided to test this principle at his gym (expecting it to fail). He got into a conversation with a stranger and was amazed by how quickly and effectively he was able first to pace and then to lead them. In his words, he became a believer!

Record how the interaction went, specifically:

- **What did you pace?** (E.g., tone of voice, gestures, facial expressions, word cues, etc.)

  ____

  ____

- **How did you pace it?** (Did you match or mirror? What exactly did you do?)

  ____

  ____

- **How did it feel?** (Did you feel comfortable? Was the exercise effortless or challenging?)

  ____

  ____

- **What were the results?** (How did the interaction go? Did you notice their willingness to follow?)

  ____

  ____

Chapter Seven

Horse Sense

> No one can tell, when two people walk closely together, what unconscious communication one mind may have with another.
>
> —ROBERT BARR, **"AN ALPINE DIVORCE"**

On September 4, 1904, *The New York Times* reported on an amazing German horse named "Hans," who had been taught by his owner, Wilhelm von Osten, how to count, figure fractions, identify different kinds of coins, and more. [77] Hans could tell you what day of the week it was by tapping his foot once for Sunday, twice for Monday, and so on. He could also identify colors by stamping his foot, and he could recognize people and spell their names by selecting the appropriate letters on a blackboard. Hans regularly demonstrated his incredible skills before the public, with different people asking him questions, astonishing experts and laypeople alike.

Intrigued, German authorities created a commission to determine whether Hans was extremely clever or whether there was some trickery involved. The members of the "Hans Commission" observed the horse very closely before concluding there were no tricks involved and that Hans was, indeed, exceptionally clever.

Hans amazed the world for several years until a psychologist named Oskar Pfungst proved he was an ordinary horse with a singular special talent: he could "read" people. Pfungst discovered that Hans gave the correct answer 89% of the time when the questioner knew the answer—and only 6% of the time when the questioner was in the dark about the correct answer. Why?

---

77 Edward T. Heyn, "Berlin's Wonderful Horse: He Can Do Almost Everything but Talk–How He Was Taught," *The New York Times* (September 4, 1904). Available online: https://timesmachine.nytimes.com/timesmachine/1904/09/04/101396572.pdf

Rather than being psychic, like most people thought he was, Hans was instead very good at detecting minute, unconscious changes in the posture and expressions of the people questioning and watching him. These changes told him whether to continue tapping his foot or to perform other behaviors accordingly.

Pfungst conducted more studies during which he discovered that he too could correctly answer questions 90% of the time just by watching the minute, inadvertent clues given by the people who were quizzing him. And when Pfungst reversed positions so that he became the questioner, he found that he also gave off tiny cues *even when he attempted to suppress them.*

If a horse can pick up on tiny changes in posture, facial tension, and other unconscious "signals," think of the phenomenal influence these signals can have on *us* as humans. Consider how much communication is going on even when we're silent, as well as how much our physical bodies can either support or undermine our efforts to persuade others when we *do* speak.

While listening to what people say is certainly important, Hans the horse shows us there is a whole range of communication being carried out beyond the words we utter. People communicate constantly, and a great deal of that communication takes place outside of spoken or written words. This can include facial expressions, eye contact, tone of voice, touch, our overall appearance, and countless other subtle gestures such as nodding our head or waving our hands.

Although the intentions of our communication may generally be positive, the impacts we have can be very different from our intentions. Case in point: even if you say nothing, you are communicating. You cannot *not* communicate. Think about it—just sitting there, saying nothing, with a blank expression on your face sends a message that someone looking at you will interpret, even if only subconsciously.

Consider a situation in which you need to have a challenging conversation with your partner. Have they made eye contact with you or are they distracted by their phone? Are they facing you or have they turned away? Are they sitting with their arms crossed? Are you reading into their behavior or assuming what their behavior means? We often mistakenly read into people's communication and claim to know their intentions.

While it's important to be aware of another person's physiology, there is also a danger in "reading into" it too much and attaching our own meaning to it.

One of the pitfalls of communication—and where it often starts to break down—is when people "mind read." Rather than engaging in such mind reading, it's best to ask clarifying questions and differentiate between information that is sensory-based (that which we observe using our senses) and non-sensory-based (attributing meaning or intent to the communication without any evidence) to ensure that your understanding of the communication is clear and accurate.

For example, if someone is sitting with their arms crossed, we might assume that they are closed off. In fact, their shoulder may be sore, they may just be more comfortable sitting that way, or a million other things may be going on that we're unaware of. The sensory-based part of the communication is simply that they are sitting with their arms crossed. There is a danger in reading into and interpreting the meaning or intention behind that non-verbal communication because, all too often, our interpretation is inherently flawed. That's why clarifying communication is so important! You'll be more effective at understanding another person and their Current State when you pay attention to all these cues, both verbal and non-verbal, while also carefully avoiding mind reading.

> **Key Concept:**
> We respond to the totality of a person's communication. Beyond simply the words that they use, their tone and physiology have a major impact on what's communicated. Remember to stay focused on sensory-based information and ask clarifying questions to avoid the mind-reading trap.

More than a century after Oskar Pfungst studied Hans the horse, scientists are still working toward a deeper understanding of the impact of our body language on communication. Rana el Kaliouby is a computer scientist who is teaching computers how to read people. The app that she is developing can tell how you're feeling emotionally—just from the look on your face![78]

"Our human face happens to be one of the most powerful channels that we all use to communicate social and emotional states, everything from enjoyment,

---

78 Rana el Kaliouby, "This app knows how you feel–from the look on your face." *TEDWomen* (May 2015). Available online: https://www.ted.com/talks/rana_el_kaliouby_this_app_knows_how_you_feel_from_the_look_on_your_face

surprise, empathy and curiosity," says Kaliouby.[79] Even in today's tech-dominant world and with the rapid development of Artificial Intelligence (AI), teaching a computer to read facial expressions is challenging, although it's something that humans (and some horses) can do quite well, with little thought. Kaliouby goes on to explain that each movement of a facial muscle is known as "an action unit." Humans have 45 action units (which include things like a brow furrow or a lip corner pull) and we combine them to express hundreds of emotions. "Teaching a computer to read these facial emotions is hard, because these action units, they can be fast, they're subtle, and they combine in many different ways," she says.[80]

Can you identify the action units that go into a simple smile or frown? Probably not—and yet you intuitively interpret facial expressions all the time to help you determine what another person is feeling and thinking. In fact, your mind expertly navigates these action units more efficiently than Kaliouby's computers. What's more, you regularly act and make decisions based on other people's facial expressions without even realizing it.

The conclusions you draw are based on your previous experiences and on your unique model of the world, and these conclusions may or may not be an accurate interpretation of how the other person is feeling or thinking at that moment. Still, with practice, when you slow down and pay close attention to the physical signs of communication and look beyond what a person is saying, you can learn so much more about their Current State.

Our eyes, for example, move very quickly and subtly; they are extremely telling and are an important part of a person's facial expression because they give us clues as to "how" (rather than "what") another person thinks.

THE EYES ARE ONLY CLUES (RATHER THAN DETECTORS)

Some people think the eyes act as a lie detector, that you can tell if a person is lying because their eyes will move a certain way. This is false. For example,

---

79 Kaliouby, "This app knows how you feel." Available online: https://www.ted.com/talks/rana_el_kaliouby_this_app_knows_how_you_feel_from_the_look_on_your_face

80 Kaliouby, "This app knows how you feel." Available online: https://www.ted.com/talks/rana_el_kaliouby_this_app_knows_how_you_feel_from_the_look_on_your_face

if, as you look at someone, their eyes move to your left, either vertically or horizontally, this generally means they are constructing something. They *might* be fabricating an elaborate excuse—or they might be constructing a way to relay something to you in the most honest and efficient manner possible. Thus, it takes more than eye movements to reveal a lie.

> The eye obeys exactly the action of the mind.
>
> –RALPH WALDO EMERSON

A person's eyes move around in distinct patterns when they are accessing information stored in the brain. These eye movements can give important clues about how that person processes information (visually, auditorily, or kinesthetically), especially when we consider them in combination with the person's word choices. To make it easy for you as you learn about these eye patterns, let's look at them from *your* perspective, that is, what you will see as you face another person. So, for example, if you're speaking to a right-handed person and their eyes go up and to *your* right, they're remembering pictures (visual processing). If their eyes move down and to *your* left, they're accessing kinesthetic information such as emotions, feelings, and sensations.

Suppose you're talking to a couple of friends who recently visited the ruins of the Acropolis, in Athens, Greece, and you ask them about the trip. One partner's eyes move up and to your right before speaking, which means they're mentally recalling a visual representation of their trip before describing the ruins to you. The other partner's eyes move down and to your left indicating that they're reliving the emotions, feelings, and sensations associated with the ruins before replying. There's an excellent chance the first person will describe the ruins using visual words and phrases such as, "the staircase *looked* insurmountable," or "I had *seen* the ruins in pictures, but I didn't realize how significantly they were crumbling until I *saw* them in real life." Meanwhile, the second person will describe the experience using kinesthetic words and phrases such as, "I *felt* awestruck thinking about how old the ruins are!" or "There were so many people, the *energy* was exhilarating."

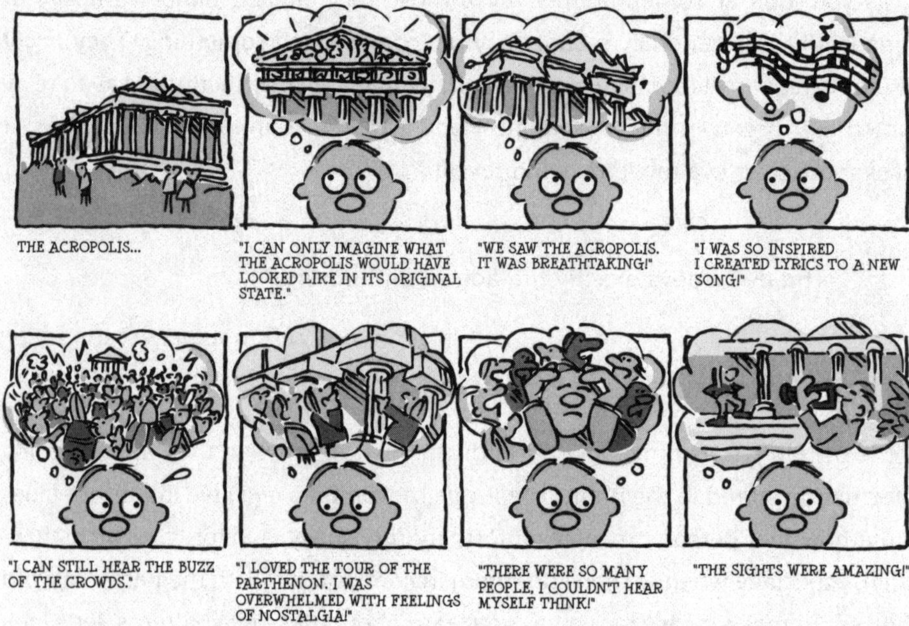

The following diagram illustrates the various eye patterns and what they indicate. The diagram is representative of a normally organized right-handed person (in general, "normally organized" means the person has experienced no severe physical or mental trauma). Note that for a left-handed person the eye patterns would be mirrored (left would flip to right and right would flip to left in the following examples).

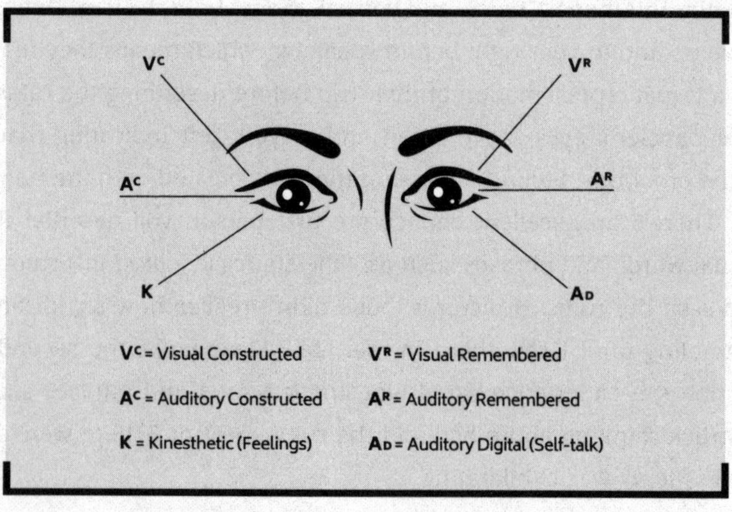

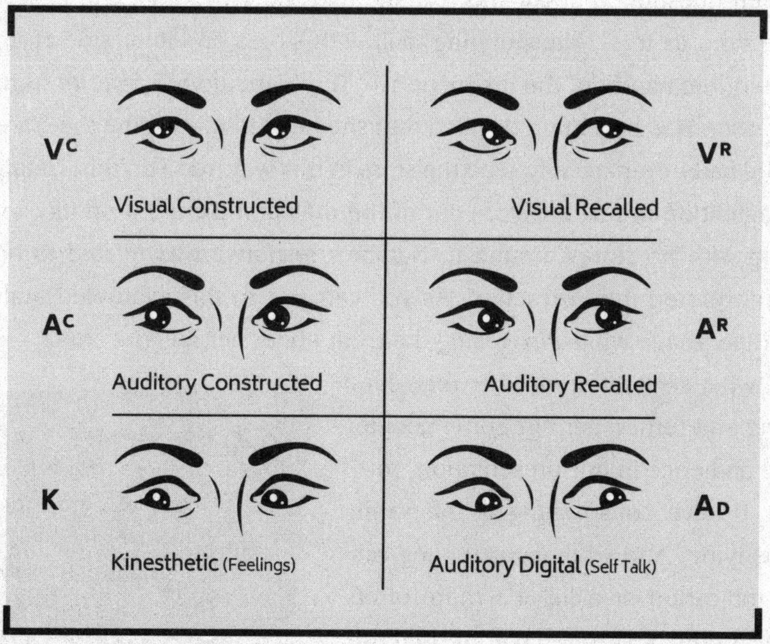

For example, say that a right-handed person's eyes move up and to your left as they collect their thoughts. We can tell that they are visually constructing a thought. If their eyes move to the left or right on the horizontal, they are remembering things in terms of sounds.

On one occasion, Natalie and I were presenting to a team of senior managers; we were discussing that we all have what we refer to as strategies, or "mental recipes," for everything we do. We explained to the audience that observing the different directions in which an individual's eyes move as they speak can reveal a great deal about how that person is thinking. During a demonstration, a member of the audience, in an attempt to uncover Natalie's strategy for shopping, asked her to think about her favorite store. Natalie is very visual, so her eyes immediately went up, first to the right before moving to the left.

As we've discussed, if you're facing a person, eye movement up and to the right indicates a visual recall, and up and to the left indicates a visual creation or construct. So, like you, the audience member (and the whole room) knew Natalie was making pictures in her head. The burning question on everyone's mind was, "Why did Natalie recall first and then construct? Was she telling a lie?"

When questioned about this, Natalie told the group that she pictured her favorite store as it is, in a shopping mall with stores on either side of it. Then, because of the nature of the instruction—"Think about your *favorite* store"—for some reason Natalie's brain decided that she needed to imagine the store on its own. She had never actually seen the store in this way, so to do this, Natalie used her imagination to pull the store out of the mall and picture it on its own, free-standing with no stores around it. Natalie's response was related to how her brain interpreted the instruction. As you can see, in this example Natalie constructed an image while *also* telling the truth about her favorite store.

So, what's the difference between constructing and remembering? Some people, like the audience in our presentation, mistakenly believe constructing is the same thing as lying. And while constructing *can* be an indication of a lie, it's more often that the brain is simply creating or constructing information rather than recalling it. For instance, if you're asked to visualize an elephant you may remember a photo or an elephant that you saw in real life and imagine what that elephant looked like. In this case your eyes will move up and to the right.

> **Key Concept:** The eyes give important clues about how a person's mind is processing information and about "how" they think. Once you know that, you can shift your language to match how they think and, as a result, become more persuasive.

If you're asked to visualize an elephant with purple spots, though, your brain will probably have to construct that image. As you create the image, it's likely that your eyes will move up and to the right initially as you first recall the image of an actual elephant that you've seen before, and then up and to the left as your mind creates a new visual with the added polka dots.

In this case, the eyes moving up and to the left indicate that the brain is constructing a visual image rather than revealing someone's level of honesty. You may have noticed that the one position missing in these diagrams is eyes straight ahead, moving neither up/down nor right/left. This typically means the person is thinking visually and the information is right there at the surface, making it very easy to access.

EXPONENTIAL X

Studies suggest that 55% of the impact of communication between people stems from physical cues—that is, the way a person stands, gestures, smiles, scowls, breathes, and so on. Another 38% of the impact of our communication is attributed to vocal tone—voice volume and timbre, rate of speech, and emphasis on certain words. Together then, physiology and tonality make up a total of 93% of the impact of the communication between people! That leaves only the final 7% attributed to words themselves (and that includes sounds like grunts and groans, which are hardly "words").

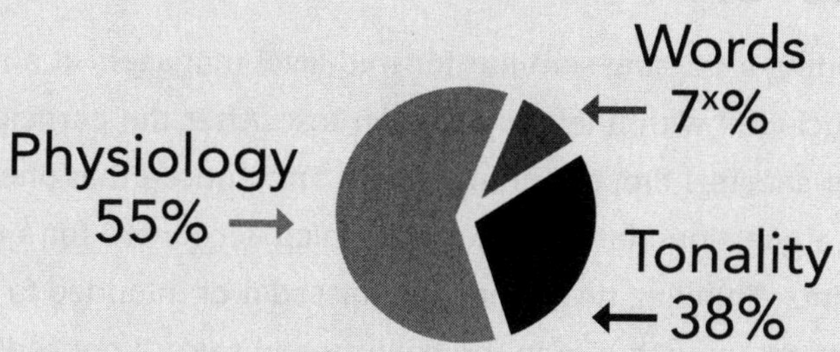

Communication is broken down into **three areas of impact**

Although only 7% of the impact of our communication is attributed to words, it's more accurate to say that words account for "seven to the exponential X percent" of communication. That may sound odd until you consider that words are labels that we use to represent experiences.

Suppose, for example, we are having a conversation, and you say the word "vacation." On one of our last trips, I had a great time exploring Croatia on a sailboat with Natalie, so the word "vacation" for me triggers an explosion of positive emotions, stories, visuals, and more in my head. That's the "exponential X" power of your words setting off a strong and positive reaction in me.

If, on the other hand, I had been mugged while on the vacation and Natalie had spent the entire time sick with the flu, the word "vacation" would release a flood of negative emotions and stories in my mind.

Knowing the "exponential X" value that a person has unconsciously placed on various words can help you guide their feelings, which will in turn help you influence their behavior.

The power of communication is in knowing that some of the experiences represented by words are positive, some are negative, and some remain neutral. The use of certain words, whether deliberate or unintentional, can bring up all the pictures, sounds, feelings, tastes, and smells attached to these experiences.

THE X-FACTOR

I was once leading a training seminar for mid-level managers at a major corporation that concluded with a lengthy written test. After the participants turned in their answer sheets, I flipped through them and noticed that one of the managers had left a question blank, a question which accounted for a considerable number of points. Thinking he might have missed it or intended to go back to it but forgot, I caught up with him in the hallway and said, "I noticed you skipped one of the questions. You may not care about missing it, I just want to point it out in case you intended to loop back and answer it but forgot."

His face turned beet red, and he practically screamed at me, "How dare you accuse me of not caring?!"

> Words need to be crafted, not sprayed. They need to be fitted together with infinite care.
>
> –NORMAN COUSINS

Wow! I had accidently triggered one of this individual's very negative "exponential X" phrases. As he was retiring within the next month, he may have believed that my "you may not care" comment was an insinuation that he was partially checked out because he was at the end of his career. In the context of deleting, distorting, and generalizing, it's possible that he distorted and generalized my comment to mean he wasn't a caring person, on top of the other emotions he was experiencing at the time. The point is that it was a negative "exponential X" phrase that likely released a flood of negative meanings, pictures, sounds, and feelings attached to one or more disempowering experiences in his life. (Notice, I'm doing a little bit of mind reading myself—it's part of being human!)

We stumble around the "exponential X" power of words all the time because we never know what the "exponential X" words or phrases will be for people. That's why it's so important to choose words carefully and to pay close attention to their impact.

Key Concept:
The words you use can either build or break rapport, and they often do so inadvertently. To be an effective persuader, you must be aware of the impact of your words. Rather than assuming others will interpret them the same way you do, pay close attention to the effect your words have. And be aware of any of your own "exponential X" reactions that may pop up based on the words that others use.

WORDLESS MINDS

What does the mind do with all this communication, with the words it hears or reads, with the sounds, sights, physical feelings, tastes, and smells it constantly receives?

While many people believe that the mind processes and stores this information in the form of words, the truth is that everything the mind absorbs is actually processed and stored in the form of sensory information (pictures, sounds, feelings, tastes, and smells) as opposed to words. The brain converts this sensory information into words, which are simply labels we use to identify and make sense of our own thoughts, feelings, and experiences and then to convey them to others as we interact. Words also help us elicit experiences and reactions from others.

Let's say someone cuts you off on the highway and sends your car into a spin. Your mind processes this horrible experience in sensory terms: the *feel* of your hands gripping the wheel as you swerve, the *sound* of screeching tires, the *sight* of other cars spinning by, the *emotion* of fear. Later, you'll use words to make sense of the experience, to describe it to yourself and others, as in, "Some jerk cut me off and sent me into a spin, which almost got me killed!" These words are so clear that they seem to be the stored information. Actually, these words are merely labels used to represent and make sense of the sensory input, that is, the stored sights, sounds, feelings, tastes, and smells. We'll look at the importance of these senses and sensory-rich storytelling more in Chapter Nine.

> Every person's map of the world is as unique as their thumbprint. There are no two people alike. No two people who understand the same sentence the same way... So, in dealing with people, you try not to fit them to your concept of what they should be.
>
> –MILTON ERICKSON

Even when you receive information primarily in the form of words, your mind processes it in terms of sensory input. Imagine you're attending a lecture about Viking warfare and their invasion of other lands. As the professor speaks you conjure up images of fierce warriors, you imagine the sights, sounds, feelings, tastes, and smells experienced by those they invaded. The word "Viking" here serves as a label for the sensory information related to these warriors that is stored in your brain.

LABELS AND CLUES

So, if "Viking" is a label we use to represent the sensory information associated with those fierce warriors, the question becomes, "Do we all represent the word 'Viking' in the same way in our imaginations?" In other words, if someone says the word "Viking," do I see the same pictures, hear the same sounds, experience the same feelings, and recall the same smells and tastes as they do?

It's possible that the way I think about or imagine "Vikings" is close to the way you do—and just as likely that it is very different. So different, in fact, that for one person "Viking" might be largely a *visual* word linked to numerous images of warriors, with just a few sounds and feelings, and tastes and smells may be absent from awareness. For another person it might be more of a *sound* word tied to battle cries and clanking swords, with just a few pictures and feelings. For a third person, "Viking" may be predominantly a *kinesthetic* word tied to feelings of adrenaline at the thought of new territories explored.

We each use all of these representational systems to various degrees and in different ways. For example, one person might be *mostly* visual, *moderately* auditory, and *slightly* kinesthetic, while another person might be mostly kinesthetic, moderately visual, and slightly auditory—really, any combination is possible! It's also important to note that although these three are the most common processing systems, smell and taste also play a role in how some people process information. It's generally accepted that in Western cultures, the visual processing system is dominant in about 60% of the population, the auditory in 20%, and the kinesthetic in the remaining 20%. Of course, what is dominant will change from culture to culture and throughout different periods in history, which is why it's essential to keep in mind that these statistics are merely an approximation based on a certain culture and context.

Key Concept: We all experience the world in a sensory manner and process information in the form of pictures, sounds, feelings, tastes, and smells. Each of us favors one of these processing channels. We tend to be most at ease when communicating with a person who shares our dominant or primary representational system, and who processes experiences similar to the way we do.

Let's think back to the Rudyard Kipling quote: "All the people like us are We, and everyone else is They." Those who have yet to be exposed to the principles in this book typically assume that others will use the same representational systems in the same ways as they do, even though that's clearly far from the truth, as Indira discovered in talking with her daughter.

Knowing whether a person is primarily visual, auditory, or kinesthetic helps you understand how they think. Keep in mind we are talking about *how* they think rather than *what* they think. This is very helpful to the persuasion process because if you know how they think you can communicate in the manner they find most "friendly." This ties back to providing emotional fulfillment and helping to build rapport.

CRACKING THE CODE

> A word is not a crystal,
> transparent and unchanging;
> it is the skin of a living thought
> and may vary greatly in color
> and content according to the
> circumstances and time in which
> it is used.
>
> –OLIVER WENDELL HOLMES

Key Concept: When you're aware of a person's dominant or primary representational system and adjust your language to match theirs, you demonstrate that you understand their model of the world and you provide them with a deeper experience of being understood, which thereby increases rapport.

Determining whether someone's preferred representational system is visual, auditory, or kinesthetic is simple: pay attention and listen carefully to what they say and notice whether the bulk of their words are more visual, more auditory, or more kinesthetic. This is quite easy to do with a little practice. Review the word list on the next page and soon you'll be able to readily identify a person's dominant or primary representational system.

Visual	Auditory	Kinesthetic	Unspecified
an eyeful	afterthought	all washed up	change
appear	be all ears	boils down to	conceive
appears to me	be heard	catch on	consider
beyond a shadow of a doubt	blabbermouth	chip off the old block	decide
bird's eye view	call on	come to grips with	distinct
catch a glimpse of	clear as a bell	concrete	experience
clear	clearly expressed	control yourself	insensitive
clear cut	deaf	cool/calm/collected	know
crystal	describe in detail	feel	learn
dawn	dissonance	firm foundations	motivate
dim view	earful	get a handle	perceive
envision	give an account of	get a handle on	process
flashed on	give me your ear	get a load of this	sense
focused	grant an audience	get hold of	think
foggy	harmonize	get in touch with	understand
get a perspective on	hear	get the drift of	
get a scope on	hear voices	get your goat	
hazy	hidden message	grasp	
hazy idea	hold your tongue	hand in hand	
horse of a different color	idle talk	hang in there	
illuminate	inquire into	hard	
imagine	keynote speaker	heated argument	
in light of	listen	hold it	
in person	loud and clear	hold on	
in view of	make music	keep your shirt on	
look	manner of speaking	know-how	
looks like	mellifluous	lay cards on the table	
make a scene	pay attention to	make contact	
mental image	power of speech	pain in the neck	
mental picture	purrs like a kitten	pull some strings	
mind's eye	question	scrape	
naked eye	resonate	sharp as a tack	
paint a picture	rings a bell	slip through	
picture	silence	slipped my mind	
reveal	sound(s)	smooth operator	
see	state your purpose	solid	
see to it	tattle-tale	so-so	
short sighted	to tell the truth	start from scratch	
show	tongue-tied	stiff upper lip	
showing off	tune in/out	stuffed shirt	
sight for sore eyes	unheard of	tap into	
staring off into space	unhearing	throw out	
take a peek	utterly	too much of a hassle	
tunnel vision	voice an opinion	topsy-turvy	
under your nose	well informed	touch	
up front	within hearing	unfeeling	
view	word for word		
well defined			

You'll have noticed that the fourth group of words on this list is "unspecified." This consists of words which are separate from visual, auditory, or kinesthetic systems. People hearing these words tend to interpret them as belonging to their preferred system. Regardless of whether you are predominantly visual, auditory, or kinesthetic, unspecified words and phrases will sound "right" to you and help give you the feeling of being understood.

Each of us occasionally uses unspecified words unintentionally. You can tap into the persuasive power of unspecified words by using them intentionally to appeal to an entire group of people with different representational systems all at once. Politicians do this all the time, saying things like, "We all want to *experience* change," and "We *understand* that we need to..." The words "experience" and "understand" feel comfortable to everyone because we each interpret them through the unique filter of our primary representational system.

Key Concept:
The words a person uses offer clues as to how they are thinking and processing information at any given moment in time. By actively listening and paying attention to their word choices, we gain insight into their unique model of the world.

The better you, the persuader, are at communicating in all of the sensory modalities, the better you will be at matching your communication to another person's dominant or primary processing style. Remember the Law of Requisite Variety from Chapter Six? The more flexibility you have in how you communicate and in matching someone's primary processing style, the easier it is to build rapport and provide them with the experience of being understood. Ultimately, this will trigger a sense of emotional fulfillment in them and increase the likelihood that you will be able to influence them toward the Desired State.

Remember!
The Law of Requisite Variety
The person who has the most mental, emotional, and behavioral flexibility will ultimately have control over a system or situation.

GO BEYOND

As we've seen, we're constantly communicating, even when we're silent, and a great deal of communication takes place outside of our awareness, beyond the literal meaning of words. The totality of a person's verbal and non-verbal communication reveals a lot about them, so we must be mindful of the importance of picking up on these cues when interacting and communicating with others. As you continue to learn how to decipher cues in others' communication effectively, you'll be able to build rapport by pacing their experience of the world.

> People immediately feel more comfortable and in rapport with someone who's responding to them in the same language representations as they've communicated at that point in time.
>
> –MICHAEL BROOKS

Find three friends who have each had an interesting experience recently, such as a starting a new job, moving to a new city, or getting married. Then, ask each one to describe their experience to you.

Watch their eye movements and listen carefully to the words they use. Then, look at the eye and word charts from this chapter. Are they primarily visual, auditory, or kinesthetic in their communication? From their eye movements and word choices, you'll be able to recognize their preferred representational system and adjust your communication accordingly. You'll also note that while they're explaining their experiences, they are likely using different ways of remembering and describing them. As you continue to listen carefully, you'll discover that their unique descriptions will tell you how they process things mentally. This can also give you insight into what their strategies or mental recipes are for doing various tasks—in other words, the sequencing and ordering that they go through as they make decisions and carry out behaviors. For example, is their sequence visual, auditory, then kinesthetic or maybe they start with kinesthetic and then move to auditory followed by visual? Or maybe it's some other sequence entirely?

Chapter Eight

The Million Dollar Question

> If I had an hour to solve a problem and my life depended on the answer, I would spend the first fifty-five minutes figuring out the proper questions to ask. For if I knew the proper questions, I could solve the problem in less than five minutes.
>
> –ALBERT EINSTEIN

At the turn of the twentieth century, Albert Einstein asked the question, "What if I rode a beam of light across the universe?"[81] This simple yet ingenious question set his imagination on a quest, and in 1905, he published his Special Theory of Relativity, which argued, among other observations, that "the speed of light is unchanging."

Einstein's quest brought him to new understandings in the realm of physics, specifically that while the laws of physics appear the same to all observers, "there is no fixed frame of reference in the universe. Everything is moving relative to everything else."[82] Einstein's seemingly simple question further guided him to challenge Newton's Three Laws of Motion, proving that they were only approximately correct and that they broke down "when velocities approached that of light." [83]

In 1915, Einstein's constant questioning led him to develop his General Theory of Relativity, which "showed that Newton's Law of Gravitation was also

---

81 Warren Berger, "Einstein and Questioning: Exploring the inquiring mind of one of our greatest thinkers," *A More Beautiful Question* (2012). Available online: http://amorebeautifulquestion.com/einstein-questioning/

82 Nora Taylor Redd, "Einstein's Theory of General Relativity," *Space.com* (November 7, 2017). Available online: https://www.space.com/17661-theory-general-relativity.html

83 Eric G. Blackman, "Albert Einstein and the Theory of Relativity." Available online: http://www.pas.rochester.edu/~blackman/ast104/einstein.html

only approximately correct, breaking down in the presence of very strong gravitational fields."[84]

Einstein's theories of relativity presented entirely new ways of thinking about and viewing the world, and they completely changed the study of space, time, mass, energy, and gravity.

Beyond his impact on the field of physics, Einstein is also well known for his thought experiments. When he was sixteen years old, he imagined himself chasing a beam of light, and asked, "What would happen if you chased a beam of light as it moved through space?"[85] Einstein's thought process demonstrates the power of the **"As If" Frame**—thinking *as if* you could chase a beam of light moving through space or *as if* you could catch up with that beam of light. If you could, what would happen?

In working through his thought experiment, Einstein proposed that if we could, in fact, do this, we might be able to see the beam of light frozen in space. Considering what we know of physics, it would then cease to be light at all, in which case, it would change our understanding of time itself. Curiously, many of Einstein's thought experiments entertained questions about the nature of time.

Einstein's simple yet profound questions sent his imagination on a series of quests, and over time they sparked quests in others too. Have you ever wondered why time seems to pass more slowly or more quickly at different moments in your life? Einstein's theories led to the discovery of a phenomenon called **time dilation** or **distortion**, an experience that also occurs in trance or hypnotic states. Time dilation or distortion shows that our perception of time is situational and contextual, and that time varies or passes at a different rate from person to person. In other words, "A fast-moving observer measures time passing more slowly than a relatively stationary observer would."[86]

You likely experience this phenomenon in your own life when time seems to pass slowly when you're bored or uninterested in what you're doing, and it appears to pass more quickly when you're really invested in or enjoying something. For example, if you're standing in line for a movie, ten minutes might

---

84 Blackman, "Albert Einstein and the Theory of Relativity." Available online: http://www.pas.rochester.edu/~blackman/ast104/einstein.html

85 Walter Isaacson, "The Light-Beam Rider" *The New York Times* (October 30, 2015). Available online: https://www.nytimes.com/2015/11/01/opinion/sunday/the-light-beam-rider.html

86 Blackman, "Albert Einstein and the Theory of Relativity." Available online: http://www.pas.rochester.edu/~blackman/ast104/einstein.html

seem like forever, whereas if it's a great movie two hours can fly by and feel like five minutes!

Einstein's theories and thought experiments generated new questions for others, which in turn led to further intellectual investigations and numerous scientific breakthroughs. Great thinkers throughout history have shared Einstein's keen sense of curiosity; several centuries earlier, Leonardo da Vinci had "an insatiably curious approach to life and an unrelenting quest for continuous learning," as Michael J. Gelb says in his book, *How to Think Like Leonardo da Vinci*.[87]

While most of us aren't quite on the same level as Einstein or da Vinci, Michael Gelb explores da Vinci's approach to creativity, thought, and questioning and argues that readers can apply da Vinci's techniques in their own lives. After all, "your brain is much better than you think," Gelb writes.

So, what thought processes did Einstein and da Vinci have in common? And how is it possible for you to train your brain to think like them?

The kinds of questions we ask guide our thoughts, emotions, and actions. In fact, questions determine the direction of our thoughts and what we focus on or pay attention to. "Great minds ask great questions," Gelb says. "The questions that engage our thoughts on a daily basis reflect our life purpose and influence the quality of our lives. By cultivating a da Vinci-like open, questioning frame of mind, we broaden our universe and improve our ability to travel through it."[88]

Here's how it works:

The mind has a system for filing information, much the same as we would store information in a filing cabinet in different folders. Where a physical filing cabinet is limited by its size, the unconscious mind can store almost unlimited amounts of information. And the better the "files"—or memories—are organized, the easier it is to access the information. Effective questions can act as your access codes to the information.

Whether you ask a question of yourself or someone else, the mind goes on a quest to find a response. For example, if you ask, "Why are you unhappy?" you'll send an individual's mind on a quest to search for the reasons behind

---

87 Michael J. Gelb, *How to Think Like Leonardo da Vinci* (Dell, 2000).

88 Gelb, *How to Think Like Leonardo da Vinci*, p. 55.

their unhappiness. If you continue to probe in this way, asking a question like, "What else makes you unhappy?" the person will keep thinking about negative things which continues to reinforce their state of unhappiness rather than shifting them to a more desirable state. Each question sends a person's mind on a quest, enabling us to elicit historical memories and information, allowing us to uncover Current State thinking, beliefs, and values, and giving us the opportunity to engage and guide the individual toward the Desired State.

Consider for a moment how many of us neglect to approach thinking from a meta perspective, and actually fail to think about our own thinking. How many questions do you ask yourself and how do those questions cause your mind to filter information in a way that you're unaware of? For example, if I ask myself, "Why am I always forgetting...?" the question brings to mind all the reasons why I continue to forget, whereas if I ask myself instead, "What's a better way to remember...?" I can create strategies for stronger memory retention.

> **Key Concept:**
> A question is a kind of tool that serves several functions. Questions enable us to access stored memories and information and to assist others to do the same. Questions also allow us to discover and clarify another person's Current State, and to engage and guide them toward a Desired State.

HABITS OF MIND

You can improve your daily habits of thinking by being more aware of the questions you ask yourself and the presuppositions inherent within them. For example, think about questions like "What else could go wrong today?" which presupposes that things have already gone wrong and will continue to do so, versus, "How do I make today even more enjoyable and fulfilling?" which presupposes that today has already been enjoyable and fulfilling and will be even more so. Over time, this awareness will prompt you to ask questions more strategically.

Most of us are quite unaware of our own thinking because the majority of our thinking occurs outside of our conscious awareness. In recognizing the power of effective questions, we gain a greater appreciation for the fact that we can all determine the direction of our own thoughts. When we're actively engaged in the thinking process, we have control over it. By asking effective questions, we engage the imagination and guide it on a quest, potentially interrupting and shifting thought processes.

Eric Schmidt, CEO of Google from 2001 to 2011, said, "We run this company on questions, not answers."[89] Indeed, this is true for the rest of us as individuals as well. We ask—and are asked—questions all day long. Casual questions, personal questions, business questions, friendly and not-so-friendly questions, innocent questions, leading questions, and many more. Curiosity is inherent in our humanity and asking questions does more than provide us with the answers we seek; questions can ignite our innovation and are a powerful persuasion tool.

Several years ago, I had the opportunity to speak with Art Fry, who helped develop the Post-it® Note for 3M. Fry explained that Post-it® Notes were the serendipitous result of a question 3M researchers had asked themselves back in the late 1960s: "What new substances or processes can we discover and develop?"

In 1968, 3M chemist Spencer Silver was tasked with coming up with "bigger, stronger, tougher adhesives." While he failed to create such an adhesive, what he found instead was a new adhesive that would stick to all kinds of things with the side effect that it only stuck *a little bit*. A "low-tack" adhesive, it clung lightly to another surface and could be removed without causing damage or leaving a residue. Yet no one at 3M could figure out how this low-tack adhesive could be used—until Fry, who was the "new products" guy at 3M, asked the right question.

"In essence my job was to continually ask questions like, 'How can we solve the customers' problems with these technologies we know about?'" Fry told me. When he heard about Silver's new adhesive, he was intrigued. So, he attended one of the 3M forums where Silver and other researchers presented their findings, learned about this strange and apparently useless adhesive, and filed the information away in his mind.[90]

---

89 Paul Sloane, "Ask Questions: The Single Most Important Habit for Innovative Thinkers," ***Innovation Management*** (December 9, 2008). Available online: https://innovationmanagement.se/2008/12/09/ask-questions-the-single-most-important-habit-for-innovative-thinkers/

90 Paul Rosenthal, "Art Fry's Invention Has a Way of Sticking Around," Lemelson Center, Smithsonian (June 13, 2008). Available online: https://invention.si.edu/podcast-art-frys-invention-has-way-sticking-around

Then one night, Fry was at a church choir practice where he typically used little pieces of paper as bookmarks in his hymnal. Unfortunately, these little papers had an annoying habit of falling out, which prompted Fry to say to himself, "I wish I could have a bookmark that would stick to the page without ripping it up. How could I do that?"[91]

He remembered Silver's low-tack adhesive and began to wonder if it could be used to create a bookmark that would stay in place *and* keep the book pages pristine. The rest is history.

> The truth is that good ideas, noble intentions, brilliant inventions, and miraculous discoveries go nowhere unless somebody forms a team to act on them.
>
> –LAURIE BETH JONES

From start to finish, Post-it® Notes were the result of asking—and answering—inventive questions.

Although retired when we spoke, Art Fry continued to work with young researchers at 3M, teaching them to ask questions like: "I wonder how we can solve problems for people in ways that have never been thought of before?" and "How can we solve their problems with these technologies that we know about?"

MOVING BEYOND INNOVATION

We've seen that resourceful questions are critical for innovation; they're also essential for uncovering a person's model of the world and identifying their Current State. A well-thought-out question reveals information about a person's Current State motivations, assumptions, beliefs, and values. Asking questions demonstrates to someone that we are interested in them and allows us to gain information that will enable us to provide them with the experience of being understood.

---

91 Art Fry, personal communication, April 3, 2013.

Paul Sloane, author of *The Leader's Guide to Lateral Thinking Skills* and *The Innovative Leader*, suggests that "with prospects, with clients, at school, at home, in business, with our friends, family, colleagues, or managers we can check assumptions and gain a better appreciation of the issues by first asking strategic questions."[92] Sloane reinforces this point by recounting a story:

> When Greg Dyke became Director-General of the BBC in 2000, he went to every major location and assembled the staff. They came expecting a long presentation. He simply sat down with them and asked a question, "What is the one thing I should do to make things better for you?" Then he listened. He followed this with another question, "What is the one thing I should do to make things better for our viewers and listeners?" He knew that at that early stage he could learn more from his employees than they could from him. The workers at the BBC had many wonderful ideas that they were keen to share. The fact that the new boss took time to question and then listen earned him enormous respect.[93]

Questions, then, are more than just requests for information. Asking the right questions is part of a larger process that can help you strengthen rapport, as Greg Dyke did with his employees and the BBC's audience.

WHERE ARE YOU GOING? LEADING THE MIND

When your boss asks, "What is the one thing I should do to make things better for you?" your mind looks for the things that need improvement, that can be made *better*. Rather than offering an impartial analysis of the company, or a list of all the good and bad things that have been done, your mind will actually search for ways the company could improve—even if everything *already* seems good.

The mind typically fails to analyze the quality of the question it is asked because at a conscious level we tend to be lazy. Acting like a biological search

---

92 Sloane, "Ask questions: The Single Most Important Habit for Innovative Thinkers." Available online: https://innovationmanagement.se/2008/12/09/ask-questions-the-single-most-important-habit-for-innovative-thinkers/

93 Sloane, "Ask questions: The Single Most Important Habit for Innovative Thinkers." Available online: https://innovationmanagement.se/2008/12/09/ask-questions-the-single-most-important-habit-for-innovative-thinkers/

engine, the mind performs a search based upon the exact question asked rather than evaluating whether or not the question is useful. For example, if someone asks, "How much better are you feeling today?" your mind searches for information about feeling better. Regardless of how you may have been feeling before the question was asked, your brain is now engaged to go on a quest to search for and pay attention to "feeling better." That quest is the mind's automatic and powerful response to a question. As persuaders, we can shape this quest by guiding the mind in the desired direction and encouraging the person to think the desired thoughts.

> **Key Concept:**
> As you know, where our thoughts go, our feelings and behavior invariably follow. This makes the questions we ask ourselves and others a powerful persuasive tool.

FOCUS ON THE JOURNEY, RATHER THAN THE DESTINATION

The use of the word "quest" (which is related to the word "question") can be traced back to the twelfth century, where it appeared in French as *quête*, "the act of seeking," and medieval Latin as *questa*, meaning "search or inquiry."[94]

The origin of the words "quest" and "question" is important because it debunks the idea that a quest is strictly about the destination, goal, or target, or that a question is only about the answer. Instead, like an "expedition by a knight or company of knights to accomplish some prescribed task, such as finding the Holy Grail," the journey that a quest or question takes you on is as important as the destination itself.[95]

As we apply this concept to the mind, it becomes increasingly evident that it's important to ask questions to spark a shift in thought, and that it's useful to ask questions at any point in the ***Think* → *Feel* → *Do*** process.

In his book on da Vinci, Michael Gelb postulates that creativity and curiosity are the impetus for greatness. The extraordinary ways in which da Vinci looked

94 "quest." *Online Etymology Dictionary*. Available online: https://www.etymonline.com/word/quest

95 "quest." *Collins Dictionary*. Available online: https://www.collinsdictionary.com/dictionary/english/quest

at things inspired creative questioning, which in turn resulted in inventions and masterpieces that were far ahead of his time.

When we look at the power of questions to ignite creativity, we realize that they are extremely useful in engaging and shifting the mind from the Current State, where it's usually stuck, to the Desired State, often resulting in a "Eureka!" moment.

As a business and life strategist, I find that many individuals are stuck in their Current State, limited by their thinking. When corporations, and the individuals within them, seek to resolve issues and provide solutions, questions are often the most powerful tool they have to do so. Among other things, questions can assist us to:

1. Understand the Current State
2. Focus on and clearly define a goal
3. Find compelling reasons for accomplishing the goal
4. Identify resources including previous experiences to support our current goals
5. Tap into resources and imagine the goal has already been achieved at that later point in time
6. Determine the steps required to successfully move in the direction of achieving the goal at that point in the future
7. Determine what evidence allows us to know we're moving in the right direction and succeeding as we move toward the goal

When we use questions strategically to engage the mind in a quest where it searches for options, we empower the mind to move beyond limited thinking to engage in creative thinking. In his book *The Opposable Mind*, Roger Martin describes individuals who have the ability to consider two or more disparate ideas in their minds simultaneously and to synthesize them into one idea that is greater than the sum of its parts. Martin refers to this skill as integrative thinking.[96] By refusing to default to standard protocols or to accept either/or limitations, integrative thinkers ask questions that challenge the norms, enabling them to tap into their creativity to solve seemingly insurmountable problems.

QUESTIONS AND THE THINK → FEEL → DO PROCESS

If you think to yourself, "There's no way to accomplish this task," you will feel discouraged. By asking yourself a question like, "If I were to go about mapping out a strategy for successfully completing this task, how would I do that?" you can send your imagination on a quest, and your feelings are likely to change from discouragement to inspiration and motivation. This quest causes your mind to shift to a presupposition of success, and the resulting mental shift itself is likely to trigger emotional changes.

> Instead of attempting to learn from observing the actions of leaders, I prefer to swim upstream to the antecedent of doing: thinking. My critical question is not what various leaders did, but how their cognitive processes produced their actions.
>
> –ROGER MARTIN, **THE OPPOSABLE MIND**

Questions can even impact a person's physiology, which, as we know, is also tied into their emotional state. For instance, if you were to be more confident, how would you be thinking? Standing? Breathing? Alternatively, how would you be thinking, standing, or breathing if you were depressed? Think of your shoulders: are they back and straight when you feel confident and slouched when you feel depressed? Notice that these questions engage the imagination to consider the physical feelings that go along with the state. As you consider both

96 Roger L. Martin, *The Opposable Mind: Winning Through Integrative Thinking* (Harvard Business, 2007).

the state and the physical sensations associated with that state, you are likely to shift your body accordingly and thereby experience the state more intensely.

To facilitate an increase in your confidence I would begin to coach you by asking, "If you were to feel more confident, what and how would you need to be thinking? What would your body feel like? How would you be standing, breathing, or moving in order to experience that confidence now?" As you actively engage your imagination and enter into that state holistically, fully associated, being present in that moment in time, notice how you experience an increased sense of confidence now.

> **Key Concept:** Questions are critical during the entire **Think → Feel → Do** process because they influence the person's thoughts, emotions, and behavior. That's why it's worth investing the time to *choose your questions strategically*.

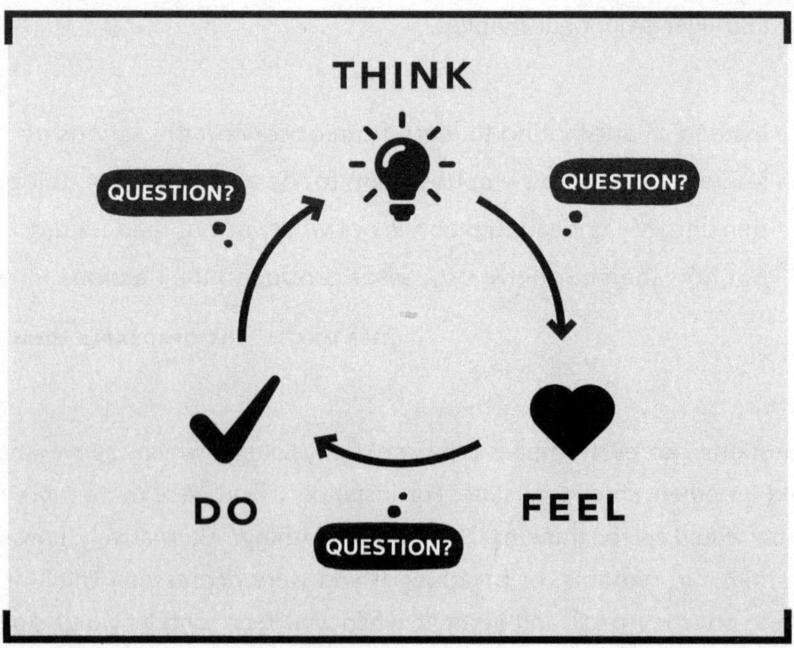

When engaging and guiding the mind with a question, your objective is generally either to uncover and clarify the Current State or to shift the mind from the Current State toward the Desired State. That's why it's critical to ask questions strategically, particularly in the context of the Desired State, otherwise, as mentioned in Chapter One, you will find yourself like Alice, lost in Wonderland:

> "Would you tell me, please, which way I ought to go from here?" Alice asked.
>
> "That depends a good deal on where you want to get to," said the Cat.
>
> "I don't much care where—" said Alice.
>
> "Then it doesn't matter which way you go," said the Cat.
>
> "—so long as I get SOMEWHERE," Alice added.
>
> "Oh, you're sure to do that," said the Cat, "if you only walk long enough."[97]

Different questions take us on different journeys, and the one given is that we're sure to arrive *somewhere*. Arriving at the Desired State requires asking the right questions at the right time and, just like anything in life, it takes practice to do this strategically and effectively.

HARNESSING QUESTIONS

There are many types of questions you can use to uncover a person's Current State and to guide their imagination on a quest that will shift them toward the Desired State. Let's go over a few of the most common ones.[98]

---

97 Lewis Carroll, ***Alice's Adventures in Wonderland*** (Macmillan, 1865), Chapter 6. Available online: https://www.adobe.com/be_en/active-use/pdf/Alice_in_Wonderland.pdf

98 The following descriptions have been adapted from Ian Rowland, ***The Full Facts Book of Cold Reading,*** 4th Edition (Ian Rowland, 2005). Available online: https://issuu.com/crl826/docs/ian_rowlands-full_facts_book_of_cold_reading

Direct questions. Simple, direct questions are the type of question that we tend to be most familiar with. An example is, "What's the best place to vacation?" The answers to these questions may provide information about the person's beliefs, values, criteria, and much more.

Embedded questions. An embedded question hides a question inside a statement. To create an embedded question, simply preface the question with phrases like, "I'm curious...," "I don't know whether...," "I'm interested to know...," or a similar opening phrase that turns the question into what appears to be a statement, all the while causing the person to respond as if you had asked them a direct question.

Tag questions. Tags are short questions added to the end of a sentence, such as, "Isn't it?" "Are you?" "Didn't he?" "Won't you?" and "Can she?" The reason for using a tag question is that they make it difficult for the listener to disagree with your statement, don't they?

Reverse questions. A reverse question is a statement with "do you?" or "don't you?" attached. Reverse questions appear to be much like tag questions. The difference is that a tag question makes it difficult for a person to disagree with your statement while with the reverse question, the goal is to get information in a way that allows you some wiggle room if there's resistance to the question. Then, you can test the waters and see if it's worth continuing in that direction. Reverse questions are very often used in the psychic entertainment industry during cold readings for psychics to go on a fishing expedition as to whether or not to continue the "reading" in a given direction. Sneaky, aren't they?!

Open and closed questions. Open questions invite a person to provide information and to elaborate. Closed questions, on the other hand, can be answered in a word or two, such as "yes" or "no."

Closed questions with conversational postulates. A conversational postulate is a request for action that masquerades as a closed question. It produces a behavioral response (rather than a verbal one), while avoiding the resistance that might result from a direct question. In essence, it's an instruction disguised as a question. For example, "John, is it possible to open that window?" will probably prompt John to go over and open the window. While he could answer the question with a "yes" or "no," his brain is more likely to interpret the question as an instruction or request to open the window, and he'll respond by following that as an assumed instruction. Test this out for yourself with your friends and family and see how well it works.

Vanishing negatives. A vanishing negative is a question disguised as a statement with ambiguous tone and phrasing. In other words, when there's a "not" in the context of a statement, the "not" ends up disappearing because the brain fails at processing the negation and, therefore, it's perceived as a question. For instance, when you say to someone, "You're not considering another option, are you?" their mind ignores the word "not" and focuses instead on the idea of other potential options.

We commonly use all these different types of questions to draw out information from other people. We employ direct questions to obtain basic information about someone, such as their name and where they live, and embedded questions when we want more detailed information about their family life or the kind of work that they do ("I'm interested to know more about your job"). We may use any combination of questions as they all assist us to determine a person's Current State so that we can build rapport, understand their mental map, and engage and guide them to a Desired State.

Unfortunately, questions are sometimes used to take advantage, too. As mentioned earlier, psychic entertainers are famous for using questions to surreptitiously obtain information. In fact, they rely heavily on tag and reverse questions to fish for information because it allows for an "out" if the psychic is wrong and ensures that the audience thinks the psychic is reading their mind, when the reality is, they are simply probing for additional information.

While each type of question is useful on its own, the effects are more subtle and impactful when different types of questions are combined, or when questions are used in conjunction with other persuasive techniques, like storytelling. Recall the Law of Requisite Variety—the more flexible we are with regard to the types of questions that we ask, the more likely we are to collect all the information required to shift an individual toward the Desired State.

Remember!
The Law of Requisite Variety
The person who has the most mental, emotional, and behavioral flexibility will ultimately have control over a system or situation.

I love the way that *Alice's Adventures in Wonderland* uses many of these questions in creative ways to draw the reader in. Consider that when Alice asks the Cheshire cat, "Would you tell me please, which way I ought to go from here?" she's asking a direct question—she wants to know exactly which way to go. When she wonders other things like, "I suppose I ought to eat or drink something or other, but the great question is, 'What?'" which type of question is she asking? And what is the effect of that question?

USING QUESTIONS STRATEGICALLY

Although you might think it's a good idea to just "come right out with it" when searching for information, some people are uncomfortable with questions that put them on the spot. These can include direct questions like, "Do you have the monthly report ready?" or "Did you like my presentation?" which may make someone feel pressured or interrogated. If this is the case, you'll need to work at lowering resistance by asking more strategic questions.

Key Concept:
Strategic questions help to establish and maintain rapport, lower resistance, elicit information, uncover beliefs and values, reveal a person's mental map and strategies, and guide others to think thoughts that lead to the Desired State.

One way to lower resistance is to "hide" a question inside a statement by using an embedded question. Remember, an embedded question in a statement turns a direct question into an indirect one and eliminates the other person's feeling of being interrogated. With a foundation of rapport in place, when you do ask questions, make sure to do so from a state of genuine curiosity because others will sense your sincerity and, as a result, they will likely be more open to responding to you and sharing information.

TIP

To create an embedded question, simply preface a question with an opening phrase that turns it into a statement, such as:

- I'm curious... ("I'm curious if you have a preference as to where we go for dinner.")
- I don't know whether... ("I don't know whether you'd like to go for a swim or not.")
- I'm wondering if ... ("I'm wondering if you can help me paint the baby's room.")
- I'm interested to know... ("I'm interested to know more about this job position.")

The statement should be delivered with an up-inflected "questioning tone," which will transform what seems like a casual declaration into an embedded question.

USING TAGS STRATEGICALLY

Remember, tags are short questions added to the end of a sentence, such as:

- … isn't it?
- … aren't you?
- … did he?
- … doesn't she?

Tag questions can act as catalysts to encourage the mind to continue moving toward the Desired State while minimizing any tendency to go backward. By tagging a small question to the end of your statement, you make it very difficult for the other person's mind to disagree. Instead, the unconscious mind finds it easier to accept the suggestion or statement once it's been linked to a tag.

TIP

In addition to lowering resistance, tag questions allow you to test rapport. In a sense, you're leading the other person with the tag question. See if they follow by giving you a verbal "yes" or "no," or watch for head nodding or shaking that indicates an unconscious "yes" or "no."

Some tag questions are positive ("… do you?") and some are negative ("… don't you?"). Here's a simple rule for using them: if the main part of the statement is *positive* the tag question should be *negative*, and if the main part of the statement is *negative* the tag question should be *positive*.

For example, "**You realize** (positive) how much you've learned, **don't you** (negative)?"

Or,

"**You haven't** (negative) begun to discover all the benefits, **have you** (positive)?"

Sprinkling tag questions and embedded questions into conversation keeps things flowing and allows you to maintain rapport while guiding a person's imagination to think desired thoughts.

Key Concept:
The Law of Requisite Variety also applies to the art of questioning. The more flexible we are in being able to ask a variety of different types of questions, the more insight we'll gain into a person's model of the world.

USING OPEN AND CLOSED QUESTIONS STRATEGICALLY

You may have already learned how to use open and closed questions. Closed questions can be answered in a word or two, such as "yes" or "no." Open-ended questions, on the other hand, invite a person to share their perspective and provide additional information.

Asking open-ended questions is a powerful tool that encourages people to talk and, whether deliberately or inadvertently, to reveal their beliefs, mental strategies, and other valuable information, all of which is very useful in understanding their model of the world.

While most of us are taught that open-ended questions are preferred, you can also effectively use closed questions in some scenarios. In fact, closed questions can be a great way to get someone thinking the thoughts that lead toward a specific desired result. A highly effective way of doing this is by using the **conversational postulate** that we discussed earlier.

A conversational postulate is essentially a request for action masquerading as a closed question. Conversational postulates produce *behavioral* responses (rather than verbal ones), while avoiding the resistance that might result from a direct question. For example, if you are sitting in a waiting room at your dentist's office and you say to someone opposite you, "Excuse me, would you mind passing me that magazine?" technically it's a closed question. While the person may choose to answer literally with a "yes" or "no," in reality you will most likely elicit an unconscious behavioral response where they accommodate by passing the magazine to you. Notice that with a conversational postulate you are more likely to take action, aren't you?

See what I did there?

Key Concept:
A question can take many different forms. The more flexibility we employ in how we ask questions, the easier it is to draw information from someone while avoiding having them feel uncomfortable by thinking we're interrogating them, and the better able we are to shift them from their Current State to a Desired State.

USING VANISHING NEGATIVES STRATEGICALLY

Keep in mind as well that the brain fails to process negation, so when we use vanishing negatives in a question, people often fail to recognize it as a question. Using vanishing negatives allows us to ask a question without the other person realizing they've been asked one.

For instance, imagine you're at a social gathering and you see someone you recognize, although you're not sure how to place them. In order to figure it out, you might ask, "You look familiar. You don't work in the medical industry, do you?" You can then calibrate the correctness of your guess, regardless of how the person answers. If they answer "No," you would say, "That's right, I didn't think so!" If they answer "Yes," you would say, "That's right, I thought you did." You appear to have been right in your claim no matter how they respond.

In a different scenario, you might hear a car salesperson ask, "You're not interested in any specific model, are you?" and again, regardless of how the person responds, the car salesperson appears to have been right in their claim.

HOW YOU ASK IS IMPORTANT

Analogue Marking is a technique that has a similar effect to bolding, italicizing, or underlining words in a written document. Analogue marking helps you highlight something of greater relevance and notifies the unconscious mind to pay particular attention to the marked information.

In my own training, I remember hearing a story about Milton Erickson that really stuck with me. As a student, Erickson paid close attention to the tone, cadence, facial expression, repetition, and other forms of analogue marking that his professor used unconsciously in each lecture. Erickson then highlighted in his notes the specific content that his professor had analogue-marked, judging this information to be the most relevant.

When Erickson used these notes to study for his exam, he performed very well. In fact, his grade on the exam was so high that his professor accused him of cheating, suggesting that Erickson had gotten his hands on a copy of the exam ahead of time. How else could his answers be so similar to the professor's?

When questioned, Erickson admitted that he knew what would be on the exam while maintaining that he was innocent of cheating. He argued that he had simply made specific note of the material being covered whenever the professor changed his tone, placed greater emphasis on certain details, or repeated information. Like a poker player who can read an opponent's "tells," Erickson was aware of his professor's unconscious analogue marking and assumed—correctly—which course material would appear on the exam.

Erickson proved his technique and cleared his name by producing his notes for the year, which matched the content on the exam. His teacher accepted the explanation, and Erickson received one of the highest exam marks ever granted in the course.

While Erickson's professor used analogue marking unconsciously, we can consciously analogue mark any aspect of our communication that we want to stand out as being more relevant or important. This can be done in a variety of ways including using gestures and other body movements to subtly draw the unconscious mind's attention to a specific component of our communication. Analogue marking also uses vocal tone, cadence, and volume to get someone's unconscious mind to pay special attention to certain words or ideas. For example, you can speak faster or slower, louder of softer, or use a neutral or dynamic tone of voice.

It is critical that analogue marking be done skillfully and subtly, since even small changes in gesture and tone have a powerful impact on what a person pays attention to and perceives as being most relevant. No matter how you choose to analogue mark, it's a way of punctuating or highlighting various pieces of communication and of guiding a person's mind to focus on the desired elements.

ASKING THE RIGHT QUESTIONS

As Albert Einstein suggested, asking the right questions is the key to success. The question now is... how do we know *which* question is the right one to ask?

Terry Heick, founder and director of TeachThought, believes the answer lies in what you want the question to accomplish. Are you asking a question to cause a person to reconsider a position? To re-examine what they think they already know? To assess their understanding? Or, to discover something new?[99]

In other words, are you asking the right questions at the right time and in the right context to uncover the Current State, or are you interrupting a train of thought and distracting from the mind's quest? Are you engaging, guiding, and shifting the imagination toward the Desired State? Do your questions spark creativity and ingenuity in yourself and others? When you ask a question, are

---

99 Terry Heick, "Why Questions Are More Important Than Answers," ***Teach Thought*** (June 12, 2012). Available online: https://www.teachthought.com/critical-thinking/why-questions-are-more-important-than-answers/

you focused on the answer or are you gaining information about the journey that the question takes a person's mind on?

It's important to realize that even with an open-ended question, you can still send someone down a rabbit hole. It all depends on context. For example, if you ask someone a question like, "Why are you dissatisfied?" even though it's an open-ended question, their mind will more than likely follow many different paths that reinforce all the ways that they're currently dissatisfied. A better question might be, "What would make you satisfied?" (even though this still presupposes an existing level of dissatisfaction). The most effective question, though, would be something like, "What would *increase your satisfaction*?" Here, you build in a presupposed level of satisfaction, and you have the opportunity to practice analogue marking as you shift the person toward the Desired State and send their mind on a quest to *increase their satisfaction*. Always consider the context in which you ask a question as well as your intention behind the question. The idea is to *elicit* information cleanly about an individual's Current State and then to *instill* thoughts, ideas, and emotions as you engage and guide them toward the Desired State.

Keep in mind, too, that when we ask questions rapidly one after another, we deprive the other person of the quest, or the search, their mind needs to go on. Instead, ask the question, and then allow the person you're speaking with time to go on the quest and return with information before you decide what your next question is going to be—or if another question even needs to be asked.

> **Key Concept:** Always remember that when you ask a question, you send the imagination on a quest. Make sure you evaluate whether the quest is desirable and refine your questions accordingly.

Has someone ever asked you a question that seemed ambiguous and created confusion as you searched for the answer? Sometimes we may ask a question that causes a person to search internally at a deep level in their mind to retrieve information relevant to answering it. This deeper internal focus of attention is known as a **transderivational search**. Asking questions that require these deeper level searches causes a person to become more introspective, creating a light trance state as the person looks inward to find the answer. Given that trance is essentially an internal focus of attention, it reminds me of what Milton Erickson said, "Anything that assumes trance causes trance."

For example, imagine I've asked you, "What if you were to think of a memory, something of significant meaning to you, something you've experienced in the past?" Then I say, "Consider what relevance that memory has now as you move forward in your life?" Notice the ambiguity in these questions. A memory from when? A year ago? Your childhood? These questions simultaneously ask you to go into your past, to bring a memory into the "now," and then to move it into the future and consider its relevance there. Your mind isn't sure how to answer these questions and, as a result, you must go on a deeper internal quest to make sense of the questions and also to search for what the answers might be. While you are in this state, you are more susceptible to persuasion and influence.

When it comes to questions, this is just the beginning. In the next chapter, we'll look at another essential persuasion technique—storytelling—and we'll consider how to use questions within stories to draw others into the ***Think* → *Feel* → *Do*** process, always with the goal of engaging and guiding them toward the Desired State.

Let's think back for a moment to Einstein's thought experiments. Like Einstein, you can use questions to activate your creativity. When you're in "the zone," doing something you truly enjoy, rather than thinking too much about it or questioning it, you just do it. Everything you're doing simply comes together—it just *works*.

Like Einstein and da Vinci, you likely have some habitual thought processes and questions that you ask yourself and others. To help you cultivate a more da Vinci-like frame of mind and train your brain to think more like these geniuses, go ahead and challenge yourself to create your own thought experiment. Create a set of specific questions that send your mind on a quest. A quest leading where? Well that all depends on your Desired State. Like Alice in Wonderland, if you're unclear as to your destination, any road will take you there. Make sure your questions are designed to engage and guide your mind in the direction of your Desired State and, as you proceed in that direction, continue to modify and refine your questions in order to tap into your resourcefulness and ensure your success. Examples of specific questions include "What would make it easier for me to remember…" and "If there was a way to accomplish it, where would I start?"

Chapter Nine

The Persuasive Power of Stories

> Stories are how we think. They are how we make meaning of life… Stories are how we explain how things work, how we make decisions, how we justify our decisions, how we persuade others, how we understand our place in the world, create our identities, and define and teach social values.
>
> –PAMELA RUTLEDGE, **"THE PSYCHOLOGICAL POWER OF STORYTELLING"**

I've said it before and it's worth saying again: anything that we vividly imagine, our bodies will respond to as if it is real. Hence, stories can cause our neurons to fire the same way they would if we were actually performing the action that we are imagining.

In order to test out this idea, let me tell you a story:

> Imagine yourself opening the airtight door of your home's refrigerator. As you hear the magnetic release of the door and your eyes adjust to the fridge's bright light, you are immediately drawn to a lonely lemon resting unassumingly on the shelf. You reach in to take the perfectly formed lemon off the top shelf, noting its beauty as you feel the weight and coolness of it in your hand and observe the bright yellow pop of color and the dimpled texture of its skin. You hear the magnetic suck of the fridge door as you close it and turn toward your kitchen counter with the cool lemon in hand. You gently roll the lemon on a cutting board that's been placed on the counter, preparing its succulent juices to be released. Reaching for your favorite knife from the knife block, you feel the weight of it in your hand as

> you effortlessly cut through the bright yellow lemon. Some of the juices escape, running in a neat stream along the cutting board as you carefully slice the lemon again, making a slight tap as the steel blade of the knife hits the smooth cutting board and the lemon falls soundlessly into quarters. Picking up a piece of the glistening lemon you see the juicy inner texture and light-yellow pulp. As you raise the piece to your mouth, the sweet lemon scent ignites your senses. Saliva starts to trickle against your tongue as you anticipate the tangy, sour flavor. When you finally bite in, the burst of tart juice fills your mouth entirely.

Notice that as you associate into the story of the lemon, the same parts of the brain that would respond if you were really eating a lemon are activated and, in fact, your mouth is likely to start watering.

Did it work for you?

We refer to this as **associating into** the story. As you read the above scenario, the sensory language invited you to imagine that you were actually there in the kitchen biting into that lemon, and so your body responded as if the experience were real by salivating. On the other hand, if you had simply watched a person in a movie reach into a refrigerator for a lemon and cut it up, you would be disassociated or disconnected from the experience, which would create a more neutral reaction.

Here's the science behind this response. When you're listening to a story, two parts of your brain—Broca's area and Wernicke's area—automatically respond. These areas comprise the gray cells that work on processing language and speech—the expressive and receptive language areas of the brain. They're the same parts of the brain that are activated when you have a conversation with a friend, watch a movie, or read a book.

Biologist John Medina, author of *Brain Rules*, argues that "we don't pay attention to boring things."[100] So, we often fail to pay conscious attention during routine tasks like driving home. It's also what is likely at work when we are held hostage during a boring PowerPoint presentation or one too many Zoom calls.

---

100 John Medina, ***Brain Rules*** (Pear Press, 2014), p. 11. Available online: https://facultylibrary.dmcodyssey.org/wp-content/uploads/2016/11/Brain-Rules-by-John-Medina.pdf

While we may make it through the ordeal, the information being presented fails to sink in.

The bottom line is that stories are powerful influencing tools because they *engage the imagination* and *guide the listener* on a journey. As they do, they trigger neurological and emotional responses and our bodies act as though the experiences in our imagination are, in fact, our reality.

STORIES OR FACTS?

During the first decade of the twenty-first century, many African countries faced numerous crises. Headlines from the BBC News website from 2002-2003 alone give an indication of the kinds of troubles the continent faced: famines in Southern Africa and Malawi, and outbreaks of malaria and Ebola in Kenya and the Congo respectively.[101]

Many charitable organizations around the globe were eager to help, yet they had to clear numerous hurdles, including gaining the attention of potential donors, persuading them to care, and finally convincing them to act and open their wallets. The efforts of these organizations took the form of everything from mass marketing appeals to telethons, from blind email blitzes to door-to-door solicitations.

Which approach do you think produced the most donations?

Researchers at the Wharton School of Business asked this question and compared the effectiveness of two different methods of asking for donations.[102] One approach was to describe the horrible situation using facts and statistics:

> Food shortages in Malawi are affecting more than three million children. In Zambia, severe rainfall deficits have resulted in a 42 percent drop in maize production from 2000. As a result, an estimated three million Zambians face hunger. Four million Angolans—one-third of the population—have been forced to

101 See, for example: "Famine stalks Southern Africa." ***BBC News*** (February 19, 2002). Available online: http://news.bbc.co.uk/2/hi/africa/1830296.stm; Raphael Tenthani, "Malawi 'on the brink of starvation,'" ***BBC News*** (February 12, 2002). Available online: http://news.bbc.co.uk/2/hi/africa/1817258.stm; "Kenya hit by malaria epidemic." ***BBC News World Edition*** (July 8, 2002). Available online: http://news.bbc.co.uk/2/hi/africa/2116136.stm; Pascale Harter, "Congo Ebola outbreak confirmed," ***BBC News*** (February 18, 2003). Available online: http://news.bbc.co.uk/2/hi/health/2776719.stm

102 "To Increase Charitable Donations, Appeal to the Heart–Not the Head," ***Knoweldge@Wharton*** (June 27, 2007). Available online: http://knowledge.wharton.upenn.edu/article.cfm?articleid=1767

> flee their homes. More than 11 million people in Ethiopia need immediate food assistance. [103]

Touched, donors in this group offered to donate money to help alleviate the suffering.

With a second group, statistics were tossed aside, and the potential donors were told this story about a seven-year-old suffering from famine:

> Any money that you donate will go to Rokia, a seven-year-old girl who lives in Malawi in Africa. Rokia is desperately poor and faces a threat of severe hunger, even starvation. Her life will be changed for the better as a result of your financial gift. With your support, and the support of other caring sponsors, Save the Children will work with Rokia's family and other members of the community to help feed and educate her, and provide her with basic medical care. [104]

The people in this group offered to donate twice as much as the first group. Stories beat statistics hands down!

As Annette Simmons points out in her book, *The Story Factor*, stories are a filter through which facts are given meaning. "A good story helps you influence the interpretation people give to facts. Facts aren't influential until they mean something to someone," she explains. "A story delivers a context so that your facts slide into new slots in your listener's brain. If you don't give them a new story, they will simply slide new facts into old slots."[105]

Key Concept:
Although facts are important, on their own they rarely persuade. Facts need to be carefully framed within the context of a story because their narratives frame what we perceive to be reality.

---

103 "To Increase Charitable Donations." Available online: http://knowledge.wharton.upenn.edu/article.cfm?articleid=1767
104 "To Increase Charitable Donations." Available online: http://knowledge.wharton.upenn.edu/article.cfm?articleid=1767
105 Annette Simmons, *The Story Factor* (Basic Books, 2006), p. 51.

THE MAGIC OF A GOOD STORY

There are many types of stories, from invented to ready-made, simple to complex (like a story within a story), ambiguous stories, and stories that begin at the end. For our purposes, stories also include fairy tales, myths, legends, and metaphors (i.e., "time is a thief") as well as similes and analogies (i.e., "a baby's brain is like a sponge").

> What happens is of little significance compared with the stories we tell ourselves about what happens. Events matter little, only stories of events affect us.
>
> –RABIH ALAMEDDINE, **THE HAKAWATI**

Moving beyond the *types* of stories, the true magic of storytelling lies in understanding what stories really are: a window to a person's world view. Stories are a tool to help you understand a person's values, beliefs, and model of the world. Ultimately, stories are a powerful strategy that we use to persuade others and shift them from their Current State to a more Desired State.

One particularly moving example of this is how the author J.R.R. Tolkien, a devout Catholic, guided his friend and fellow author, C.S. Lewis, a resolute atheist, toward Christianity, through their mutual engagement in telling and writing stories.[106]

In Tolkien's essay "On Fairy-Stories," he discusses two different kinds of belief. A primary belief, writes Tolkien, is when someone tells you a story that you know is true. When you know it's fictional and yet it's so well told that you find yourself drawn in, the story itself commands what Tolkien calls secondary belief.[107]

The stories that evoke secondary beliefs are often stories exploring grand human themes, such as good triumphing over evil, stories of victory, of escaping

---

106 Tim Keller, "C.S. Lewis and J.R.R. Tolkien on the Power of Fiction," *YouTube* (June 19, 2017). Available online: https://www.youtube.com/watch?v=WoAE15gtEzg

107 Verlyn Flieger and Douglas A. Anderson, *Tolkien on Fairy-Stories* (HarperCollins, 2008).

death, and of eternal love that overcomes death. While we understand that evil does at times appear to prevail, that death is inevitable, and that we sometimes lose the ones we love, Tolkien points out that all human beings want to believe the opposite—which is why these secondary beliefs are truths that can feel more real than "real" life.

C.S. Lewis agreed with Tolkien's thesis regarding secondary beliefs, although he argued that as beautiful as they were, they were still lies. Their debate continued throughout their friendship, and over time, Lewis shifted his religious beliefs, famously saying: "I believe in Christianity as I believe that the Sun has risen, not only because I see it, but because by it, I see everything else."[108]

You can use storytelling strategically to form primary and secondary beliefs, like Tolkien and Lewis. Or you can use storytelling to pace a person's Current State and guide them to the Desired State. One way to do this is to use a person's own "story" as a starting point. Our own story is any story we tell ourselves as we attach meaning to things. We're constantly telling ourselves stories about events, people, and what things mean in our lives. These stories are sometimes referred to as our narratives. You can start with another person's narrative, modifying their storyline to reframe their beliefs and values as you move them toward the Desired State.

Take Adah, for example. When we sat down together, I started the conversation the same way I do with all my coaching clients. "You came here for a reason, what do you want to accomplish during our time together?" I asked. She told me that she was there because "her relationship with her husband wasn't as good as it used to be." Adah believed that her husband didn't love her anymore because he often raised his voice when speaking with her, and his responses were short and snippy. She said her husband used to be patient, kind, and more caring when he spoke to her. Adah's belief about her husband's feelings toward her were intertwined in this story she told herself.

I began by reframing her story, and asked, "In what context could your husband raise his voice and speak in a short and snippy way to show you he loves you?" Adah responded that there was no scenario in which he could speak

---

108 C.S. Lewis, "Is Theology Poetry?" (1944) (Samizdat University Press, 2014). Available online: http://www.samizdat.qc.ca/arts/lit/Theology=-Poetry_CSL.pdf

this way while showing he loved her because "he never used to speak like that when we first got married."

I then asked, "What if you were in the basement of your house, and the house was on fire? Your husband yells at you from the top of the stairs, as loud as he can, 'Honey, get out of the house *now*.' Does that short, snippy, loud statement mean he loves you in this context?

She thought about it and said, "Yes, I suppose it does."

"So that means it *could* be that he loves you even though he speaks to you this way?" I asked. Adah agreed. I had created a paradox where short and snippy communication could be reflecting feelings of love. Once we had reframed her story in this way, we were able to get to the real issue and began working on how Adah and her husband could improve their communication with each other, with the goal of bringing them closer to how they communicated when they were first married.

Occasionally, rather than reframing a story, or telling a story yourself, just saying a few words or showing a picture may be all that is necessary to lead listeners to *create stories in their minds*—and these are often more effective than any stories that you tell.

Take a look at the picture below. What story do you tell yourself about it? Who are the characters? What is the motivation? What is the action? What do you feel about all of these?

No matter how you leverage stories, the fundamentals of a persuasive story remain the same:

1. It's relevant to the situation. You can ensure this by first mapping out the person's Current and Desired States.
2. It paces the person's Current State with regard to their existing beliefs, values, and experiences.
3. It engages and guides the person toward a Desired State by modifying or updating their various beliefs and values as you reframe their story.
4. It uses sensory-rich details throughout.
5. You ask strategic questions to disassociate the individual from and/or associate them into the story.

Key Concept: It's worth noting that by engaging *all* of the senses, a story provides your listener with the opportunity to fully experience and "live the story" as you're telling it. The more sensory-rich it is, the more likely the person is to associate fully with the storyline and, therefore, the more emotionally compelling and persuasive they will find it.

STORIES AT WORK

Given the oral storytelling traditions observed across cultures, stories appear to be hard-wired into our DNA. In a guest blog post on *Scientific American,* Jag Bhalla writes that "it is in our nature to need stories. They are our earliest sciences, a kind of people-physics. Their logic is how we naturally think. They configure our biology, and how we feel, in ways long essential for our survival."[109]

Stories perform several different functions. They can:

- Capture our imagination and hold our attention
- Bring facts to life by giving them context and relevance
- Evoke emotions which drive our behavior
- Confirm or alter our world view

109 Jag Bhalla, "It Is in Our Nature to Need Stories," *Scientific American* (May 8, 2013). Available online: https://blogs.scientificamerican.com/guest-blog/it-is-in-our-nature-to-need-stories/

Whether short or long, simple or complex, real or fairy tales, prepared or spontaneous, stories have many persuasive uses throughout the ***Think* → *Feel* → *Do*** process.

STORIES INCREASE RELATABILITY

Stories are often used to facilitate getting to know someone or letting someone get to know us, as I did in the introduction of this book. Speakers often introduce themselves by telling a story to create a frame of relatability. When I give a talk, I typically begin by telling the audience that I was diagnosed with a learning disability in the second grade, then failed and was held back a year. This story about me lets the audience know that I have had challenges, just like many of them, and have struggled to transform myself from a "learning-disabled" kid into a successful, knowledgeable speaker. It also shows that I'm willing to reveal my vulnerable side, which breaks the ice and establishes rapport between us.

I know of another speaker who introduces himself with a recitation of his lengthy resume that ends with something like, "I have a PhD, an industry award of excellence, and a note from my mother." The list of his achievements tells the story of his accomplishments, while the joke turns the initial story into another one: he's self-deprecating and funny.

THE STORYTELLER WHO CREATES A NEW CONTEXT

Mei, a medical science liaison for a pharmaceutical company, was faced with highly publicized negative reports about a side effect of one of her company's medications. Coincidently, her own mother-in-law was a participant in one of the clinical studies of this medication and had suffered from this specific adverse event. While this sounds like a double-whammy, Mei cleverly reframed the story, telling the concerned doctors who prescribed the medication, "Yes, my mother-in-law suffered from this adverse event when she was on the medication. But if you asked her if it was worth having this side effect to extend her life long enough to attend our wedding, she would say, 'Yes, absolutely!'"

Stories bring facts to life and change their interpretation by putting them into a new context—in other words, stories have the power to reframe facts. In this case, the story of the medication's side effect was reframed in the much larger context of its overarching benefits.

HEART OVER MIND

Remember the story of seven-year-old Rokia? Her story was aimed at the emotions rather than the intellect because emotional stories are often more successful than rational ones. Another study published in the *Harvard Business Review* found that among customers, emotional fulfillment was more important than rational fulfillment and led to a greater sense of overall satisfaction.[110]

In other words, the feeling that you're getting a good product or deal, or that the salespeople and the company they represent are taking good care of you, is worth far more than the data that they provide you about the features, benefits, costs, warranties, and so on, of their product. This is a major reason that storytelling is so important and effective.

Stories can also serve to help overcome doubts, increase feelings of safety or security, create feelings of concern, or generate fear. For example, a doctor might tell a little story about a patient who didn't watch their blood sugar, developed

---

110 John H. Fleming, Curt Coffman, and James K. Harter, "Managing Your Human Sigma," ***Harvard Business Review*** (July 2005). Available online: https://hbr.org/2005/07/manage-your-human-sigma

diabetes, and wound up needing to have a foot amputated. A "cautionary tale" such as this one can be very powerful in moving the listener toward the desired result (modifying behaviors to protect health outcomes).

THE STORIES WE TELL OURSELVES

While we use stories to persuade others, we also frequently tell stories to ourselves. In fact, it's fairly common for our minds to fill in missing information by creating a story. Perhaps a usually friendly co-worker doesn't smile at you when she enters the room, and soon you're telling yourself that she's frowning at you because she's mad about something you said.

What's the reality of the situation? The co-worker may have been frowning at you. Then again, her expression may have been something other than a frown. Perhaps she was grimacing because she had heartburn or was thinking about her income taxes. The possibilities are nearly endless.

In his book, *The 7 Habits of Highly Effective People*, author Steven Covey tells the story of a man and his young children on a subway.[111] The man seemed to be lost in thought and was ignoring his loud, misbehaving children. Other passengers cast angry glances his way, thinking he was a terrible father and a jerk who didn't care if his children annoyed everyone else. When someone finally said something to him, the man explained that his wife had just passed away and he and his children were on their way home from the hospital. All at once, everyone in the subway car had a change of attitude. Suddenly they were sympathetic, understanding perfectly why the children were misbehaving and why their father was barely noticing.

> **Key Concept:**
> Stories can be either empowering or disempowering; they help us to achieve our goals, or they stand in our way. This means that all stories—the ones we tell ourselves or others, as well as those that are told to us—ultimately impact our lives.

The other subway passengers told themselves two very different stories in a short period of time: first, that the man was an irresponsible father, and second,

111 Stephen R. Covey, *The 7 Habits of Highly Effective People: Powerful Lessons in Personal Change* (Free Press, 2004).

that this poor man and his children needed sympathy and help. The passengers invented the first story based on their interpretation of the behavior of the man and his children, while the second was based on the man's explanation. One story was false, and one was true, yet each was equally powerful in the feelings it evoked in the passengers.

We constantly tell ourselves stories, stories about ourselves and stories about other people, to help us understand and explain situations, events, and the world itself. These stories become the foundation of our beliefs, and they can both propel us forward and hold us back (think, for instance, of "I'll never run a mile in four minutes").

Remember!
Remember back in Chapter Three when I spoke about the power of the Reticular Activating System (RAS)? Stories have the power to strengthen or weaken our beliefs and values by engaging the RAS to filter information that either supports, conflicts with, or potentially even changes, our model of the world.

WHY ARE STORIES SO POWERFUL?

Why are stories infinitely more effective than facts and statistics? Annette Simmons explains, "facts need a context of when, who, and where to become truths... A story is a very good representation of what is true because it can weave the relational aspects of facts with space, time, and values."[112] Just as questions send the imagination on a quest, so do stories. Our brain then engages within the context of this journey and searches for evidence that supports the storyline.

The RAS is the attention center in the brain. It is a very powerful and complex collection of neurons which serve as a point of convergence for signals from the external world and from your interior environment. In other words, it is the part of your brain where the world outside of you and your thoughts and feelings from "inside" of you, meet.

112 Simmons, *The Story Factor* (Basic Books, 2006).

The RAS, operating based on our beliefs and values, draws our attention to certain things and gets our minds to ignore other things. Essentially, it contributes to how our brains filter information—what gets filtered in and what gets filtered out.

> If everything I perceive is based on what I already know, how will I ever perceive anything new? If I never perceive anything new, how will I change? How will I grow?
>
> —WILLIAM ARNTZ, **WHAT THE BLEEP DO WE KNOW!?**

Think back to the story I told you earlier about eating a lemon. You were probably salivating by the time you finished reading it, weren't you? The incredible fact is that the mind and body respond to stories the same way they respond to events that actually happen to you. Stories influence us holistically, affecting even our beliefs and values, which is why they have the potential to impact us as effectively and powerfully as firsthand experiences.

The stories we tell ourselves, which may include beliefs, values, and so on are also subject to **confirmation bias**, which is what happens when we unconsciously seek evidence to support our stories and confirm our beliefs. For example, if you tell yourself the story that your co-worker is angry over something you said, then your mind will seek to confirm and support that belief by looking for evidence or facts that validate that story.

Does this remind you of the Barnum Effect?

The Barnum Effect comes into play when a story being told is intentionally vague so that a person applies their own

> **Key Concept:** When someone embraces your story as their own, you've taken a big step toward the desired outcome. Your objective is for them to have "Aha!" moments and when they say things like, "That's interesting, I've never thought of it that way before!" then you know you have influenced their thinking, setting in motion the **Think → Feel → Do** process.

beliefs to it in order to make it true. Stories support beliefs, which is why they are so powerful. As Simmons says, "A good story helps you influence the interpretation people give to facts. Facts aren't influential until they mean something to someone. Providing facts without story leaves too much to chance."[113]

Stories are also powerful as tools of persuasion. You can leverage them to persuade others to hire you, adopt your ideas, buy your product, or otherwise follow your lead to the Desired State.

HOW TO PERSUADE WITH STORIES

Stories have the potential to shift a person from their Current State to a Desired State. This shift is accomplished by placing questions strategically throughout your story in a way that includes and engages the listener. If you ask the right questions at the right points in the story, then the person will find themselves involved in the storyline and will engage emotionally in the story. It's this engagement in the story that triggers and leverages the ***Think → Feel → Do*** process.

Using questions to engage and associate the listener into the storyline means that they actively become a part of the story, which evokes an emotional reaction. Stories that persuade people will engage their imaginations to enter into the storyline.

Many years ago, I remember listening to an interview on the radio with author Stephen King in which he was asked how he invents the ideas for his horror novels. His response was, "I go there in my imagination, and I write about what I'm experiencing." Likewise, when King's readers go to that place in their own imaginations, it triggers the emotions and evokes the responses that make his stories so powerful.

Keep in mind that stories often use someone else's voice to say the things you would like to convey in a way that might seem more palatable or less threatening coming from someone else. Stories also allow you to introduce potentially sensitive topics while minimizing resistance. Milton Erickson used this technique, which he referred to as **extended quotes**, to bypass resistance with his patients. For instance, he would often recount a metaphor that paralleled his

---

113 Simmons, *The Story Factor* (Basic Books, 2006).

patient's Current State or experience in order to engage and guide them to a Desired State through the story.

Essentially, extended quotes allow you to make a suggestion to somebody about themselves without using them in your example. Allowing them to move through someone else's experience is less threatening than if the story were directly about them. It also makes it easier for the person's unconscious mind to identify with the lessons connected to the story that are most relevant to them.

We've already looked at how to create a story to shift a person from their Current State to a Desired State. Next, let's look at what kinds of stories can be most effective.

While it's possible to make up a story on the spot, sometimes it's best to prepare one ahead of time. In other instances, it is useful to begin with a simple on-the-spot story to create rapport when an opportunity arises, then move on to a ready-made story to make your point and lead the person toward the Desired State.

You will want to associate the individual into the storyline when your goal is to engage their emotions. In contrast, there will be other times when you'll want to disengage their emotions and you can accomplish this by disassociating them from the storyline. This is achieved by using the right language and asking the right questions—the same skills you've been learning so far!

Questions are critical to storytelling because they can associate a listener into or disassociate them from the story depending on your intention. They can also clarify or update a belief and may even change an individual's internal story by reframing it. Asking questions is extremely effective in challenging a person's thinking and reinforcing or shifting their beliefs.

As if!

You can add "as if" presuppositions to your story to associate someone into it or disassociate them from it. Some examples of these are:

- Just suppose…
- Hypothetically…
- Imagine…
- If you were to be…
- In a perfect world…
- What if…

Reflect back on the story of the lemon. Notice that I used sensory-rich language to associate you into that story. In fact, there are several ways to use language to associate a person into or disassociate them from a story. For example, you can use "as if" language to disassociate someone from a story by saying things such as, "If you were a fly on the wall watching this interaction…"

This type of "as if" language provides a different perceptual position which helps remove the person from being in the event firsthand; they're now in the role of an observer, watching themselves in the event, disassociated from it completely. This has the effect of neutralizing their emotions around the event.

Alternatively, you can associate a person into a story by using "as if" language to guide their mind to imagine that they are fully living the experience, seeing it through their own eyes, hearing it through their own ears and fully experiencing it themselves. This triggers their emotions around the event.

Before choosing to use associative or disassociative language, first decide whether or not it's desirable for the emotion(s) to be magnified or diminished. Once you know that, then you can choose to use associative language to trigger and amplify the person's emotions or disassociative language to neutralize their emotions.

It's important to understand the distinction between association and disassociation. Within the context of persuading and influencing—particularly in the areas of sales or marketing, for instance—you may want to trigger a positive or negative emotion to an event or competitor depending on the context. Within the realm of psychology, we often look to disassociate an individual from an event or recollection that is traumatic or disempowering because it neutralizes the emotion connected with the negative memories.

A prime example of the power of disassociation is with those who suffer from post-traumatic stress disorder (PTSD). Generally, people with PTSD are fully associated into their negative memories and, therefore, neurologically and emotionally continue to relive the traumatic events of their past over and over again. One of the methods for treating PTSD is to help people change how their past experiences are encoded in their nervous systems. This can be accomplished in part by teaching them how to disassociate, so that instead of associating into the memory and reliving the event as though it's happening again, they can frame the memory in a disassociated way and neutralize the emotions connected to it.

Assisting people suffering from PTSD is a very important use of associative/disassociative language. This technique extends beyond therapeutic contexts, though. Salespeople leverage the power of association to guide potential customers to imagine that the desired outcome has already materialized. For instance, a real estate agent might ask "Hypothetically, just suppose you were to move in today, which bedroom would you give to your son?" or "If you were to paint these walls any color, what color would make you feel most at home?" Insurance salespeople, on the other hand, might use a negative "as if" frame when they say things like, "What if you don't have insurance and your house burns down?" The listener's mind imagines a negative event, experiences negative emotions, and takes preventive action.

Here are some other examples of associative and disassociative language patterns:

Associated Language	Disassociated Language
This experience is...	*That experience could...*
How does this currently make you feel?	*As you look back on how you felt when...*
Looking at it from your perspective...	*If you were a fly on the wall...*
Be in this conversation and hear it through your own ears...	*As you imagine yourself overhearing a conversation like that...*
Feel as you do now...	*How else do you think you could have felt...?*
As you reexperience that memory now...	*Consider what could happen if...?*
Experience the reality of that now...	*Look at yourself in the future...*
I'm thinking...	*One might think...*

Being aware of and using associative or disassociative language enables you to move the listener into and out of the emotional dynamics of the narrative as you guide them through the story or situation.

When you're engaging someone in a story for the purpose of shifting them from a Current to a Desired State, it can be helpful to include these five elements:

1. *Another person*—a stand-in for the listener (a friend/client/customer/boss/employee/ spouse).
2. *A similar state*—the other person's mental/physical/emotional state was the same as the listener's Current State.

3. *Your idea*—your idea/product/service/technique was presented as the best solution to the other person, who accepted it.
4. *Positive outcome*—great results occurred because the other person accepted your idea/product/service, and they are happy having made that choice now.
5. *A question that leads the person into the future*—the question gets the listener to imagine the great outcome that will result by accepting your product/idea/plan now.

Keep in mind that these points allow us to pace and lead from Current to Desired State as well.

In a seminar on the use of stories and metaphors that I attended many years ago, co-presenter John Grinder shared a story about a little boy who would only speak in a whisper. Rather than looking for subconscious causes to explain why he avoided using his "full" voice, the boy's therapist told him a fairy-tale about a little frog who would only "ribbit" in a small voice, never in a big voice. Once the little frog moved to a pond where the big frogs lived, he began ribbitting loudly, just like they did.

"There was another little frog who didn't ribbit like the big frogs," Grinder continued. "When do you think this little frog will start ribbitting like the big frogs?"

The little boy replied, "On my birthday."

And indeed, on the boy's very next birthday he began speaking in a full voice.

The therapist used the fictional story of the frog to pace the boy's current experience (only using a small voice), then moved the boy's thinking toward the desired outcome (using a full voice). The boy understood, subconsciously, that the story was all about him, and responded with the desired behavior. Your story can be fictional or based in reality—as long as it achieves the desired result.

> Wisdom comes from experience, but experience is not enough. Experience anticipated and experience revisited is the true source of wisdom.
>
> –JOHN GRINDER

THE ILLUSION OF CHOICE: THE DOUBLE BIND

As we've discussed, Milton Erickson was a master at using trance-like language and double binds to guide his clients to a Desired State by giving them the illusion of choice. I heard he once said to a client: "I think your unconscious mind knows more about this than your conscious mind does. And if your unconscious mind knows more about this than your conscious mind does, then you probably know more about this than you think you do." Ericksonian **double binds** are sentences that suggest to your listener to do one of two things—this is actually an illusion of choice because either option is the direction you want them to go. An example of this is if a hypnotist says to a client, "Would you like to enter trance now or would you like to try to keep your eyes open for a little longer?" Regardless of what the client chooses, they are still ultimately led into a trance state. Another example is asking a child, "Do you want to go to bed now or watch five minutes more of your video before you go to bed?" Either way, the child will go to bed.

Restaurant waitstaff often use this approach when they ask, "Will you be having a drink now or with your dinner?" before you've had a chance to say whether or not you'd even like a drink. It's an illusion because no matter which option you choose, the persuader will be satisfied. The server isn't really concerned *when* you have a drink, they just want you to order one. With this question, the server invites you to imagine having a drink, something like, "Hmmm, I'd love to start this fantastic meal by having a refreshing gin and tonic with my appetizer." Or perhaps you may say to yourself, "I remember how nice it was last time we were here when we had that Gewürztraminer with the lobster." What you imagine about enjoying a drink is more powerful than anything the server could tell you. And in the end, with a little luck, they may end up selling you both!

Additionally, beginning a story with the ending (or a few possible endings) in mind is another way of associating the listener into the Current State and guiding them toward a Desired State. If you construct a story with the Desired State in mind, the story is going to lead toward that end outcome. Many movies make use of this tactic in their storytelling. The creators of these films had to first ask themselves, "What's the end outcome that I want from this story? What's the Desired State?" And then they had to build a story that works to associate the listener and move them toward that Desired State.

Two prime examples are the movies *Fight Club* (1999) and *Forrest Gump* (1994). These movies both begin with the ending and take the audience back through the events and experiences of the characters leading up to the opening sequence. Throughout these films, the audience is absorbed by the leading characters' stories—the highs and lows of their lives, their thoughts and emotions, their struggles and triumphs—and by the end the storyteller (in this case, the movie director) has gradually shifted the assumptions the audience may have held at the beginning of the movies toward something entirely different.

> Telling stories is the best way to teach, persuade, and even understand ourselves.
>
> –"THE POWER OF STORIES" COLLECTION, **PSYCHOLOGY TODAY**

Beginning with the ending closes the door on the idea that the Desired State might fail to happen; it has *already* happened. This is true in the movies—and also true in the case of ordering a drink with dinner and the child going to bed. In each scenario, the person is guided toward believing that they have options, although to some extent the ending has already been decided for them. Like the "as if" approach, beginning with the ending primes an individual's mind to believe the desired outcome is "real" and it's just a matter of working out the details.

PERSUADERS ARE NATURAL STORYTELLERS

As persuaders, we need to be able to tell stories and, while telling a good story may seem like magic, it's actually scientific and formulaic. Let's look at a tried-and-true formula from one of the best in the business. Pixar Animation Studios tell great, award-winning stories. Emma Coats, a former story artist at Pixar, is credited with cracking the "Pixar code" and, in doing so, she developed a template for a new type of pitch that is irresistible.[114] Simply put, Coats postulated that each and every Pixar movie "shares the same narrative DNA, a deep structure of storytelling that involves six sequential sentences:

1. Once upon a time... (Back in the beginning...; Historically...; When I first met you...; There once was...)
2. Every day... (People typically...; It was common for...; We often found...)
3. One day... (Then things changed...; Then a new product came to market...)
4. Because of that... (Resulting in...; Which led to....)
5. Because of that... (Then that caused...; Which further prompted...)
6. Until finally... (And now...; Currently...; The new reality is...)"[115]

Using Coats's formula (in bold), let's look at the plot of Pixar's *Finding Nemo* (2003) as an example:

> **Once upon a time** there was a widowed fish named Marlin who was extremely protective of his only son, Nemo. **Every day**, Marlin warned Nemo of the ocean's dangers and implored him not to swim far away. **One day** in an act of defiance, Nemo ignored his father's warnings and swam into the open water.

114 Daniel H. Pink, *To Sell Is Human: The Surprising Truth About Moving Others* (Riverhead Books, 2013).

115 "Pixar Story Rules (one version)," *The Pixar Touch* Blog (May 15, 2011)/. P 171. Available online: http://www.pixartouchbook.com/blog/2011/5/15/pixar-story-rules-one-version.html

> **Because of that**, Nemo was captured by a diver and ended up in the fish tank of a dentist in Sydney. **Because of that**, Marlin set off on a journey to rescue Nemo, enlisting the help of other sea creatures along the way. **Until finally** Marlin and Nemo found each other, reunited, and learned that love depends on trust. [116]

This formula can help anyone to create an influential story. No matter what form it takes, or how short or long it is, a story is an incredibly powerful persuasive tool. It's also possible for stories to be made even *more* effective by combining them with additional persuasive techniques such as making and triggering connections. Keep reading as we explore the power of connections in the next chapter.

116 "Pixar Story Rules (one version)," ***The Pixar Touch*** Blog (May 15, 2011). Available online: http://www.pixartouchbook.com/blog/2011/5/15/pixar-story-rules-one-version.html

1. Identify two stories that have impacted your beliefs (for example, from a book, a movie, a biblical story, or a story about your family history). For each story pinpoint the belief that was shaped. Think of a way that you could alter the story to shift your beliefs.
2. Identify one story that you've told yourself today. Perhaps that story is about how you'll complete a project ahead of schedule, or perhaps it's about what will happen if your child chooses one university or another. Maybe it's even a story pertaining to your own capabilities and what you can and cannot accomplish. Can you differentiate the facts from your own beliefs within the story?
3. Use the "Pixar Code" to write your own persuasive story.

   Once upon a time… *(or you could say: Back in the beginning…; Historically…; When I first met you…; There once was…)*

   Every day… *(or you could say: People typically…; It was common for…; We often found…)*

   One day… *(or you could say: Then things changed…; Then a new product came to market…)*

   Because of that… *(or you could say: Resulting in…; Which led to….)*

   Because of that… *(or you could say: Then that caused…; Which further prompted…)*

   Until finally… *(or you could say: And now…; Currently…; The new reality is…)*

Chapter Ten

Making, Breaking, and Reinforcing Connections

> Magic is hidden in the language we speak. The webs that you can tie and untie are at your command…
>
> –RICHARD BANDLER AND JOHN GRINDER, **THE STRUCTURE OF MAGIC**

Around 1900, a young man by the name of Edwin Burket Twitmyer was conducting research for his doctoral dissertation at the University of Pennsylvania. He was interested in the ways the patellar tendon reflex—the reflex that causes your leg to jerk up and out when a doctor taps your knee with a little rubber hammer—behaved in different circumstances. During the course of his study, he tapped lots of knees and stumbled across an interesting phenomenon.

Twitmyer would ring a bell to let subjects know that he was about to tap their knees. Ring, then tap. At one point he accidently hit the bell and, even though he did not tap the subject's knee, their leg jerked up and out.

Intrigued, Twitmyer decided to see if this was a one-time idiosyncrasy or if there was something behind it. With a little more experimentation, he learned that once the connection between the ring of the bell and the strike of the hammer was established in a subject's mind, the knee would jerk when the bell rang, even in the absence of the hammer striking. Indeed, several of his subjects found it impossible to prevent their knees from jerking up when the bell rang, regardless of how hard they attempted to keep their legs still.

Now, you've likely never heard of Edwin Twitmyer; few people have. The reason is that around the same time, in Russia, a professor named Ivan Pavlov was conducting similar stimulus-response experiments with dogs. Pavlov had started to notice that the dogs in his research lab would begin to salivate upon merely hearing the footsteps of his assistant arriving to deliver their food. The dogs had begun to associate the footsteps with the delivery of their food and salivated in anticipation of it. This relationship between the footsteps and the food may have been serendipitous, yet Pavlov's important observation of the dogs' association led to further experimentation with stimulus-response connections.

Next came Pavlov's famous experiment, in which he used a bell to condition the dogs' responses. He began by simply ringing the bell. As you might guess, the dogs did nothing. Then, Pavlov started ringing the bell right before the dogs were fed. Ringing the bell before feeding the dogs created a conditioned response: the dogs began salivating anytime they heard the ringing of the bell. Pavlov had made a positive connection in the dogs' nervous system between the bell and the food, so much so that the dogs expected to be fed when they heard the bell ring! This functioned in the same way as the connection that originally had the dogs salivating in anticipation of the food when they heard the assistant's footsteps.

Pavlov subsequently conducted similar experiments with dogs and a sleeping drug. The dogs were injected with the drug, and they fell asleep. After this happened several times, the dogs fell asleep as soon as they saw the needle—the link between the syringe and sleeping was that strong. These are prime examples of **classical conditioning**, responses that involve the creation and reinforcement of connections between things or objects that previously had no real relationship to each other.

Working separately, Pavlov and Twitmyer both demonstrated how strong these connections can be—they can even change the way the body behaves! We'll explore the body's physiological response to connections throughout this chapter. First, though, let's look at how skillfully the mind can make simple connections.

During a training session with a group of physicians, I decided to play with the power of connections. As I did with you in Chapter Three, I casually said to a participant, "You're probably unaware of how your feet feel inside of your shoes right now," while making a simple gesture toward his feet. As the training continued, I intentionally circled back to this connection by saying only, "As we discussed earlier…," and gesturing to his feet. The participant instantly smiled and responded, "Yeah I know… my feet inside of my shoes." As the session continued, any time I would gesture toward this gentleman's shoes it would fire off or trigger the association, and he and others would grin. This demonstrated to the audience how easy it is to create a link and connect a thought, feeling, or action to a simple gesture, just as Twitmyer and Pavlov had done with the sound of a bell.

There are many examples of how simple it is to create connections, intentionally or unintentionally. I focus a lot of my work in the medical and pharmaceutical industries where I have seen firsthand the creation of connections, which is why there are so many of these examples in this chapter. It is important to understand that connections are made in a wide range of fields, as well as in people's personal lives. Marketers, for example, often very purposefully make connections between the products they are selling and positive emotions and memories. In other instances, marketers may intentionally—or unintentionally—create negative connections, too.

CAN CONNECTIONS CHANGE HOW THE BODY RESPONDS?

Imagine your doctor has just prescribed a new medication. The doctor tells you how you will benefit from taking it and explains some of its known side effects. Do you focus on the knowledge that the medication will provide benefits or are you left anticipating side effects that may occur? Wherever your mind leads you, your expectations and experiences will follow. The power of the connections our brains make, and our subsequent expectations, are demonstrated through the placebo and nocebo effects.

You've likely heard of the **placebo effect** within the context of medicine. The placebo effect is the term used when a patient experiences a beneficial outcome "produced by a placebo drug or treatment, which cannot be attributed to the properties of the placebo itself and must therefore be due to the patient's belief in that treatment."[117] The **nocebo effect**, on the other hand, is a lesser-known phenomenon that is also sometimes referred to as a "negative placebo effect." With the nocebo effect, a patient's expectation of a negative or harmful effect *increases* the chance that they will experience that negative or harmful effect.

You may be aware that pharmaceutical companies test their drugs against a placebo, which is an inert treatment generally made up of a safe, inactive substance rather than active ingredients. To pass clinical trials, the company

117 Placebo effect," *Lexico*. Available online: https://www.lexico.com/definition/placebo_effect

must prove that their drug is significantly more effective than the placebo in the study.

Now, imagine again that your doctor has prescribed you a medication. With the placebo effect, you connect the medication to the benefits that the doctor described. You expect that the treatment will work and you, in fact, believe it will work. Your body unconsciously focuses on manifesting those positive outcomes based on the connection you've made between the drug and your expectation that the drug will benefit you.

With the nocebo effect, you connect the medication to the side effects that the doctor warned you may occur. If the doctor tells you those side effects are headache and nausea, this builds an expectation that you will experience headaches and nausea. Your body unconsciously manifests those negative outcomes based on the connection you've made between the drug and the expectation that the drug will cause these specific adverse events.

The placebo and the nocebo effects show how, intentionally or unintentionally, we make positive or negative connections. The two words are Latin, with *nocebo* meaning "I will harm" and *placebo* meaning "I will please." In both cases, the doctor's phrasing of the relative benefits or side effects of the drug creates the expectation of either a positive or a negative outcome.

> Whatever we plant in our subconscious mind and nourish with repetition and emotion will one day become a reality.
>
> –EARL NIGHTINGALE

In the example of a doctor prescribing a medication, the subtle difference between the two is that a placebo effect is an expectation of an improvement in symptoms (a positive event) whereas a nocebo effect is an expectation of an adverse side effect (a negative event). Of course, we know that whether an actual benefit or side effect is experienced is due to the chemical properties of the drug. Still, in the case of a placebo or a nocebo effect, the way the positive or negative effect is communicated can create an expectation within a person's mind that can outweigh the chemical properties of the drug itself and is likely to become a self-fulfilling prophecy.

In the 1950s, a man known as "Mr. Wright" developed a cancer of the lymph nodes, complete with large tumors in his chest, neck, and groin, as well as a milky fluid that continually collected in his abdomen and had to be drained off every two days.[118] Treatments for cancer were relatively primitive back then, so doctors had little hope for his recovery.

When Mr. Wright heard about a clinical study being conducted on a new drug called Krebiozen for his form of cancer, he begged his doctor to enroll him. Although the doctor knew that Mr. Wright's cancer was too far advanced for the drug to be effective, he agreed. And so, Mr. Wright began to take Krebiozen—and had a positive response! His tumors shrank rapidly, and the response was so incredible that all signs of the cancer disappeared within two weeks.

It was an amazing cure. Until, that is, the results of the study were released. Apart from Mr. Wright, the medicine had helped essentially no one and the researchers had concluded that it was worthless. Mr. Wright's "cure" was, in fact, a powerful placebo response. His belief that the medication would cure him appeared to have stimulated his immune system to the extent that it had beaten back the cancer. Of course, this placebo effect is just one potential explanation for Mr. Wright's amazing physical response.

> A drug's usefulness is a direct result of not only the chemical properties of the drug, but also the patient's belief in the usefulness and effectiveness of the drug.
>
> –HENRY BEECHER

Once Mr. Wright learned the results of the study, his faith in the drug was destroyed. The placebo effect vanished, and his tumors and other symptoms returned. While modern medical ethics would prohibit a physician from doing this today, his doctor had a nevertheless clever idea: he told Mr. Wright that a brand new, more powerful version of the medication had been developed and that he, personally, could administer it. Mr. Wright was thrilled. The doctor gave

118 Bruce H. Lipton, *The Biology of Belief: Unleashing the Power of Consciousness, Matter and Miracles* (Hay House, 2011).

him the improved medication—which was an inactive substance—and within a few days Mr. Wright's tumors had *again* shrunk and his other symptoms subsided. Mr. Wright's amazing recovery was once more due to the placebo effect, which is a persuasive example of the power of belief to impact biological functions.

Another powerful example of the body's biological response to the imagination is seen in two works by Norman Cousins, *Anatomy of an Illness as Perceived by the Patient: Reflections on Healing and Regeneration* (1979) and *Head First: The Biology of Hope and the Healing Power of the Human Spirit* (1989). Upon his return from a stressful trip abroad in 1964, Cousins, an American political journalist and editor, was diagnosed with ankylosing spondylitis, a crippling and irreversible degenerative disease of the spine. He suffered almost constant severe pain as well as near paralysis of his legs, neck and back. His doctor suggested that the illness would be terminal within a matter of months. Cousins, however, disagreed and hypothesized that because he had been well prior to his stressful trip, stress must have contributed to his illness. He further proposed that if stress had *caused* his illness, then positive emotions should relieve his symptoms and possibly even reverse his diagnosis.

> Drugs are not always necessary, however, belief in recovery always is.
>
> —NORMAN COUSINS

So, Cousins checked himself out of the hospital, surrounded himself with a continuous stream of things he thought were funny and positive (like comedic films and television shows), and ended up changing his mental focus and bolstering his more empowering beliefs about his ability to regain his health—to the point that he altered the outcome of the disease. When even morphine failed to provide relief from the pain, Cousins reported: "Ten minutes of genuine belly laughter had an anesthetic effect and would give me at least two hours of pain-free sleep."[119] His condition improved steadily, and he gradually regained the use

---

119 Norman Cousins, *Anatomy of an Illness as Perceived by the Patient* (W.W. Norton & Company, 1979, 2016), p. 11.

of his limbs. Cousins was back on his feet within six months and, two years later, he returned to work full-time. He subsequently joined the faculty of UCLA as an adjunct professor in the Department of Psychiatry and Biobehavioral Sciences, researching the connection between mental attitude and health.

As exemplified in the cases of Mr. Wright and Norman Cousins, human beings are created in such a way that our thoughts and beliefs can be powerful enough to affect our bodies and galvanize us to fight disease. These are just two of many instances that demonstrate the interdependence of mind and body. While these connections have been most widely studied in the context of medicine, we can also employ variations of the placebo and nocebo effects to instill positive or negative expectations in others in many situations outside the context of medicine. We've seen clear illustrations of just how strong the mind-body connection is and how careful we must be with our communication because of the dynamic influence it has on beliefs and expectations. As persuaders, our goal is to engage and guide a person's imagination toward a Desired State because we know that once the desired thoughts are in place, feelings and behavior will follow. Let's look at some other ways to accomplish the task of engaging minds, guiding emotions, and driving behavior.

CONNECTIONS ARE POWERFUL AND LASTING

Do you remember where you were when the 9/11 attacks on the World Trade Center happened? Do you recall the language and images from the news stories as the events of that day unfolded? What about the sounds and sights of the things and people around you when you first learned of the attacks? Although there were, of course, many negative connections to the events of that day, there were positive connections as well, including the emotional stories of families reuniting, messages of hope from survivors, and the positive associations to all the people who helped and offered support to total strangers and entire communities.

Depending on how old you are, you probably also know exactly what you were doing when the Berlin Wall fell, when humankind first walked on the moon, or when President John F. Kennedy was assassinated. Memories of these significant events are likely seared into your mind—and those "stored memories" will remain there forever, springing to life any time you hear, read, or think about these significant events.

Over the years, everybody accumulates numerous positive and negative "stored memories" which, when activated, cause specific reactions. You may smile at the smell of pumpkin pie because it triggers the stored memory of dinner at Grandma's, or you may feel fearful at the sight of a large dog because it triggers a memory of being bitten, and so on. Psychologists use the term "anchors" to describe these links between events, memories, and reactions. To keep it simple, I call them **connections**, and remind people that these powerful persuasive tools are readily at our disposal. Pavlov and Twitmyer first discovered how easily these connections can be established through linking basic stimuli and responses. In many ways, their research into classical conditioning was the foundation for understanding how to make connections between apparently unrelated things.

> **Key Concept:**
> When properly leveraged, connections link a sense like a touch, sight, sound, taste, or smell that is associated with one thing to something else in the mind. Making positive connections in a person's mind, and eliminating negative ones, is a very powerful persuasive strategy.

As a masterful persuader, you, too, must learn how to make these connections intentionally. With carefully chosen words and actions, you can use connections to speed the process of shifting a person to a Desired State by:

- Making helpful new connections in the brain which you can trigger later
- Breaking or separating undesirable existing connections that stand in the way of the Desired State
- Reinforcing helpful existing connections

CONNECTIONS CAN BE POSITIVE OR NEGATIVE

It's easy to create and reinforce connections, both positive and negative. Remember the example of Mr. Wright and the trial cancer medication with the placebo effect? When the clinical study proved the drug to be ineffective, his doctor created a new, positive connection for Mr. Wright regarding the "improved and more powerful" medication—despite knowing that he was actually giving Mr. Wright an inactive placebo. The doctor could just as easily have created a negative connection for Mr. Wright instead, by telling him that the "medication" he was taking would upset his stomach or cause dizziness.

We also frequently see positive and negative connections being created in advertisements. Think about a television commercial for a medication, for example, which plays happy music and shows positive imagery while a long list of side effects is read quietly in the background. The happy music and positive images are intentionally used to stimulate your senses and create an emotional connection between the brand and a positive memory or sensation, hoping that will override any misgivings you may have about the potential side effects of the medication.

> **Key Concept:** Positive and negative connections can be created and reinforced in many ways, using words, sounds, actions, pictures, smells, symbols, and more. These are powerful persuasive tools that make us more effective as we shift others toward a Desired State.

We're all familiar with the acumen that large corporations and their marketing teams demonstrate in creating positive and negative connections. Individuals are also naturally adept at making emotional associations and creating sensory connections to other people, places, and things. We see these connections at work every day. Think of the real estate agent who advises a home seller to bake cookies before their open house, which serves to create a sensory connection between a house and a *home*.

Take a moment to reflect on the many positive and negative connections you have created throughout your life based on scents, images, tastes, sounds, feelings, or the language that was used at the time. You likely have many memories tied to a scent or an image as they tend to produce very strong connections.

LEVERAGING CONNECTIONS

The marketers behind brands understand that people make emotional connections to things. You've probably noticed that when celebrities get into trouble they are immediately dropped by their sponsors. Think of what happened to Tiger Woods's sponsorships when he was caught cheating on his wife, to model Kate Moss when photos of her doing cocaine were published in a London tabloid, or to actress Lori Loughlin when she and her husband were implicated in the 2019 college admissions cheating scandal.

These celebrities lost sponsorships, work projects, and lucrative endorsement deals. They were "dumped" because the positive connection established between them and the public—which the sponsoring companies were willing to pay millions to take advantage of—had turned negative, and companies wanted to distance themselves and their products from any sort of negative association.

When there's a positive feeling created by having celebrities endorse a product, it builds a strong psychological connection that changes the way people behave toward the product. Think back to Pavlov: when he rang a bell, the dogs in his lab salivated as though food was actually there. Pavlov had created a connection between the sound of the bell and food that was neurologically strong enough that the bell ringing triggered the physical response that the actual stimulus (i.e., food) would have evoked. What psychologists, marketers, salespeople, and those in many other fields have learned is that it's possible to use connections to their advantage in the context of their story, their brand, or their offering. Of course, the more frequently a stimulus and a response are paired, the stronger the neurological connections become.

As persuaders, we can use this knowledge to reinforce or break connections, too. When the 2008 Great Recession hit the American auto manufacturing industry, these companies looked to the U.S. Congress for financial aid. This meant the car manufacturers had to attend hearings before the House Financial Services Committee in Washington, D.C., in November 2008.

Unfortunately for these auto executives, they decided to fly to D.C. in their private jets—their *very expensive* private jets. That created, in the minds of tens of millions of Americans, a connection between "car company CEO" and "extravagant rich guy."

Realizing their mistake, the next time the CEOs had to go to D.C., they drove hybrid cars in the hopes of breaking the existing connection between "car company CEO" and "extravagant rich guy," and simultaneously creating a new one between "car company CEO" and "regular guy who cares about the environment."

Did it work? Do you think car company CEOs are "regular guys who care about the environment"?

> **Key Concept:**
> Be deliberate with the connections you create, reinforce, or break.

There are many ways to make, reinforce, or break connections with words, tones, gestures, repetition, music, scents, images, and so on. As a persuader, you will come across certain connections that are disadvantageous. A pharmaceutical sales representative was once given the unenviable task of convincing physicians that spinal problems in patients were caused by factors other than his company's medication. He diligently visited each doctor to explain why this medicine was *not* the cause of these problems.

The pharmaceutical rep emphasized his conviction and sincerity by pressing his hands together in front of his chest while saying, "Doctor, there's *no connection* between this medicine and the spinal issue." Then he offered scientific studies to prove it.

> I am very confident, I look confident, I act confident, I speak in a confident way.
>
> —MILTON ERICKSON

What this rep failed to realize was that the physical act of pressing his hands together subtly emphasized the idea of "connectedness" and reinforced the perceived association between his medicine and patients' spinal problems in the doctors he was speaking to. Since approximately 55% of the impact of our communication is attributed to our physiology, this simple gesture easily outweighed his words. Adding to his problem was the fact that the rep used the phrase "no connection." The doctors failed to process the negation and they understood this message as "connection," effectively reinforcing the belief that the medication was harmful.

So, how could this rep have delivered his message more effectively? Let's imagine instead that when speaking to the doctors, the rep had begun with his hands together to indicate a connection, then pulled them apart as he stated, "Doctor, this is a separate issue." The act of *separating* his hands would then have been connected to the idea that the effectiveness of the medication and the spinal problem are separate matters. Finally, he might have repeated the gesture of pulling his hands apart while saying, "This study confirms they are separate," in order to reinforce his point.

Remember Rapport
It's essential to remember that rapport always comes first. Making, breaking, and reinforcing connections is a powerful persuasion technique when you have rapport with an individual.

PRESUMED TRUTHS

"THE DIFFERENCE BETWEEN THE RIGHT WORD AND THE ALMOST RIGHT WORD IS THE DIFFERENCE BETWEEN LIGHTNING AND THE LIGHTNING BUG."
Mark Twain

I recently led a seminar on improving communication for a group of oncology nurses who had prepared for the session by "treating" volunteers who were acting as patients. Their one-on-one interactions were videotaped and then, during the seminar, we watched the videos of the nurses diligently interviewing their "patients" regarding their symptoms, warning them about potential side effects to medications, and explaining procedures. The nurses often said things like:

- "Some of the side effects you'll likely experience are…"
- "How much worse have the side effects been this month?"
- "Don't get too worried if your response to treatment is slow."

I complimented the nurses for being so conscientious and having good intentions. I then explained that the impact they were having was likely very different from the positive conversation that they intended. If we look at the nurses' communications above, we see that the first example assumes that side effects are likely; the second presupposes that the side effects are getting worse; and the third instills worry in the patient as well as an expectation that they are potentially slow to respond to treatment.

> **Key Concept:**
> Presuppositions are used to create certain assumptions as we engage and guide an individual toward the Desired State. Be aware of opportunities to leverage presuppositions with intention in your communication.

Remember, a **presupposition** is an idea or statement that must be taken for granted and accepted as true in order for a communication to make sense. One of the oncology nurses that I just told you about actually said to a patient, "When trouble arises…," a statement that presupposes that trouble *will* arise—the only question is when. The nurse unintentionally used the nocebo effect to instill an expectation that something negative would happen.

Presuppositions are very powerful because the mind is hardwired to accept what is presupposed without critical evaluation. In essence, a presupposition gets the mind to skip the step of evaluating a statement—as in, "Will trouble *really* arise?"—and instead jump right to an agreement and response. Statements or questions with embedded presuppositions are catalysts for directing the focus and imagination of those individuals that you want to persuade and influence. Using presuppositions, you can guide a person's imagination, emotional state, and ultimately their behavior, from where it is now (the Current State) to where you want it to be (the Desired State).

BE CAREFUL!

As with the nurses on the previous page, we need to be careful to avoid unintentionally instilling a thought or idea in a person's mind. Recall that when communicating, there is a very fine line between **elicitation** (drawing information out of someone) and **instillation** (instilling thoughts or ideas). Remember that you can create and reinforce positive or negative connections, so be strategic and leverage connections intentionally when shifting someone to a Desired State.

USE "TRY" STRATEGICALLY

Be aware of presuppositions in your everyday language and either use them with intention or avoid them. The word "try," for example, presupposes failure and strongly implants the idea in a person's mind that they are likely to fail. When you say, "Try to be on time for our meeting," the mind gets the message that it will likely *fail* to be on time. In this instance, you can avoid suggesting the idea of failure by eliminating the word "try" and crafting a communication that instead instills an expectation of success, such as, "Remember to be on time for our meeting." There are times when you might deliberately use "try" to instill an idea of failure, because it's to your advantage. For example, I once coached a client who was suffering from a phobia of spiders. After helping her work through the phobia, I said, "Go ahead and *try* to find the fear of spiders that you used to have." This implanted the suggestion that she would fail at finding

Key Concept: The word "try" presupposes failure, so avoid using it when you want the other person to succeed. If, on the other hand, you want them to fail, well.... I'll leave that one up to you!

the fear, which also presupposed that her fear of spiders was gone. You'll be amazed at the results you achieve when you use presuppositions strategically.

THE SCIENCE OF "NOT"

What's the first thing that pops into your mind when someone says, "Don't think of the number three?" The number three, of course! That's because you cannot *not* think about something.

Think about it.

The mind fails at processing negation. When you say things like, "It's not too expensive," the other person's mind deletes the "not" and focuses on "expensive," which is the idea that ends up being instilled in their brain. Saying, "Don't worry, this won't hurt," sends the message that it's time to worry *and* primes the mind to focus on pain. Isn't it interesting that the more we attempt *not* to think about something, the more the mind actually focuses on it? When I was in university, I remember my psychology professor discussing several studies, including one in which a group of study volunteers was asked to *not* think of a white bear for five minutes while a second group of volunteers was asked to think about a white bear. During each five-minute period, the volunteers verbalized any thoughts that came to mind and rang a bell when they thought of a white bear.

The results? The group instructed not to think of a white bear thought about it more often than the group that was asked to think about it!

I also remember that same professor discussing a study that dealt with the negative intrusive thoughts that plague many people. Each volunteer was asked to select a negative intrusive thought they had experienced and to keep a record of how many times it occurred during the time frame of the study. Then the volunteers were divided into three groups. One group was told to *suppress* the negative thought every time it popped up. The second group was asked to *think about* the negative thought whenever it came to mind, and the third group was instructed simply to *keep a record of* how many times the negative thought occurred. The results showed that those who *tried to suppress* their negative intrusive thoughts ended up having more of them.

The simplest way to avoid the issue of the mind failing to process negation is to use positive statements. With a little practice, it's really very easy to get into the habit of stating things in the positive by "saying it the way you want it." So, rather than saying, "Don't think this is difficult," say, "This is easy." Instead of telling someone, "Don't worry, this won't hurt," say, "Relax, this is more comfortable than you think; it will be over before you know it." As a parent, rather than saying to your child, "Don't forget about your homework," you'll get better results if you instruct them to, "Remember to do your homework." Instead of saying to a child who is climbing a tree, "Don't fall," tell them to, "Be careful." When it comes to mealtime, replace, "Don't spill your milk," with telling your child to, "Drink your milk carefully and put your glass on the table when you're done."

> **Key Concept:** Since the mind fails to process negation, it's important to say it the way you want it. Once you've mastered this foundational principle, you can then deliberately and strategically apply it with intention to instill a negative where appropriate.

Stating things in the positive, or "saying it the way you want it," is one of my foundational techniques. I want to make it clear that avoiding stating things in the negative is very different from giving people negative feedback or saying something negative. It's okay to give negative feedback and you still want to state it in the positive. Here's a simple example. Say I went to a new restaurant, and I had a bad experience. I may say something like, "I was disappointed with the new restaurant I went to last week. The service was terrible, and the food was mediocre." This is a negative commentary stated in the positive and, as such, it leaves my listener thinking that my experience was disappointing, which it was. Now imagine that I instead say, "The new restaurant I went to last week was not very good. The service didn't meet my expectations and the food wasn't fresh." This time I've stated my negative review in the negative, which opens the door to the possibility that the brain will focus on "very good," "met my expectations," and "fresh." Instead, when I provide my negative feedback stated in the positive, I more accurately and effectively communicate my intended message.

Of course, as with the word "try," you can also deliberately use negatives to implant certain ideas. If, for example, you want to convince a client that your product is best, and you want to avoid bragging, you can say, "I'm not suggesting my product is superior to all the other brands…" The client's mind will delete the "not" and be left with "my product is superior to all the other brands."

LEVERAGING THE POWER OF "BECAUSE"

What if *one word* could dramatically increase the likelihood that people will comply with your requests? A 1978 study by Harvard psychologist Ellen Langer and her colleagues demonstrated the persuasive power of the word "because" by examining the effectiveness of various phrases.[120] At a library photocopier, researchers attempted to push to the front of the line, each time offering one of three excuses:

1. "Excuse me, I have five pages. May I use the Xerox machine?"
2. "Excuse me, I have five pages. May I use the Xerox machine because I'm in a rush?"
3. "Excuse me, I have five pages. May I use the Xerox machine because I have to make some copies?"

The first request, which served as a sort of "control" question, set the bar with 60 % compliance. Compliance shot up to 94 % with the second request, "May I use the Xerox machine *because* I'm in a rush?" indicating that giving a good reason for cutting in line increases the odds of success. The fascinating finding from this study lies with the third request, which employed a nonsensical reason (everybody in the photocopier lineup was there because they had to make some copies!) and still gained 93 % compliance. Why did this nonsensical reason result in the same level of compliance as a perfectly good reason?

---

120 E. Langer, A. Blank, and B. Chanowitz, "The Mindlessness of Ostensibly Thoughtful Action: The Role of 'Placebic' information in Interpersonal Interaction," *Journal of Personality and Social Psychology* 36(6) (1978), pp. 635-642.

LEVERAGE THE POWER OF "BECAUSE".

The reason the nonsensical excuse was so successful was that the word "because" has a peculiar effect on the human mind. We tend to interpret "because" as meaning "good reasons are coming." Since our minds are primed to "believe" this, we pay less attention to the actual reasons once they are given—or even ignore the fact that they are completely nonsensical.

Interestingly, Langer and her colleagues found that the nonsensical reason was less effective when the ask was larger. They increased the number of pages to copy from 5 to 20, with very different results:

1. "Excuse me, I have 20 pages. May I use the Xerox machine?" had a 24% success rate.
2. "Excuse me, I have 20 pages. May I use the Xerox machine because I'm in a rush?" had a 42% success rate.
3. "Excuse me, I have 20 pages. May I use the Xerox machine because I have to make some copies?" also had a 24% success rate.

Key Concept: Using the word "because" leads people to gloss over the reasons for a request—or even skip them altogether—if the ask is small enough. Remember, when the reason is also tied in with a strong emotion, there is even more of a compulsion to comply and it's easier to get someone to acquiesce to your request.

The word "because" is powerful and yet, as Langer and her colleagues explain, the mind will focus on the reason following "because" more closely when the ask increases and requires more effort: "Once compliance with the request required a modicum of effort on the subject's part, thoughtful responding seemed to take the place of mindlessness, and the reason now seemed to matter."[121]

It's worth noting that what was missing in this study is the emotional significance of the reason. Langer said that the reason was essentially irrelevant as long as the request was small enough. What I have found over the years is that if the reason is tied in with emotion, and the emotion is triggered strongly enough, it creates more leverage by creating a compulsion to comply with the request.

Remember back to the study of the Harvard doctors in Chapter One recommending the less effective treatment option for their patients based on emotional framing? The way in which the statistics on patient outcomes for surgery versus radiation were framed impacted physicians' decisions regarding treatment. As with the way in which a doctor describes the benefits and side effects of a medication, word choice matters. The words "mortality" and "survival" were each connected with an emotion for the doctors in the Harvard study, and this influenced them to make treatment recommendations differentially.

ENGAGE THE MIND THROUGH THE SENSES

Have you ever wondered why there is music playing in shopping malls?

> **Key Concept:** Sights, sounds, smells, and other sensory inputs that are absorbed outside of our conscious awareness can influence our thoughts, feelings, and behaviors.

Remember in Chapter Five when we looked at Adrian North's study of music, wine, and the unconscious mind? A similar study testing the effects of sound and scent on mall shoppers was conducted by researchers from Rutgers University.[122] On different days, they played slow-tempo popular music, infused a citrus scent into the air, did both, or did nothing (with people on the "nothing" day serving as the control group).

---

121 Langer, Blank, and Chanowitz, "The Mindlessness of Ostensibly Thoughtful Action," p. 638.

122 S. Dingfelder, "Music motivates impulse buyers, not thoughtful shoppers," ***Monitor on Psychology*** 36(10), (November 2005). Available online: http://www.apa.org/monitor/nov05/music.aspx

The researchers also surveyed shoppers, asking how much they enjoyed their shopping experience, whether it was easy to find items in the mall, how much they had spent, and whether or not some of their purchases were unplanned. "While the pleasant scent and music failed to show any effect on the shoppers' reported moods, they did affect how much the shoppers spent. Shoppers who had made an unplanned purchase spent, on average, $32.89 more when music was playing than those in the control condition. When a scent was present, they spent about $8.66 less."[123] Although relatively few shoppers were consciously aware of either the music or the scent, as a group they were significantly affected by them.

> Consumer decision making and buying behavior are driven more by unconscious thoughts and feelings than by conscious ones. These unconscious forces include ever-changing memories, images, sensations, and stories that interact.
>
> –GERALD ZALTMAN, **HOW CUSTOMERS THINK**

Even tinkering with a common sound can influence people's behavior at an unconscious level. When volunteers were asked to rate the freshness and crispness of potato chips, they rated the chips more highly when they made a louder overall sound or louder high frequency sound. As the scientists who conducted this study noted, "These results highlight the significant role that auditory cues can play in modulating the perception and evaluation of foodstuffs (despite the fact that consumers are often unaware of the influence of such auditory cues)."[124]

HOW MUCH DO YOU PAY YOUR WORDS?

As we saw in Chapter One with the physicians in the Harvard study whose treatment choices were influenced differentially by the words "mortality" and

---

123 Dingfelder, "Music motivates impulse buyers, not thoughtful shoppers." Available online: http://www.apa.org/monitor/nov05/music.aspx

124 M. Zampini and C. Spence, "The role of auditory cues in modulating the perceived crispness and staleness of potato chips," *Journal of Sensory Studies* 19(5) (2004), pp. 347-363.

"survival," words matter a great deal. As persuaders and influencers, we can use language to captivate our listeners' imagination, engage and trigger their emotions, and shift their behaviors. In fact, there are particular words that enable us to spark reactions in others that seem almost magical.

Examples of some of these words are:

- Wonder
- Puzzle
- Understand
- Curious
- Imagine
- Amusement
- Consider
- Breakthrough
- Discover
- Ponder
- Intrigue
- Perplex
- Their name (a person's name is attention-grabbing to its owner!)

These words cut through the constant barrage of mindless chatter that bombards people on a daily basis and helps you to stand out as you captivate their attention and compel them to focus on their interaction with you. Notice the difference between asking, "What are you thinking?" versus, "I'm intrigued and wondering what's going through your mind right now." I'm curious, which one of these is more engaging for you? You can use this tactic to shift a person's mind toward the Desired State by using statements that are embellished by specific words.

> "That's a great deal to make one word mean," Alice said in a thoughtful tone.
>
> "When I make a word do a lot of work like that," said Humpty Dumpty, "I always pay it extra."
>
> –LEWIS CARROLL, **ALICE THROUGH THE LOOKING-GLASS**

Here are some more ways to use the words above to shift a person's mind toward the Desired State:

Instead of...	Say...
Which color do you like best?	*I'm **curious** as to which color you like best...*
There are other ways of doing this...	***Imagine** the myriad other ways there are of doing this...*
What I think is most interesting...	*The **puzzling** thing that interests me most is...*
Most people discover that the biggest benefit is...	*Most people discover, **Barry**, that the biggest benefit is...*
What we did today was...	*The most **intriguing** thing we did today was...*

Words engage the mind in many different ways. Some induce states, such as anxiety. For example, adding the words "two days left" to an advertisement will, in certain people, trigger a state of urgency, a fear that they will miss out on the opportunity if they hesitate to make the purchase quickly. Other mind-engaging words like "remarkable" and "startling" work by framing a story. For instance, the word "suddenly" gives what follows extra impact because the mind understands "suddenly" to mean "this is unexpected, so pay attention."

THIS ONE WORD CAN DESTROY RAPPORT

How do you feel when someone says to you, "You're right, *but*..." or "That's an interesting idea, *but*..."?

Used this way, the word "but" essentially means "You're wrong" or "What you're saying is irrelevant." When you're given the *but*, you feel as if you're being shut down. This makes "but" a rapport-buster that completely eradicates the experience of being understood. It negates what comes before it and it demonstrates dismissal rather than understanding. The result is a dynamic whereby the other person is likely to either disengage altogether or vehemently maintain their stance and become oppositional to your suggestions.

As a persuader, you can avoid this problem by replacing the word "but" with bridging terms such as "and," "also," "another thing worth contemplating is..." and so on. These bridging conjunctions and phrases connect your ideas to those of the other person, rather than negating their ideas, allowing you to validate their input while still making your point. In essence, you accept the individual's idea and build on it, or perhaps redirect it toward the desired outcome. As we discussed in Chapter Six, your goal is to provide the other person with the experience of being understood as you acknowledge their ideas and open their mind to other possibilities.

> **Key Concept:**
> The mind is engaged by certain words that make what you say more interesting and compelling, while other words, such as "but," are powerful rapport-busters and should be used with caution. When it comes to the words you use, be sure to choose them carefully and deliberately.

So, instead of saying, "You're right, *but* I think..." say, "You're right, *and* another thing worth considering is..." or "That's an interesting idea, *also there's the option of*..."

For example, imagine that two managers are discussing a candidate for a job. While they agree that the candidate has key qualities that would benefit the company, they are divided about the individual's level of experience. Rather than dismiss the other person's viewpoint and potentially create an emotionally charged argument, notice how using "and" instead of "but" reduces the risk of possible conflict.

Here's an example of how to use "and" in this situation to *dissuade* the other person from hiring the candidate:

- *Acknowledge and extend*: "I agree that this candidate is inexperienced, *and* I also think she's too disorganized."
- *Acknowledge and question*: "I agree that this candidate is inexperienced, *and* I question whether she has the right leadership skills that can be developed over time to effectively lead the team."

To use "and" in this situation to *support* hiring the candidate, you might:

- *Acknowledge and redirect*: "I agree that this candidate is inexperienced, *and* I believe that her flexibility will allow her to work well with and learn from the more experienced members of the team."
- *Acknowledge and disagree*: "I agree that this candidate is inexperienced, *and* I still support her because of her raw talent."

In this situation, using "and" is a powerful persuasion tool to guide the other person thoughtfully toward your desired outcome, whether you support hiring the candidate or passing them over.

Words, gestures, tonality, and the whole range of verbal and non-verbal communication are highly influential in making, breaking, and reinforcing connections. You can use the totality of the options for communication to lead a person from their Current State to a more Desired State. When it comes to words, it's important to use them deliberately. Remember, words have an exponential impact and a tremendous effect, both consciously and unconsciously, on thoughts, emotions, and behavior. As we've been discussing in this chapter, the word "but" negates everything before it, while the word "try" instills doubt and presupposes failure. Always use words mindfully because language is ultimately one of the most powerful tools available to the persuader… and it's a skill that is worth mastering!

> Like stones, words are laborious and unforgiving, and the fitting of them together, like the fitting of stones, demands great patience and strength of purpose and particular skill.
>
> –EDMUND MORRISON

In this chapter you've learned how certain words (like "curious" and "wonder") can have a tremendous impact on engaging others' minds, as well as on making, breaking, or reinforcing connections. You've also learned how the word "try" can lead to failure and "but" can undermine rapport.

Now I invite you to create your own list of engaging words. Which ones do you find yourself using already? Which ones would you like to employ more in your daily interactions?

Test a few of these words out on the next person you speak with and notice how they respond now and throughout the rest of your week or month. Observe the effect that simple shifts in your language can have. Leverage what you've learned about sensory communication and observe as people respond differently when you use persuasive language.

Chapter Eleven

SMARTen Up!

In the previous chapters, we've noted the mind's incredible ability to alter our perception of reality and even to change our own beliefs. Do you remember the story of weightlifter Vasily Alekseyev who struggled to lift 500 pounds even though he had successfully lifted just below that weight several times before? You may recall that his trainer stamped 500-pound weights with a label indicating that they were the lower weight Alekseyev knew he could lift in order to bypass his limiting beliefs and to shift his thinking about his own abilities. In this way, Alekseyev was "tricked" into realizing that he could, indeed, successfully achieve his goal of lifting 500 pounds.

When we think of goals, it's easy to set "big picture" objectives for ourselves that vary in terms of whether we can realistically achieve them. This was the case for Florence Chadwick, the first woman to swim the English Channel in both directions. In 1952, Florence set her sights on a new goal, deciding to swim across the Catalina Channel in California—another huge feat.

> On July 4, 1952, at the age of 34, Chadwick attempted to become the first woman to swim 21 miles across the Catalina Channel, from Catalina Island to Palos Verdes on the California coast. The weather that day was not auspicious—the ocean was ice cold, the fog was so thick that she could hardly see the support boats that followed her, and sharks prowled around her. Several times, her support crew used rifles to drive away the sharks. While Americans watched on television, she swam for hours. Her mother and her trainer, who were in one of the support boats, encouraged her to keep going. However, after 15 hours and 55 minutes, with only a half mile to go, she felt that she couldn't go on, and asked to be taken out of the water.[125]

125 "Florence Chadwick 1953-1964," ***Queen of the Channel***. Available online: https://www.queenofthechannel.com/florence-chadwick

Chadwick later told reporters that because she was unable to *see* her goal, she was unable to complete it. Although our own goals are often less extreme, it's easy to identify with Florence's sentiment. Think back to our discussion on association and disassociation in Chapter Nine. A very basic principle is at work here: when you have a clear picture of your realized goal in your mind, you'll have a much easier time achieving it. As you visualize and then initiate the steps toward your goal and gradually shift your thinking, emotions, and behaviors, often with the encouragement of someone else to keep you accountable and on track, you are ensuring the greatest likelihood of success.

In Chadwick's case, she persevered. She returned to the water several months later and, with her goal clear in her mind even through dense fog, she became the first woman to swim the Catalina Channel, beating the previous record by more than two hours. Chadwick's story is a clear example of why it's important to have a specific, self-initiated goal and how to achieve it using the **SMART** (**S**pecific, **M**easurable, **A**ttainable, **R**ealistic, and **T**imed) methodology, which we'll explore in the next few sections.

SMART LIKE ME

Although they lack the capacity to use language (that we can understand), when it comes to intelligence, octopuses are arguably smarter than most of us give them credit for. Jennifer Mather, a comparative psychologist at the University of Lethbridge, has found that these creatures are capable of self-initiated, planned behavior, an ability that is unique among invertebrates in the animal kingdom.

Mather has been studying octopuses since 1972 and, during her field work in Bermuda in 1984, she witnessed something truly amazing. She "watched a common octopus catch some crabs and take them back to its shelter to eat. Then it suddenly darted toward a rock about 7ft (2m) away, put it [the rock] under its tentacles and took it back to its den. The octopus did this three more times, creating a wall in front of its home. As if confident in the extra security measure, it then fell asleep behind the barrier."[126] Mather argued that this type of behavior proves that the octopus is capable of foresight and sequencing. "This

126 Nic Fleming, "Eight Reasons Why Octopuses are the Geniuses of the Ocean," *BBC Earth* (May 30, 2016). Available online: http://www.bbc.com/earth/story/20160527-eight-reasons-why-octopuses-are-the-geniuses-of-the-ocean

demonstrated to me that there was an animal with a mental image of what it wanted and one that was capable of planning," she told the BBC. "It was very far removed from the automatic stimuli-response that we were used to thinking about with animals."

Over two decades later, in 2009, Julian Finn of Museum Victoria in Melbourne, Australia, observed similar self-initiated behavior in veined octopuses.

> The octopuses were digging up discarded coconut shells from the ocean floor, cleaning them with water jets, sometimes stacking them and carrying them up to 66ft (20m) to later reassemble as a shelter. The octopuses were filmed arranging the half-shells with the pointed ends facing down, then extending their arms over them and walking in a comic fashion along the sea floor.[127]

What on earth were they doing?

The octopuses' bizarre movements, which were slow and energy inefficient, made them more vulnerable to predators. While the observers initially failed to understand that the octopuses were collecting and organizing rocks and shells for a future use, it soon became clear that these octopuses had a specific, self-initiated goal in mind, which was motivating their actions. In fact, their motivation to reach a future goal outweighed any immediate risk. As Julian Finn argues, the "octopuses were willing to accept these risks in exchange for protection in the future."[128]

As we see with these octopuses, when the motivation is strong enough, we will make the effort required to achieve a specific outcome. As persuaders, we can at the very least be as SMART as an octopus! You can help shift another person to the Desired State by ensuring that their goals, and yours, follow the SMART methodology.

THE SMART WAY TO ACHIEVE GOALS

The SMART model is one that's common in the world of education, coaching and goal setting, and it can also be used to persuade and influence others. In the

---

127 Fleming, "Eight Reasons Why Octopuses are the Geniuses of the Ocean." Available online: http://www.bbc.com/earth/story/20160527-eight-reasons-why-octopuses-are-the-geniuses-of-the-ocean

128 Fleming, "Eight Reasons Why Octopuses are the Geniuses of the Ocean." Available online: http://www.bbc.com/earth/story/20160527-eight-reasons-why-octopuses-are-the-geniuses-of-the-ocean

previous examples of Vasily Alekseyev lifting incredible weights and Florence Chadwick swimming long distances, each had a series of smaller goals and the support of a coach or coaches who helped lead them toward their success.

> If a man knows not to which port he sails, no wind is favorable.
>
> –LUCIUS ANNAEUS SENECA

Coaching is often a selfless endeavor that seeks to help others clarify and attain their goals. Coaches assist individuals to access their own internal resources and determine what other external resources and actions are required to successfully achieve specific goals. Persuading, on the other hand, is focused on your own Desired State as a persuader and on encouraging and shifting others toward that Desired State in a way that is also relevant to them based on their beliefs and values.

Key Concept: Once you understand what's important to someone, what they value and why, you can connect what you're doing or offering in a way that's more meaningful and relevant to them.

The SMART model provides a very useful framework for both coaching and persuading. For our purposes, we'll look at it within the context of persuasion as a filter through which we can refine our Desired State. In this context, rather than as a technique, we use the SMART model as a checklist with which we measure the quality of our Desired State. If our Desired State is well-defined, it will naturally align with the SMART model.

Like the researchers who studied octopuses, you can start to understand someone else's goals by observing their behavior. In contrast to the octopus, with people you have the added benefit of being able to have a dialogue and ask clarifying questions about what matters to them.

THE SMART MODEL IN ACTION

Setting a goal using the SMART model engages the Reticular Activating System (RAS), the part of the brain that plays an important role in attention. When refining our Desired State in the context of persuasion, remember that we need to ensure that we make the desired outcome relevant to the other person by connecting it to their current beliefs and values. This relevance activates their RAS and primes their mind to pay attention.

> **Key Concept:** Desired goals that are SMART in its simplest form—specific, measurable, attainable, realistic/relevant, and timed—are much more likely to be achieved than those that fail to meet these criteria.

So how do we use the SMART model to persuade effectively? Use this outline to develop an objective that is:

S — **Specific, Stated in the Positive, Sensory-Based** (Visual, Auditory, Kinesthetic, Olfactory, and Gustatory), **Self-Initiated and Self-Maintained**

M — **Measurable and Meaningful** (think about to whom it is meaningful and why)

A — **Attainable, Actionable, and "As If"**

R — **Realistic and Relevant** (think about to whom it is relevant and why)

T — **Timed, Toward the Future**

Recall that in Chapter Ten, we discussed the relevance of creating meaningful connections. As you plan and refine your Desired State with the SMART model in mind, remember to search for opportunities to make strategic connections so that what you are offering is linked to what is most meaningful and relevant to the person with whom you are working.

Think back to Paul Butler and the people of St. Lucia. By renaming "the bird" the "St. Lucia Parrot," Butler connected it to the identity of St. Lucians. "It's one of us and we protect our own" became the islanders' new way of thinking, triggering feelings of nationalism and pride with regard to protecting the parrot.

Once these new feelings were instilled, the people were motivated to act differently toward the parrot (they stopped hunting and eating the bird and destroying its habitat, and instead protected it). Keep in mind that rather than being based on what the people of St. Lucia initially wanted, the desired goal was instead to shift their thinking and actions toward the conservation of the species.

Creating meaningful connections is critical to developing a SMART objective and it is just one of the reasons that SMART goals are so effective. Let's take a more granular look at SMART goals and why they work so well in the context of persuading and influencing people.

S

Specific, Stated in the Positive, Sensory-Based (Visual, Auditory, Kinesthetic, Olfactory, and Gustatory), **Self-Initiated and Self-Maintained**

The **"S"** stands for **specific**
+ the need to ensure that the **outcome** is **stated** in the **positive** and is **sensory-based.**

M

Measurable and Meaningful (think about to whom it is meaningful and why)

When outcomes are **measurable**, you have **specific achievements** to strive for
+ the distinction of **meaningful** to the person who will be achieving the goal.

A

Attainable, Actionable, and "As If"

To **ensure success**, strive for **achievable goals**
+ two distinctions, the outcome needs to be mapped out in actionable steps and it is important to **imagine "as if" the outcome** is **already in place** at the desired time in the future.

R

Realistic and Relevant (think about to whom it is relevant and why)

For **you** as well as for **other key parties** that are involved
+ relevant for **all parties.**

T

Timed, Toward the Future

Establishing a **time frame** in which to **reach** the **outcome**
+ the **distinction** of having the outcome be **future oriented.**

S

Specific, Stated in the Positive, Sensory-Based
(Visual, Auditory, Kinesthetic, Olfactory, and Gustatory),
Self-Initiated and Self-Maintained

The **"S"** stands for **specific**
+ the need to ensure that the **outcome is stated** in the **positive** and is **sensory-based.**

The "S" in "SMART" primarily stands for **specific**, and I've expanded it in the context of persuasion to also indicate *stated in the positive, sensory-based, self-initiated, and self-maintained.*

Ideas, plans, or methods that are specific are far more powerful and likely to be accomplished and/or maintained than vague ones. For instance, if you were to tell someone you'll meet them "for lunch soon," the chances of you actually meeting are slim unless you also give them the name or address of a *specific* restaurant as well as a *specific* date and time.

When we think about this simple example in the context of persuading, we can see that if either the Desired State or our method of achieving the Desired State is ambiguous, then it's easy for us to get off track. The more specific we are in defining our Desired State and how we'll achieve it, the easier it is to stay on track and keep the other person's attention moving in that direction. Remember, the body will always move in the direction of the mind's most dominant thoughts.

As a persuader, it's important to tune in to an individual's Current State and align your desired outcome to their beliefs and values. As you connect the goal to what is relevant and meaningful to them, they are more likely to be motivated and willing to follow as you shift them to a Desired State. Recall the key point we have covered before: if you want to get someone to care about something, link it to something they already care about or that is of value to them.

For example, think back to Chapter Nine and the BBC News headlines reporting on the famines affecting many parts of Africa. You may recall the study that looked at two different approaches to obtaining donations—the first presented a collection of facts and figures, the second told a moving story of a seven-year-old girl in Malawi and her family and community who were directly affected by the events. Reflect on which approach gained the most donations and why. The second one—because the story gave donors a specific, relevant cause to care about, effectively influencing them to donate more money.

Always state your offering in the positive: *say it the way you want it*. If, for instance, you present the donors in the previous example with the goal framed as, "Don't ignore the needs of the African people," their minds initially focus on ignoring people in Africa that are in need, rather than the desired outcome of helping African people live and thrive. Instead, it's far more effective to talk about how rewarding it will feel (*toward* motivation) to help avoid unnecessary deaths (*away from* motivation) by contributing to famine relief efforts aimed at assisting Rokia, her family and other members of their community to succeed (*toward* motivation). Keep in mind that, as with any messaging like this, we have the opportunity to customize our communication to the specific audience. The better we understand those we are appealing to, the better able we are to take into consideration their beliefs, values, criteria, and motivational preferences when crafting our messages.

> The best way to get someone to care about something they don't yet care about is to connect it to something that they already care about.
>
> –CHIP HEATH AND DAN HEATH, **MADE TO STICK**

When it comes to influencing others, you may also want to present the goal in *sensory-based* terms to make it more compelling, realistic, and therefore more likely to "stick" in the recipient's mind. Since the human mind processes information in terms of pictures, sounds, feelings, tastes, and smells, translating the goal into the "language of the brain" will improve both reception and retention.

You can evoke the senses by guiding an individual to imagine what they will see, hear, and feel once they reach the Desired State. In Chapter Nine, we described associating into the experience of biting into a lemon—taking the cool, juicy lemon from the refrigerator, holding and feeling the weight of it in your hands, slowly and carefully slicing it open while anticipating the taste of the cold, tart juices. Consider using similar kinds of sensory-rich language to associate others into a story when engaging and guiding them. By engaging the senses, you are more likely to associate a person into the experience, trigger their emotions, and shift them in the direction of your Desired State.

I recently asked participants in one of my workshops, "Suppose I offered you a subscription to cable television, where would you put the first television in your home?" One woman said the kitchen. When I asked her why the kitchen, she explained that it was difficult to get her children to sit and eat, and she thought they'd be more likely to do so if there were a television in the kitchen. In probing further regarding what programs her children would watch, she reported that they enjoyed Baby Shark and then she spontaneously started to perform the associated song and dance. While she and the audience laughed about it, this was a clear example of my engaging and guiding her, and also connecting what I was offering (a subscription to cable television) to something meaningful to her (her children and mealtime) and eliciting a positive emotional state (a connection to the joy experienced when singing a song with her children).

Speaking of children, many parents good-naturedly have their own goals and ambitions for their children. You may have experienced this with your own parents, who may have wanted you to become a doctor, a lawyer, or a star athlete. Unless their goals for you truly align with your own, success is unlikely. Goals must be *self-initiated*. A goal should always be something *you* want, that *you* initiate, and that *you* can monitor and *self-maintain*. This is important to consider when it comes to persuasion and influence. The Desired State must be self-initiated and self-maintained by the person you're influencing, rather than by you the persuader. Like Paul Butler, who moved the St. Lucian people to a Desired State of respecting and valuing the St. Lucia Parrot, that usually means persuading another person (or group of people) to adopt a goal as their own (and we've already discussed many ways to do that—by tapping into motivation, by aligning a Desired State with their values and beliefs, by using effective communication techniques, and so much more).

When it's your goal rather than a goal someone else has for you, you're much more likely to be successful in taking ownership, responsibility, and accountability for that goal. Doing so helps you maintain an internal locus of control (which we'll discuss in Chapter Twelve) while seeing the goal through to completion.

Remember, it's your responsibility to make sure you see your goals through to the end, and that is more likely to happen if you've set them for yourself. Many people tend to "blame" others for a goal that's not completed. You've probably seen examples of this throughout your own life. A teenager may say a member of their group was absent and so their assignment was poorly done. A co-worker may blame a missing report for a low result this quarter. In both instances, these goals lack self-maintenance. As I often tell my clients in private practice—you're putting energy into either finding an excuse or finding a way. The responsibility for accomplishing your goals lies solely with *you!*

M

Measurable and Meaningful (think about to whom it is meaningful and why)

When outcomes are **measurable,** you have **specific achievements** to strive for **+** the distinction of **meaningful** to the person who will be achieving the goal.

Goals that are presented in a *measurable* manner are easier to understand and evaluate, and therefore are more compelling than goals which lack a quantifiable component. For example, rather than setting a goal for yourself "to lose weight," set a goal to lose five pounds and ensure that you also set a time frame (see "T" on the following pages) in which to measure success. In the context of persuasion, it is critical that the goal is also meaningful to the other person as you shift them in a desired direction.

How do we make goals meaningful to others, then? This is where uncovering and understanding a person's Current State comes in. An integral part of doing this is listening carefully for their beliefs, values, criteria, meta programs, and so on—the essence of their model of the world. Houdini, for instance, was exceptionally good at doing this and one way he gauged the beliefs and values of his audience was to ask them what type of "miracle" would impress them most and why. In this way, the outcome of his performance was highly meaningful to them because it was of their choosing.

There is a fascinating story about Houdini and an illusion he performed with an old cathedral bell in Russia. Houdini, who was entertaining the Russian Tsar and other members of the country's elite, asked them to choose a feat for him to accomplish. The audience requested that he ring the bell in the old cathedral's tower. Of course, everyone there knew that twenty years earlier this particular bell's 500-pound clapper had fallen from the tower, killing a hundred people and injuring many others. Following that tragic incident, a strict decree had been issued forbidding the bell from ever being rung again. In light of this, the request seemed impossible! Yet according to reports, Houdini "miraculously" made the bell ring five times on the spot while standing within the palace, impressing the Tsar, the Grand Dukes, and everyone else in the room. The illusion was impressive and made all the more meaningful because of the value it held to those who were amazed to hear the infamous bell ring once more.[129]

Beyond the sentimental experience for the people of Moscow, Houdini's illusion is a powerful example of a well-thought-out Desired State. Even though SMART goals are a modern concept, Houdini followed a similar process. He knew what would be meaningful to his audience and planned his ruse using actionable, measurable steps (and as you keep reading, we'll disclose more about how he did it). Just like Houdini, who identified what was relevant to others and utilized that knowledge to support his success, use what you uncover about a person's beliefs and values to ensure the Desired State is both meaningful and measurable.

A

Attainable, Actionable, and "As If"

To **ensure success**, strive for **achievable goals**
+ two distinctions, the outcome needs to be mapped out in actionable steps and it is important to **imagine "as if" the outcome** is **already in place** at the desired time in the future.

Attainable goals are more credible than unrealistic ones. If you're a fitness coach, for example, and you promise an out-of-shape potential client that he will look like wrestler and actor Dwayne "The Rock" Johnson in a few months, there's a good chance he'll laugh in your face. If, on the other hand, you say that you'll help him increase muscle mass and lose fat tissue by a plausible percentage within a reasonable period of time, the client will be more likely to

129 Dean Carnegie, "New Twists on Houdini's Russian Tour," ***The Magic Detective Blog*** (March 10, 2012). Available online: http://www.themagicdetective.com/2012/03/new-twists-on-houdinis-russian-tour.html

accept your offering. You can do this by using the *as if* technique that we've already covered. Imagine the goal "as if" a committed outcome is already in place—and ensure that the outcome is actionable.

Let's return again to Vasily Alekseyev, the Russian weightlifter who struggled to lift 500 pounds. Lifting 500 pounds was, in fact, *attainable*, as proven when his trainer, by subtly tweaking the weight stamps on his bar, managed also to tweak Alekseyev's mindset. Alekseyev was able to accomplish this feat and break the 500-pound barrier—it simply needed to be attainable in his mind.

It's important to be aware that what qualifies as an "attainable goal" will vary from person to person, depending on their previous experiences and their Current State, including factors such as their beliefs and values. By gaining a deeper understanding of an individual's Current State, we are better equipped to give them the experience of being understood as we assist them to map out a Desired State that is most appropriate for them.

In Chapter One we introduced the ***Think → Feel → Do*** process. Consider how important the "Do" is in achieving a Desired State. We can think about and feel inspired to do something, yet if we stop short of acting on it, then nothing happens! It's helpful to reinforce a commitment to an objective with an attainable plan and actionable behavioral steps as part of our SMART checklist. In this way, we ensure that there is follow through and actionable movement that shifts us in the direction of our Desired State.

R

Realistic and Relevant (think about to whom it is relevant and why)

For **you** as well as for **other key parties** that are involved
+ relevant for **all parties.**

Recall what you have learned so far about uncovering a person's Current State, including their beliefs, values, criteria, and meta programs. When a goal is *relevant* to someone, when it applies to what they're currently thinking and doing, or when it seems relatable to something in their life now or in the future, it will be easier to influence them to change their thinking. When you make the goal relevant for them and help them experience the Desired State as meaningful and *realistic*, they are much more likely to follow you.

For example, imagine that you're training an employee to become a senior manager in your organization. It's unrealistic to expect the employee to start making strong management decisions and leading the company right away. As a good leader you will work with them to enhance their skillset and experience over time—months, or even years. As the employee advances in their current role, having realistic timelines and measurable goals relevant to their Current State will foster their skills, and their confidence in themselves, as they transition to the more senior management role.

As you can see, it's important that the goal and outcomes are realistic and relevant for all parties.

T

Timed, Toward the Future

Establishing a **time frame** in which to **reach** the **outcome**
+ the **distinction** of having the outcome be **future oriented.**

Finally, as a persuader you must establish a *time* frame in which to reach your desired outcome. A goal that will be realized "someday" or "eventually" is lacking a commitment to a timeline and is likely to lead to disappointment and failure.

Consider this. A person looking to switch career paths and become a freelance artist may say they want to make that change within the next few years. In order for this person to have a solid commitment to the plan, it is essential that they have an exact time frame in place that has measurable steps (i.e., sourcing art materials by the end of the month, leasing studio space and completing ten pieces of art within six months, creating an online portfolio by the end of the year, liaising with local galleries or buyers early in year two, selling five new paintings by the end of the second year, etc.).

In the absence of a timeline that is manageable, goals can feel far off. For instance, imagine that you are a student, and you want to pay off the remaining balance of your student debt, which is $8,000, within the next twenty-four months. To make this goal realistic, you'll need to set aside about $333 (plus interest) each month to contribute toward the debt. With an exact time frame and dollar amount in place, you can take responsibility for reducing how much you spend on other items so that you are able to put the necessary amount of money toward paying down your debt within the set time frame.

This also applies to the example of the employee becoming a manager that we just looked at. If you say that you eventually want this employee to lead the company, what defines "eventually"? A year from now? Five years? Giving the employee a time frame such as one or two years is both realistic and time-bound.

SMART MAKES SENSE

Remember the story of Houdini's bell ringing illusion? You may be wondering how he pulled it off. Interestingly, his method follows much of the SMART model. Although no one knows his true intent, in all likelihood Houdini's very *specific* goal to make the bell ring (or make others believe it could ring again) was geared toward his audience and was chosen simply because this feat would seem impossible to them. Houdini discovered in advance how meaningful ringing the bell would be for this group of dignitaries and that in itself provided a very unique opportunity—all he needed were the proper tools to make the "miracle" a reality.

Houdini used the strategic placement of an assistant within viewing distance of the window in the room where he began his ruse. He then had the assistant watch and wait for his signal from the window—a simple flip of a white handkerchief. When the assistant saw the signal, he fired an air rifle at the bell in order to make it ring. In addition to being *actionable* and *attainable* in this way, Houdini's goal was also *realistic* and *relevant*, extremely *well-timed,* and highly *sensory-based* considering that he used the flicking of the handkerchief to create a visual cue that was virtually simultaneous with the audible ringing of the bell.

What appeared to be an incredible feat of magic to his bewildered audience was, essentially, a brilliant sequence of steps that led to an overall well-formed SMART outcome and Houdini's Desired State of amazing his audience was successfully achieved.

THE ECOLOGY OF PERSUASION

In addition to being SMART, a well-formed outcome also takes into consideration the overall **ecology** of the situation. Many people are familiar with the word ecology as a scientific term that biologists use to describe a relationship between an organism and its environment. In the field of linguistics, the term "ecology" is applied to human systems (which include family, work relationships, school, friendships, and community). In the context of being a persuader, this means you must have an awareness of and sensitivity to the impact any modification has on the entire system.

It's important to proceed with respectful caution because changes made within a human system will affect that system in other areas. An ecological choice is one that aims to have a positive impact on the whole system. And it's also important for *you* to genuinely believe that any desired change in a person's thinking, state, and behavior is the best thing for them. *Always remember to consider ecology when mapping out your Desired State.*

Think of a human system as being like a bus route. When we make a change to the beginning of the route by adding a new stop, there are implications for the rest of the route, and arrival and departure times will change. While adding a stop may be beneficial for passengers in a select area, how will it impact other passengers who will be requesting bus transfers and who will need arrival and departure times to coordinate with catching other routes? If these passengers miss their transfers, how will the other routes be affected? As you can see, one seemingly small change can have a widespread effect.

When we refer to ecological goals, choices, and changes, we're considering how existing systems will be affected and whether the goal, choice or change will be positive and healthy for the entire system. Being ecological requires us to be aware of existing values and to identify conflicting values, as we'll discuss below.

It is critical to note that the benefit of employing an ecological approach within the context of persuasion is that it encourages consideration of the *full impact* of any potential change in the ***Think → Feel → Do*** process. **Cartesian coordinates** are a great way to harness the power of questions as you help the person you're persuading work through the ***Think → Feel → Do*** process on their way toward the Desired State.

Based on Cartesian logic, these mathematical applications, as shown in the diagram below, introduce different "what if" type questions to prime a person to think about the positive and negative consequences that are connected with their decisions.[130]

In the context of persuasion, we can use Cartesian logic to go beyond the typical pro/con list that many people use when making decisions. Each of the four quadrants of a Cartesian plane is a valuable way of encouraging someone to think outside of the box and to evaluate a decision in new contexts. With this process we systematically consider, from different perspectives, various thoughts and perceptions about the decision and all its potential outcomes. This evaluation is holistic and ecological because it looks at the broader impact(s) of the decision.

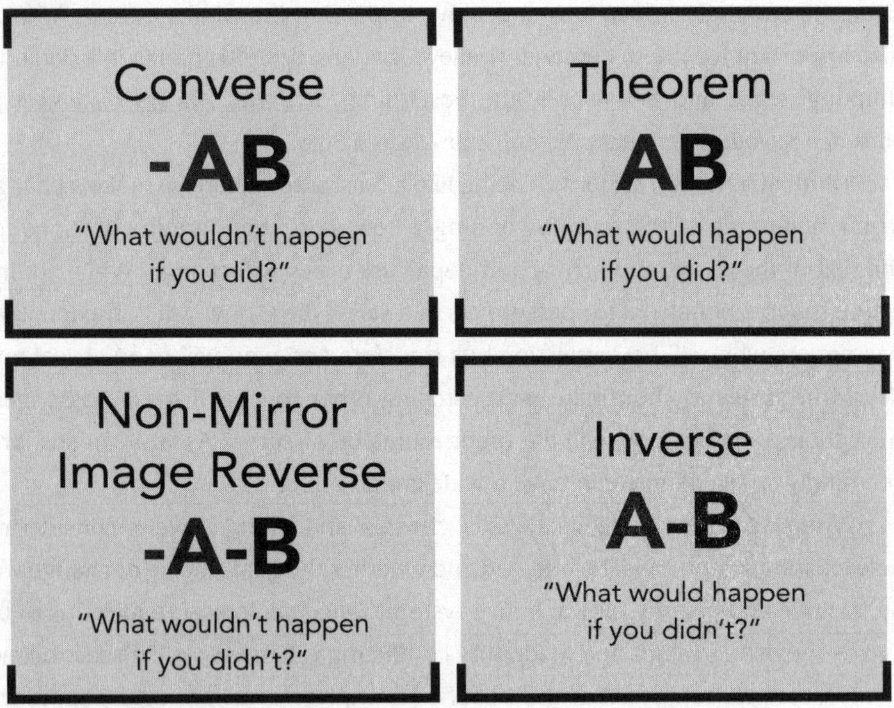

Adapted from Tad James, Tad James, "Prime Concerns: Using Quantum Linguistics to Increase the Effectiveness of the Language We Use." ©1989, 1994. Used with permission.

130 Cartesian Coordinates and diagram adapted from Tad James, "Prime Concerns: Using Quantum Linguistics to Increase the Effectiveness of the Language We Use." ©1989, 1994. Used with permission

USING CARTESIAN COORDINATES TO ADDRESS CONFLICTING VALUES

I once counselled an executive named Martin who had been offered a prestigious promotion and a nice bump in salary. Unfortunately, the promotion required him to move to Dubai. The new position would be great for Martin's career, his wife, Josie, was supportive, and he wanted to take it, yet he was conflicted. His main concern was thinking that by taking the job he would essentially be "abandoning" his two college-aged sons. Martin was worried that if he brought his sons with him to Dubai, they might hate it, miss out on important educational and social opportunities at home, and perhaps feel like life was passing them by.

When I asked Martin to tell me the most important thing he could do for his sons, he instantly replied, "Help them become strong and independent." Once it was clear that he valued their independence, it was easy to help him work through his conflicting values using the Cartesian coordinates.

Here's how:

For each of the quadrants, I worked with Martin to fully consider the impact of the question. For example, one of the many questions I asked him within the Theorem AB quadrant was, "What would happen if you moved your family to Dubai?" His answer to this specific question was that his career would flourish while his sons would miss opportunities at home. I moved through the Cartesian coordinates clockwise, asking Martin the question in each quadrant in several ways such as, "What would happen if you didn't move your family to Dubai?" He replied that his career would stagnate. We moved on to "What wouldn't happen if you didn't move your family to Dubai?" Martin said that he wouldn't be able to further his career and challenge himself. Finally, I asked, "What wouldn't happen if you did move your family to Dubai." Here, Martin said his sons would miss out on being able to graduate from a Canadian university, which had been a positive and life-altering experience for him. As Martin and I moved through each of the quadrants, I continued asking each question multiple times in subtly different ways to allow Martin to fully consider the impact of the decision.

Knowing that Martin felt conflicted regarding some of these outcomes, I changed the outcome and rephrased the four questions. I asked him, "What would happen if you and your wife moved to Dubai while your sons stayed home and attended a Canadian university?" In using the same process to work through each coordinate with this new outcome, Martin was able to clearly see that his move to Dubai could be good for the whole family.

He realized that he and his wife could keep their house in Canada, let their sons live there, and give them enough money to cover schooling and basic expenses. If their sons wanted anything beyond that, they could get jobs and earn money. Meanwhile, relatives who lived nearby could check on them every so often to make sure they were all right.

Martin's goal of advancing his career was now in alignment with one of his criteria for being a good father: "fostering independence." In fact, moving to Dubai helped him get *closer* to fulfilling that criterion. With the conflict resolved, he could progress freely toward the well-formed outcome.

By employing Cartesian logic, I was able to facilitate a dialogue by asking strategic questions that empowered Martin to discover an ecological solution for himself, one that took into account all the needs of his family, and which was much more powerful and effective than simply suggesting a solution.

SMART AND ECOLOGICAL

Was taking the job in Dubai an ecological decision for Martin and his family in the long term? It was. Martin continued to retain me as a resource and coach for his sons while he was in Dubai. When he visited Canada (which he did at least once a year), we always made time to get together. We kept in touch for years afterwards and Martin still believes the move was one of the best decisions he ever made for himself, his career, *and* for his entire family.

Ecological outcomes are made up of ideas, plans, or products that you are certain are best for another person. If you're an insurance broker, for example, you would offer a prospective client *only* the policies that fit their situation, rather than those that have the highest commission or are the most advantageous for you or your company. While the product you're offering

> **Key Concept:** Always check to ensure that your goals are ecological. People with integrity help others become aware of their needs and offer to help them find a genuine solution to those needs.

may be good, those with integrity choose to present others with the best thing for them at that time and in that situation.

It may be tempting at times to use persuasive techniques for self-serving purposes. History is littered with charismatic individuals who have used their talents for personal gain or to harm others: think of cult leaders and prosperity gospel TV preachers. This, of course, is highly *un*ecological. My intent in sharing these techniques is for you to use them positively in your life. Always ask yourself: "Is this truly right for the other person? Or does it just selfishly meet my own needs?"

If your solution is something other than (or at odds with) what the person needs, it's best to point them in the direction of someone else who has a better solution to those needs or for you to move on to someone who has a problem for which you do have a solution. If you force something on someone, you potentially set up a dynamic of "buyer's remorse." Instead, focus on understanding and truly fulfilling others' needs in the most meaningful ways to ensure they are satisfied. This is the principled way to work with people, and they may well promote and recommend you based upon their experience.

DEALING WITH DISEMPOWERING BELIEFS

As we've previously discussed, some beliefs are empowering while others are limiting. Empowering beliefs help you move forward, while disempowering beliefs prevent progress. In fact, disempowering beliefs can block progress toward any goal, no matter how desirable, ecological, or SMART.

It's important to listen closely to and be aware of the language an individual uses to describe their beliefs. If we detect disempowering beliefs, we can assist the individual in ecologically updating their current beliefs, transforming them into

Key Concept: Even the most carefully planned desired outcome may be sabotaged if a person has conflicting values or disempowering beliefs. To ensure success, it's imperative that our beliefs and values are congruent and that we create goals that are in alignment with them. Remember, beliefs and values are the navigational compass that guides our behavior.

more useful and empowering ones. These updated beliefs will then support the person as we help navigate them in the direction of their Desired State.

I once coached a teenager, Anton, whose parents had employed various tactics to address his rebellious behavior. The main problem was that he refused to attend school. During our first session, Anton initially presented as withdrawn and was resistant to interacting with me. My top priority, as always, was to build rapport with him by matching, mirroring, and pacing. In addition, part of my strategy for getting him on-side was to give Anton the choice to opt-out of future sessions if he wanted so long as he devoted his full attention to our current interaction for the whole hour. My offer made Anton's parents noticeably uncomfortable as they reported that I was their last resort.

When Anton agreed, I asked him why he thought his parents had brought him to see me. "Because I don't want to go to school. I have a bad memory and so there's no point in me trying in school," he replied. Before guiding Anton toward our desired outcome of getting him to return to school, I first had to address the limiting belief he held about his memory and ability to learn. The updated belief I wanted to instill in Anton was that memory is like a muscle and the more it's used the stronger it becomes.

So, I asked him, "What if I said I could teach you how to say the alphabet backward, would you believe me? Would you come back?" When Anton answered "No," as you might have guessed, I clarified by reminding him that I had asked him two questions, and he only gave me one answer. This made him laugh and add, "No, I don't believe that I can learn to say the alphabet backward, but yes, I'm willing to come back."

To his parents' relief, I had successfully established enough rapport that Anton agreed to come back. I spent the next couple of sessions with him practicing the story of ZeeWhy the Ex-Warrior as well as several other memory strategies like the mnemonic peg system and the method of loci, which are techniques that have been around since the Ancient Greeks and Romans.

Often, the reason that people fail to grow and develop is because, like this teen, they give up on their own abilities. New tasks and assignments are automatically seen as too difficult to master. To move closer to the things you want, you must first *believe that you have the capability to change*. Accomplishing change typically requires either *new knowledge* or gaining *exposure to new or more efficient strategies*, followed by the *immediate implementation* of what you have learned.

LEARN THE ALPHABET BACKWARD WITH ZEEWHY THE EX-WARRIOR

Immediate and frequent practice is essential in order for us to remember new things as we are learning them. The *secret* or *shortcut* to learning to say the alphabet backward is to create a **mnemonic** or a memory aid. A mnemonic is a fun, logical way of remembering something that may otherwise be difficult to remember.

To teach Anton to say the alphabet backward, the mnemonic that I used involved recalling five chunks of information that relate to an unusual, easy to remember story. What makes this memory aid so effective is that the story engages the imagination; Anton was likely to imagine the scenario in his mind as we went through the exercise. Let's review this mnemonic together, as I did with Anton, so you can *experience for yourself just how easy it is to learn the alphabet backward*, too.[131]

> To begin, think of a one-hundred-year-old, ex-Viking warrior named ZeeWhy. ZeeWhy's hobby is collecting cute baby alligators. Imagine that ZeeWhy is being sent to the store by his wife with a coupon. Being one hundred years old, he can barely see what's written on the coupon he is holding... or even remember why he is going to the store! ZeeWhy asks his wife (with his Viking accent), "Vut's our coupon for?" She replies, "Why, it's for milk jugs!" "Milk jugs," says ZeeWhy, "Why do we need milk jugs?" "Silly man," says his wife, "they're to feed the cute baby alligators."

To say the alphabet backward, remember these five chunks of information as your mnemonic for the sequence of letters (remember "chunking" from Chapter Three).

---

131 Adapted from Chuck Hickok, "Teaching Memory Skills" lecture series, 2010. Used with permission.

"**Z**eeWh**y**"	z, y
(the) "e**x**-**w**arrior" (asks)…	x, w
"**Vut's** ou**r** cou(**q**)**pon** (for)?"…	v, u, t, s, r, q, p, o, n
(Answer) "**Milk ju**(**ih**)**g**(s)…"	m, l, k, j, i, h, g
(to) "**fe**ed" (the) "**c**ute **b**aby **a**lligators."	f, e, d, c, b, a

Now it's your turn! If you begin with this memorable story and then practice saying the five chunks of information out loud, you can learn to say the alphabet backward in the next five minutes. To lock this technique into your long-term memory, simply practice numerous times over the next couple of days.

SO, WHAT'S THE GUY'S NAME?

ZEEWHY

WHAT DID HE DO FOR A LIVING?

EX-WARRIOR

WHAT QUESTION DOES HE ASK

VUT'S OUR COU(Q)PON FOR?

WHAT IS THE COUPON FOR?

MILKJ U(IH)GS

WHAT ARE THE MILK JUGS FOR?

TO FEED THE CUTE BABY ALLIGATORS

This simple and useful mnemonic helped Anton teach himself something he initially believed was impossible for him to learn. With my guidance—and this small mnemonic masquerading as a silly story—Anton was able to update his limiting belief about having a bad memory, replacing it with the empowering belief that memory is like a muscle and the more it's used the stronger it becomes. This updated belief in turn improved Anton's self-esteem and encouraged him to engage more fully in school.

Like this teenage boy, you can develop your memory too! Simply write the alphabet backward on sticky notes and place the notes where you are likely to see them every day. Review the story of ZeeWhy in your mind as you link it to saying the alphabet backward. As with many other things in life, once you've mastered it, you'll only need occasional practice to easily do something that others find daunting.

CHUNKING IN PRACTICE

As you reflect back on the relevance of 7 ± 2 chunks, the story of ZeeWhy the Ex-Warrior shows exactly how our unconscious mind works to process these chunks of information.

Now that you are able to say the alphabet backward, you can use the story of ZeeWhy as an empowering exercise to practice with children or adults, especially those who may exhibit limiting beliefs about their learning ability or memory.

Key Concept: Empowering beliefs act as catalysts, progressing you toward your Desired State, while limiting beliefs impede progress. Be diligent in recognizing opportunities to assist in updating or modifying a person's limiting beliefs.

As for Anton, the teen who resisted going to school? He willingly came back to our subsequent sessions, displaying a far more open attitude, and his self-esteem, engagement in school, and grades all dramatically increased. His parents, who had almost given up hope, were thrilled and referred numerous other parents who were struggling with their teenagers.

DEVELOPING A SERIES OF SMART OUTCOMES

UCLA won many national basketball championships under the leadership of John Wooden, who is considered by many to have been the greatest college basketball coach of all time. Wooden liked to say that "When you improve a little each day, eventually big things will occur."[132]

Sometimes incremental steps are required to move someone from their Current State to the Desired State. Take a person who's afraid of public speaking, for example. It's unlikely that they could make the leap all at once from their

132 Quoted by Chip Heath and Dan Health, *Switch* (Broadway Books, 2010), p. 144.

Current State of "terrified at the mere thought of speaking in front of even a small group of people" to the Desired State of "comfortable while making a presentation to the entire company." Going through a planned sequence of manageable short- and long-term goals, each with a specific, well-formed outcome, is more realistic. Think of it as a series of mini-goals, presented in a SMART manner, with each mini-goal having unique thinking, feeling, and doing components.

For instance, say you have a goal of making a certain amount of money this year. You might ask yourself a series of questions like, "To accomplish this goal, how much do I need to make each quarter?" and, "If I want to make that amount by the end of each quarter, how much do I need to make by the end of each week?" Finally, you would ask, "If I want to make that much by the end of this week, how many hours do I need to bill each day?" As you achieve your daily goals, and you stay on track for the quarter, you're also progressing toward achieving your year-end goal.

In this way, as you work through the SMART steps to achieve a Desired State, that Desired State now becomes your new Current State. You can then use this new Current State to achieve the next step which is the next Desired State. With this continual incremental progress, and by using the SMART framework as a filter or checklist, success is inevitable. In the next chapter we'll discuss how you can leverage the SMART framework combined with the techniques you've learned so far as you question confidently, challenge respectfully, and always negotiate.

In this chapter, we've explored the relevance of developing SMART goals as we help others move in the direction of a Desired State. Now, I invite you to think about your own life and evaluate the last time you set or updated your goals.

Let's assume for a moment that *anything* is possible. If you had a magic wand and could accomplish anything you desired in the next ten years, what would you want to accomplish and why? What would be SMART to accomplish over the next five years? The next month? Today? As you do this, consider various categories for your goals, like travel, health and wellness, financial, spiritual, relational, educational, personal development, and so on.

Remember in Chapter Two we discussed how often we ask ourselves "Why?" without understanding its impact? Keep in mind that the SMARTer your goal is and the stronger the "Why," the more likely you'll be able to accomplish it. Practice developing your "Why?" using the SMART checklist which will help you further refine your Desired State.

Additionally, have some fun by teaching your children, friends, or colleagues how to say the alphabet backward using the ZeeWhy the Ex-Warrior story. Notice how it boosts their self-esteem!

Chapter Twelve

Question Confidently, Challenge Respectfully, and Always Negotiate

Like most successful businesspeople, Robert Iger, former CEO and current Chairman of the Walt Disney Company, has honed his negotiation skills over his whole career. Still, when Disney announced in 2013 that it was acquiring Lucasfilm for US$4.05 billion, many people were surprised that George Lucas, the creator of *Star Wars* and the sole shareholder in Lucasfilm Ltd., would let go of his empire.

For many years, George Lucas had managed Lucasfilm entirely on his own and had successfully made his mark in the overlapping worlds of special effects technology and film. In a video interview on the Star Wars YouTube channel in 2012, he divulged that his decision to pass on the company was due in part to his wish to retire from the film business as well as a desire to pass the company along to "a larger entity which would protect it." Disney, he felt, had the capabilities, strengths, and opportunities to expand Lucasfilm.[133]

As the sole owner, Lucas could very well have retired and left Lucasfilm to continue with business as usual. The language Lucas used to describe Disney tells us that he felt that Iger and the Disney team had Lucasfilm's best interests in mind. According to Harvard Law School's *Program on Negotiation,* Lucas's decision to hand over his creative legacy to Disney was ultimately because "there was a lot of trust there."[134] The level of trust and respect established between Lucas and Iger meant

Key Concept:
Persuasion relies on building a foundation of rapport, and trust is a by-product of consistent rapport over time.

---

133 Star Wars. ***Part 1: George Lucas & Kathleen Kennedy Discuss Disney and the Future of Star Wars.*** YouTube (uploaded October 30, 2012). Available online: https://www.youtube.com/watch?v=YyqlTi7IkhY

134 "10 Top Negotiation Examples," ***Program on Negotiation Blog***, Harvard Law School (September 26, 2019). Available online: https://www.pon.harvard.edu/daily/negotiation-skills-daily/famous-negotiators-feature-in-top-negotiations-of-2012/

that the merger was more than just business, and Lucas felt that his legacy was in safe hands.

So far, we've mastered the art of developing and maintaining rapport, learned how to uncover an individual's Current State, and become skilled at using various techniques for leading them to a Desired State. There's just one step left to master: negotiating.

> Negotiation is about gaining, and you gain without necessarily making the other side lose. And that's the trick.
>
> –CHRIS VOSS

The art of persuasion almost always involves some negotiation, whether the process takes two minutes, two months, or two years. Negotiations are most likely to fall apart if we move too quickly into details without ensuring that we have alignment and agreement at a higher level. Remember we talked about pacing and leading in Chapter Six and asked, "How fast can you lead?" The answer remains, "Only as quickly as the other person is willing to follow."

Some people are hesitant to negotiate with the person they're persuading, fearing it might destroy the relationship they've built. This assumes that relationships are a "thing" that can be acquired or lost. Think back to our discussion of nominalizations. We learned that we tend to nominalize the term "relationship," treating it as if it were an abstract noun, or something we have, when it's actually a verb; as we saw with George Lucas and Bob Iger, a **relationship** is a *process* that exists within the context of two or more people who are *relating* to each other.

"I've been working with my client for six months," a salesperson once told me. "Giving him information, demonstrating the equipment, showing him the savings projections. We've gotten friendly, but we've hit a brick wall over the payment details. I'm afraid to challenge him for fear that I'll damage the relationship." Notice, in this example the salesperson is still treating a relationship as a noun (a thing that can be damaged) rather than as a verb (a process of relating).

While this salesperson's fear may be reasonable, it's unfounded. Remember it is our *rapport* and *how we relate* to another person, rather than a relationship, that allows us to lead someone from their Current State to the Desired State. This realization is a huge "Aha!" moment for many people I work with. Understanding the difference between rapport and a relationship will increase your ability to be bold and confident because you'll remember that rapport is elastic. Just as rapport can be stretched and even broken, it can also be repaired. You simply back up, re-establish it, and move ahead again using the techniques we have outlined in this book. This awareness allows you to be courageous and to challenge respectfully.

> In this world of dramatically changing customer buying behavior and rapidly diverging sales talent, your sales approach must evolve, or you will be left behind.
>
> –MATTHEW DIXON AND BRENT ADAMSON, **THE CHALLENGER SALE**

You may be familiar with Matthew Dixon and Brent Adamson's book, *The Challenger Sale*, in which they suggest that the best salespeople consistently do three critical things: **teach**, **tailor**, and **take control**.[135]

Dixon and Adamson's challenger sales approach is most effectively applied when you understand that you may choose to develop rapport with a person despite a lack of desire to be friends with them or to relate to them in a personal context. You can develop rapport with someone for the sake of doing business and, indeed, you may even establish rapport with someone that you dislike for that purpose. From neighbors to grocery store attendants to business associates, from those you see fairly often to those you see only once in a while, the rapport you establish may exist in the absence of sharing enough of the same beliefs, values and interests for you to want to relate to or with that person in any personal context.

---

135 Matthew Dixon and Brent Adamson, *The Challenger Sale: Taking Control of the Customer Conversation* (Penguin, 2011).

You may initially develop rapport with someone for business purposes and then if you choose, you may relate to them in a more personal way, perhaps inviting them to dinner and developing a "friendship" (another nominalization) because of shared beliefs, values, and interests. As you can see, the choice is yours. You may choose to relate with another person that you like or even one that you dislike and, either way, you can still maintain rapport for the sake of doing business.

Occasionally, shifting someone to the Desired State involves some negotiation as part of the process. Rather than worrying that you may break rapport, think of the negotiation as a litmus test that will show you how well you're progressing toward the Desired State.

> **Key Concept:**
> When relating to and persuading others, focus on rapport and remember that rapport is elastic and, if broken, can be repaired. This means that you can **question confidently**, **challenge respectfully**, and **negotiate skillfully** as you lead someone toward a desired goal.

For example, imagine that you've encountered a challenge in getting the negotiation process started: the person you're dealing with is cautious about sharing information and seems to toss aside your questions and comments. If they behave like this, it means you've failed to develop enough rapport—or possibly even any at all. Stop the negotiation and re-focus on building rapport. Shift to a different topic of conversation, perhaps one that has nothing to do with the situation at hand. Chat about the weather, the local sports team, or something else that will put you on common ground as you rebuild rapport. All the while, remember to pace the individual in order to enhance their experience of being understood. Remember: rapport is the key to persuasion.

STOP AND CHECK YOUR ALIGNMENT

We've already covered the many ways that we humans process and interpret information in unique ways, and we've also discussed how to identify the Current State and shift a person's thoughts, feelings, and behaviors to a Desired

State. You may still occasionally run into unexpected outcomes or disagreements, and if you do, it's likely because you have gone into details before ensuring that you are aligned with the person with whom you're negotiating.

Think back to our discussion of the Meta Model and the Milton Model in Chapter Five. We need to apply our knowledge of these models to negotiation in order to ensure alignment between all parties. Indeed, when negotiations fall apart it's often because of misalignment in understanding. If this happens, take a step back and start again.

Key Concept: If the negotiation process is stalled before it even gets started, check your rapport. If it's absent, always start by building it.

The more flexibility we have in moving up to the abstract and down into the details, the more likely we are to be successful as we negotiate. This skill relies on theories developed by linguist Noam Chomsky. With regard to communication, Chomsky differentiates between what he calls surface structure versus deep structure. For our purposes here, **surface structure** simply refers to language that is more vague or abstract, and it consists of the labels we use to represent actual experiences after we have filtered them (deleted, distorted, and generalized). **Deep structure** refers to language that reveals actual experiences, details, and specific information. As persuaders, it is vital to be able to move fluidly between surface structure and deep structure. We can move in either direction by simply asking the right questions.

What are "the right questions"? There are specific questions that can help you shift another person up into the abstractness of surface structure and down into the details of deep structure, depending on the situation you're in and the person you're persuading.

As you **chunk up**, which is a term used to describe moving an individual toward the more abstract surface structure, ask questions like:

- What is this an example of?
- For what purpose...?
- What is your intention...?

Recall the questions we looked at in the context of the Meta Model and the Milton Model. As you **chunk down**, which is a term used to describe moving a person toward deep structure, ask any Meta Model questions that recover the deeper level of meaning and reveal more of the details like:

- What are examples of this?
- What are other examples of this?
- What specifically…?
- Who specifically…?

One last thing that's worth mentioning here is that from time to time, it may also be useful to **chunk laterally** in order to find other suitable examples at that same level before proceeding toward greater detail. Lateral chunking increases our flexibility in a negotiation and may reveal other alternatives that are more agreeable as we proceed into the details.

Let's delve into a simple example of how this works. Imagine that you and a friend are both thinking you need a vacation. As you discuss the idea and begin to explore possibilities, you agree that you'd like to go on vacation together. After considering various locations, you decide that you want to travel in Canada. Eventually, you land on the Canadian Rockies—a place neither of you have been and that each of you has always wanted to visit. Further conversation leads you to agree that you'd like to go in the spring, as you've heard that that's an ideal time to visit the Rockies. Together, you decide that being away for a week is too short and two weeks is too long, so you choose a ten-day trip. With a location and time frame settled upon, you and your friend are beginning to get excited!

The next item you need to work out is how to get there. You prefer flying because it is faster than other options which means you'll have more time to spend exploring the Rockies. Your friend, though, is insistent on driving because it's more economical and because he is a nervous flyer. He also believes the journey is as much fun as the destination and is keen on having a vehicle so that you can fully explore the surrounding area when you arrive. You're not on board with driving for the reason already stated (it takes too long to arrive) and because you want to have a break from driving when you're on vacation. As your discussion goes back and forth, you realize that you have reached an impasse on the details. You are adamant about flying, while your friend is determined to drive. It appears that your vacation may be in jeopardy before it has even begun!

This is the point at which you need to **chunk back up** to your last point of agreement. Once you confirm that, yes, you agree you want to go on vacation together for ten days in the spring to the Canadian Rockies, you can then together explore other possibilities for getting there by asking questions such as, "What are other ways to get there besides flying or driving?" In contemplating other options for transportation, you consider taking a train or a bus. You're surprised that neither of you had previously thought of taking the train and it turns out that the two of you like this idea! You are happy because you won't have to spend time behind the wheel, and you both like the idea that you will be able to see things on the journey that you would have otherwise missed. Your friend is pleased that he can avoid the anxiety of flying and, given that the train will save money compared to flying, he is happy to rent a car to explore the Rockies once you arrive—a decision that you concur with. You agree that taking a train will be fun and, with this agreement in place, you can both begin to look forward again to your upcoming trip.

Fluidity is important here as you chunk up, down, or laterally. In cases where communication or negotiations seem to falter, it's useful to chunk up, moving back up into the more abstract big picture where you last had alignment or agreement with the individual. Once that alignment or agreement has been re-established, you can use tools (such as reframing) in order to chunk laterally or chunk down to move back into details, always doing so *only* as quickly as you're able to maintain agreement with the other person. Remember to maintain rapport throughout and only lead them as fast as they are willing to follow you.

Increasing your flexibility with this skill will enable you to chunk up to find common ground and agreement, and then chunk laterally or back down as needed while maintaining that agreement.

Of course, like anything in life, when you're persuading someone, things can sometimes go differently than expected. Perhaps the process is moving too fast, the wrong words have been used, or your offering has been presented in a way that conflicts with an individual's existing beliefs or values. For any number of reasons, rapport has been broken and the other person is no longer willing to follow your lead. The persuasive process has stopped dead in its tracks.

If this happens, remember that your most important tool is sticking with the persuasive process and re-establishing rapport in order to get things back on track.

> **Key Concept:** Always remember that persuasion and influence may also include some negotiation, with ups and downs, giant steps forward and little stumbles backward. It's all part of the process and you can learn from and correct any little "slip," so long as you maintain rapport, remain flexible, and stay focused on your outcome.

For instance, imagine that you're a real estate agent showing a home to a prospective buyer. As you walk her through the house, you learn that the buyer is looking for a two-story home with a fireplace, modern kitchen, and large back yard. Fortunately, that's exactly what this house has! The buyer seems quite interested, yet as you begin to ease into the financial details, you feel some resistance.

Nervous, you start rattling off the home's selling points; you do a little "sales jiu-jitsu," dropping hints about other buyers who are eager to grab this house. These techniques might work, you might happen to mention a feature that revives her interest, or she may be worried about the house being scooped up by the other buyers. Then again, she might think you're pressuring her and walk away.

Instead, return to your last point of agreement, specifically that she wants "a two-story home with a fireplace, modern kitchen, and large back yard"—which is exactly what you're selling. From this point of agreement, check your rapport, make sure it's strong, and start leading her toward the Desired State again—this time, on a different path or with a different approach that's SMART.

It's often the smallest details that can break rapport and derail communication. For example, a medical device salesperson may have sold a potential customer on a certain model, price, and various other terms. Then, a discussion about the extended warranty breaks the rapport and the buyer is on the verge of walking out.

In a situation like this, forget about starting to run through your "sales tricks." Instead, remain confident and go back to the last point of agreement—price, for instance—and start again from there. Gloss over the extended warranty, leave it out completely, or find a new way of presenting it. Just keep the rapport strong and the negotiation going.

> **Key Concept:** If you encounter disagreement when leading an individual to a Desired State, this is a sign that it's time to step back up to the last point of agreement and only move down into more detail as quickly as you can maintain that agreement.

CONSIDER MOTIVATION

Have you ever been in the middle of a conversation or a sales interaction that appears to be going well, only to watch helplessly as it falters and crumbles for what seems like absolutely no reason? It's frustrating! You had developed rapport and were pacing and leading toward a SMART outcome, choosing your words well, using stories, and employing all the other techniques we've discussed, only to see it all unravel.

Think back to Coca-Cola's marketing blunder that we discussed in Chapter Four. As was the case in that example, the root of your problem may be a clash of motivational traits: you may have been using a "New Coke" approach when a "Coca-Cola Classic" style was more appropriate.

> **Remember** we learned how to identify motivational factors? There are a number of these motivational traits that determine how people sort or filter information and make decisions, including:
>
> - Internal and External
> - Toward and Away From
> - Options and Procedures
> - Sameness and Difference

In the context of negotiation, it's important to learn to accurately recognize these motivational factors in others. Equipped with this awareness, you are then able to adjust your language in order to communicate in a way that's most relevant and motivating to the person with whom you are negotiating.

GET GRITTY

Rapport, alignment, motivation... there are a lot of factors at play in a negotiation! Science, as well as experience, shows us that perseverance and grit are also key factors. Indeed, the way children negotiate provides a clear example of the power of perseverance. As serial entrepreneur and CEO Offir Gutelzon writes: "As early as age two, children are offering to eat more vegetables at dinner if it means ice cream for dessert. By the tender age of three, kids have developed a whole arsenal of negotiation tactics. Their approaches to securing prime toys, dessert, or a later bedtime are not just child's play—they offer valuable reminders about successful negotiation tactics in any setting."[136]

> In the confrontation between the stream and the rock, the stream always wins, not through strength but through persistence.
>
> –H. JACKSON BROWN

Anyone who has spent time around children knows that when it comes to dessert or a later bedtime, children will persevere and continue their negotiations, even if they've been told "No" multiple times. Savvy children will even apply creative negotiation tactics, like carefully timing their approach, enlisting the help of a sibling or grandparent as an advocate, targeting the parent who is most likely to say "Yes" (and avoiding the parent who is most likely to say "No"), and finally, turning on their "cute factor" to play on your emotions.

While you might recognize some (or all!) of these negotiation tactics, the key takeaway lies beyond the tactics themselves, in the persistence of these tiny negotiators. Rather than feeling offended or intimidated by a "No," children

136 Offir Gutelzon, "5 Negotiation Tactics You Can Learn from Kids," *Entrepreneur* (April 21, 2014). Available online: https://www.entrepreneur.com/article/233248

are resilient, they are comfortable finding out where they went wrong, and are confident to ask again. This **grit** is a critical element to success.

In her TED Talk, "Grit: The Power of Passion and Perseverance," teacher, psychologist, and popular science author Angela Lee Duckworth shares how she became convinced through her teaching career that all her students could learn the material if they worked long and hard enough. "In education, the one thing we know how to measure best is IQ," she says. "But what if doing well in school and in life depends on much more than your ability to learn quickly and easily?"[137]

This curiosity led Duckworth on a quest to study children and adults in many different settings; eventually, she came up with other, more important, questions: "Who is successful here and why?" In various scenarios ranging from spelling bees to military cadet training, and in looking at people from teachers working in tough neighborhoods to salespeople in private businesses, she and her colleagues focused on predicting who would succeed.

"In all of those different contexts, one characteristic emerged as a significant predictor of success," Duckworth notes in her TED Talk. It wasn't social intelligence, good looks, physical health, or IQ. It was simple, old-fashioned grit! "Grit is passion and perseverance for very long-term goals. Grit is having stamina, sticking with your future day in and day out, not just for the week or month but for years, and working really hard to make that future a reality," Duckworth says.

> **Key Concept:** As you engage and guide someone toward a Desired State, remember that grit is one of the most important underlying factors of your success.

Duckworth has made a career out of studying grit, particularly in high schools where she has noticed that kids with more "grit" are more likely to graduate. When asked how to build grit, she references an idea developed at Stanford University by Carol Dweck called the **growth mindset**, or the belief that the ability to learn isn't fixed—it can change with effort. Dweck explains that when

137 Angela Lee Duckworth, "Grit: The Power of Passion and Perseverance," *TED* (April 2013). Available online: https://www.ted.com/talks/angela_lee_duckworth_grit_the_power_of_passion_and_perseverance

children understand how their brains grow when faced with a challenge, they're more likely to persevere because they see failure as a temporary condition.

Like these children, you, too, can learn to persevere in your negotiations with others. Just remember that any unexpected outcomes or disagreements are temporary, and you can skillfully shift the process using the techniques you've been mastering throughout this book.

SETTING BOUNDARIES

Until now we've been focused on the person we're persuading. In the process of persuading, though, it's also important to look inward and evaluate your own goals and boundaries. In negotiations—as in life—there are occasionally situations in which another person attempts to manipulate you or guilt you into doing something for their own selfish gains. In these instances, it's necessary to clearly know what your boundaries are and how to maintain them.

> One of the things that any negotiator needs to get better at is to be able to gently say "no."
>
> –CHRIS VOSS

All too often we feel guilted into things, thinking that we "should" do them rather than doing them because we want and choose to. Our modal operators of impossibility and necessity come into play here. **Modal operators of impossibility** are words like, "cannot," and "do not," while **modal operators of necessity** are words like, "should," "have to," and "must." These modal operators are partners that often appear together, and they reflect our feelings and thoughts. For example, a parent may say (or think), "I *have to* volunteer at the school fair, but I *don't* think I'll be able to find the time." In the case of modal operators of necessity, they limit our choices, increase feelings of pressure and, ultimately, increase our level of stress.

Wondering how these modal operators relate to stress? The "shoulds" and "musts" in our lives decrease our agency and control while increasing the internal demands that we place on ourselves, and the result is that our stress is increased. As a way of empowering people to manage their stress effectively, I often teach them what I call the **Stress Management Equation**.

One of the issues that comes up over and over again when I'm working with clients, especially business owners, is the question: "How do I avoid the burn out?" I created the Stress Management Equation to help clients understand and manage stress. I've tested this equation with thousands of individuals in corporations around the world and it works! In fact, I encourage you to download this equation from our website **www.SolutionsInMind.com** and put it up in your home and workspace. Anytime you're feeling stress that's higher than what you deem to be useful, simply re-evaluate this equation.

Here's how it works.

Start by looking at **demand**. What is creating a demand in your life? In the context of that demand, there are always two factors. First, there are the internal demands you place on yourself with the "shoulds," "have tos," and so on. Next, there are the external demands placed on you by others (bosses, business partners, colleagues, spouses, children, etc.). Turning your "shoulds" and other modal operators of necessity back into choices helps you control the internal demands. The boundaries that you set help you control the external demands.

Next, let's look at **control**. As there was with demand, control has internal and external factors. Examples of internal controls include your own thoughts (for example, the meaning that you attach to events), attitudes, language, emotional states, and behaviors. Then there are external things which you may or may not be able to control, like the weather, a late flight, or a cancelled meeting. Together, these internal and external demands and controls contribute directly to the levels of stress you experience.

You have likely noticed that in this equation, stress is managed relationally by the amount of demand divided by the amount of control.

> Forces beyond your control can take away everything you possess except one thing, your freedom to choose how you will respond to the situation. You cannot control what happens to you in life, but you can always control what you will feel and do about what happens to you.
>
> –VIKTOR FRANKL, **MAN'S SEARCH FOR MEANING**

Now it's your turn! Make a list of the internal and external demands and controls in your life. Assign a number to each, with **0** being "No demand" or "No control" and **10** being the highest demand or the highest control. Once your list is complete, divide the demand by the control. Notice how your level of stress is impacted.

The secret to reducing stress is lowering the demands in your life while also increasing the control you have over things. If we take a look at the left side of the equation, we can better understand the role that demand plays. If your stress is higher than what's useful, then focus on reducing the internal demands you place on yourself or re-evaluate your boundaries, setting new ones that will protect you from the external demands being placed on you.

Setting boundaries is a powerful way to reduce your stress because when you lower the demands placed on you, your stress will go down accordingly, even if the right side of the equation (control) stays the same. Alternatively, you can choose to keep demand as is and instead focus on the right side of the equation to increase your control in order to reduce your stress.

Let's look more closely at how to do this. Keep in mind that external factors are the only variables that can sometimes be outside the realm of your control, so instead focus on the things you *can* control. Internally, you can control the meaning you're attaching to events, and you can also control your own thoughts, emotional responses, attitudes, behaviors, and so on. Consider if any of the factors that seem outside of your control may be more within your control than you think. When you decrease the demand that you place on yourself with "shoulds" and realize that you are in control of your thoughts—including the meaning you attach to any given event—you'll see a proportional reduction in stress.

How many times have you felt pressured to cave into someone or something because they kept pestering you or because you felt guilty for saying "no"? Set your boundaries with the Stress Management Equation in mind, knowing that it's perfectly fine—and indeed healthy!—to hold firm on your own boundaries. The technique we'll look at in the next section is designed to empower you to let go of guilt and be comfortable and confident holding firm on your own boundaries.

> **Key Concept:** Maintaining an internal locus of control and reinforcing your boundaries are key factors in reducing your level of stress.

HOW TO DISAGREE WITHOUT BEING DISAGREEABLE

For many of us, maintaining our boundaries is one of the most challenging parts of any negotiation because we want to be pleasant, agreeable, and liked. In business negotiations in particular, we are often concerned with the risk of losing a client or a sale by creating any kind of tension. It is likely, though, that you will disagree with someone while negotiating, especially if you jump into too many details too quickly or if you happen to encounter someone who is attempting to manipulate you for their own ends.

As I've said, as you move into details in any negotiation you may end up with points of disagreement. In these instances, continue to communicate as you maintain your boundaries. While the negotiation may be stalled, you can continue to maintain rapport and your boundaries by **agreeing in principle** and **restating your purpose**. This technique empowers you to acknowledge what another person wants while maintaining your own boundaries, and while it is exceptionally useful in negotiations, it also works remarkably well in day-to-day life.

To agree in principle, simply repeat what the person is saying to you in order to confirm that you are listening to them and that you do understand them even in the absence of agreeing with them. As you do so, remember to watch their eye patterns, consider their language, listen for predicates, and use the other techniques we've discussed so far. Agreeing in principle in this way allows you to maintain rapport.

To restate your purpose simply reinforce, through your language, your intention, objective, or boundary. You can feel empowered and confident to do so while being completely free from having to justify or explain your boundary to the other person.

> If you are going to fight, don't let them talk you into negotiating. But, if you are going to negotiate, don't let them talk you into fighting.
>
> –ABRAHAM LINCOLN

The purpose of agreeing in principle and restating your purpose is to maintain your resolve while preserving rapport. This enables you to have a difference of opinion while holding firm on your overall objectives and boundaries.

Let's look at an example: your child is attempting to manipulate you into giving them candy before dinner even though they know the house rule is that they may only have candy after they have eaten dinner. An effective way to respond to this would be to acknowledge their request and agree in principle that they want candy, while continuing to hold the boundary of giving them candy only once dinner is done. You can say something like, "I know that you want candy now, *and* I will give you a candy once you've finished your dinner."

If the child continues to pressure you by stating that their friend's mother lets him have candy before dinner, you can again agree in principle while restating your purpose by saying, "I understand that Connor's mother may let him eat candy before dinner *and* you can have candy when your dinner is finished." Your child might proclaim that it isn't fair and start throwing a temper tantrum, in which case you can still maintain your boundary by calmly saying, "I realize that you think it's unfair *and* as I said, you can have candy when your dinner is finished."

You can clearly see here that regardless of what the child says, you can easily agree in principle while effortlessly maintaining your stance. Keep in mind that the moment you give in, the child has gained control.

Next, let's apply this technique to a business-related example. Imagine a customer is attempting to use an expired coupon. You can refuse to accept the coupon by saying something like, "I appreciate that you would like to use the coupon *and* our policy is to only accept coupons within the allotted time frame." The customer may then reply, "I want to speak to the manager," hoping they'll get a different response from someone else. It remains easy to continue to agree in principle and restate your purpose by responding, "I understand that you want to speak to the manager, *and* she will agree that the coupon may only be used on the dates listed."

> **Key Concept:** Rather than risk breaking rapport by flat-out disagreeing, continue giving others the experience of being understood, even as you maintain your boundaries, by agreeing in principle and restating your purpose.

Still, they might persist, adding, "I'll write a bad review on Google," in which case you can come back with, "I understand you have the option to write a bad review, *and* our policy remains that the coupon may only be used on the dates listed."

The final result might be the customer threatening to walk away altogether, saying, "If I can't use this coupon, I'll take my business elsewhere." In this case, you can continue to maintain your boundary by responding, "I understand that you could take your business elsewhere, *and* the coupon may only be used on the dates listed. We trust you will *keep coming back* because we value and appreciate your business!"

How many times do you have to agree in principle and restate your purpose? As many times as the person repeats their request. Much like the lighthouse pictured below, standing resolute against the waves, regardless of how many times someone attempts to weaken your resolve, using this technique allows you to stand firm on your principles, restate your purpose, and uphold your boundaries, all while maintaining rapport.

During this type of interaction, you are completely free from having to explain why your boundaries are what or where they are. You can refuse to give your child candy or to honor a customer's expired coupon if that's what you choose to do. Rather than giving in, you can recognize the situation, remain firm with regard to your position, and maintain your sense of empowerment and your boundaries simply by agreeing in principle and then restating your purpose. Remember, this technique is different from negotiation because it enables you to hold firm rather than be drawn into negotiating your boundaries. Abraham Lincoln had a good point about maintaining intentions, don't you think?

CLARITY IS POWER

The art of negotiation involves skillfully applying the valuable knowledge you've gathered through the totality of your life experiences along with the powerful persuasive techniques that you've learned as you've worked through this book. Keep in mind that, as da Vinci said, knowledge is just the first step. The differentiating edge comes by practicing and integrating these techniques until they become second nature.

> Knowing is not enough; we must apply. Being willing is not enough; we must do.
>
> —LEONARDO DA VINCI

As you do so, strive for clarity. Whether your negotiation takes two minutes (like when you negotiate what your child will wear in the morning) or many years (like the sale of Lucasfilm to Disney), it is critical to remain crystal clear: clear about the other person's Current State, their Desired State, the motivational factors at play, and the techniques that are most appropriate at any given moment. The more clarity you have, the better able you will be to question confidently question, challenge respectfully, and negotiate skillfully all while leading an individual toward the desired goal. And, when someone is attempting to persuade or manipulate you for their own self-serving purposes, greater clarity will give you the power to stand your ground and to maintain your boundaries.

Finally, as always, keep the Law of Requisite Variety in mind. Where negotiation is concerned, whoever has the most flexibility and clarity has the strongest position for success.

We've reflected a great deal in this chapter on how agreeing in principle and restating your purpose helps you maintain your boundaries—recall the examples of the child who wanted candy and the customer who wanted to use an expired coupon.

Think of a situation you recently faced in which you may have felt pressured into doing something you didn't want to do. Whether it was in your personal life with a friend or family member, or at work with a co-worker or client, write down a few scenarios and alternate ways you could have maintained your boundaries by agreeing in principle and restating your purpose. I encourage you to practice this technique because the more you practice, the better prepared you will be for any future situations in which others may "try" to encroach upon your boundaries (and yes, "try" presupposes that they will fail!).

Chapter Thirteen

Influence in Action

On January 7, 1918, Harry Houdini stood in the middle of the Hippodrome Theater in New York City. He paced back and forth in front of the audience as they waited impatiently for his act. Houdini began with the story of an elephant named Jennie who belonged to the Powers Performing Elephants troop, a regular show at the Hippodrome. Jennie, though, was more than a regular elephant. She was special, Houdini said. Jennie was the daughter of Jumbo, P.T. Barnum's most famous elephant.[138]

Like Houdini's audience, you've probably heard of Jumbo the elephant, whom P.T. Barnum claimed was the largest elephant ever to have lived. Jumbo was also the inspiration for the Disney movie *Dumbo*, as well as many spinoffs, including Tim Burton's more recent live action movie *Dumbo*.[139] What the Disney and Burton movies glossed over was the harrowing mistreatment and abuse that Jumbo suffered during his time at Barnum's circus.

Naturalist David Attenborough investigated the life of Jumbo for a 2017 documentary called *Attenborough and the Giant Elephant*, which revealed the animal's heartbreaking story.[140] Jumbo was presented to Barnum's circus audiences as a calm, gentle giant, and historical documents reveal that behind the scenes Jumbo's handlers fed him alcohol to keep him calm in front of crowds.[141] While there is no evidence that Jumbo ever lashed out at people, he would apparently go into a rage at night, likely due to pain from a horrible toothache.[142] Attenborough's team closely examined Jumbo's remains and found evidence of a poor diet, years of mistreatment and neglect, and what likely would have been a life of constant pain.[143]

---

138 John Cox, "100 years ago Houdini vanished an elephant," ***Wild About Harry*** (January 7, 2018). Available online: https://www.wildabouthoudini.com/2018/01/100-years-ago-houdini-vanished-elephant.html

139 Emma Pietras and Harriet Williamson, "Tortured Giant," ***The Sun*** (November 19, 2018). Available online: https://www.thesun.co.uk/news/5067407/the-alcoholic-elephant-dumbo-film/

140 Stephen Dunleavy, ***Attenborough and the Giant Elephant*** (2017). Documentary.

141 Pietras and Williamson, "Tortured Giant." Available online: https://www.thesun.co.uk/news/5067407/the-alcoholic-elephant-dumbo-film/

142 Pietras and Williamson, "Tortured Giant." Available online: https://www.thesun.co.uk/news/5067407/the-alcoholic-elephant-dumbo-film/

143 Pietras and Williamson, "Tortured Giant." Available online: https://www.thesun.co.uk/news/5067407/the-alcoholic-elephant-dumbo-film/

While Houdini (or his audience) could never have known the full extent of the neglect that Jumbo endured at P.T. Barnum's circus, it is likely that he had heard of Jumbo's tragic death, which happened when Houdini himself was just eleven years old.[144] Jumbo died in September of 1885 when Barnum's circus was performing in St. Thomas, Ontario. Barnum claimed that Jumbo sacrificed his life to save a smaller elephant, Tom Thumb, by running onto the tracks in front of an oncoming train. Photographs that Attenborough and his team uncovered at the Elgin County Museum in Ontario tell a different story.[145] After the show, Jumbo and Tom Thumb were being loaded into the circus train when a freight train came up behind Jumbo and, unable to stop, hit and killed him.

Records also show that Jumbo was quite ill when he died. He was suffering from what was described as a wasting disease, although at the time he was a relatively young elephant in his twenties.[146] While today Jumbo is a distant memory, the story of his mistreatment is looked upon by many as the spark that helped spearhead the modern animal rights movement.[147]

In 1918, Jumbo's story and P.T. Barnum's circus would still have been fresh in the minds of Houdini's audiences—for many, Jumbo and his death would have been one of the notable news stories of their lifetime. So, as Houdini stood in front of his audience at the Hippodrome Theater that January, he spun a story about Jennie, Jumbo's daughter, establishing the connection between Jennie and Barnum's Jumbo, who had been advertised as the largest elephant on earth. This connection would make what Houdini did next even more amazing.

Based on accounts by John Cox, a notable Houdini expert, Jennie was led into the rear of a large cabinet that was decorated to look like a circus wagon, visually reinforcing the connection to Jumbo and Barnum's circus. The cabinet was closed and with the effort of thirty men, turned toward the audience. When Houdini gave the command, the back and front of the cabinet were opened, and the audience could see through the cabinet to the back of the stage. Jennie was gone.[148]

---

144 "Harry Houdini," Wikipedia (modified November 3, 2020), https://en.wikipedia.org/w/index.php?title=Harry_Houdini

145 Pietras and Williamson, "Tortured Giant." Available online: https://www.thesun.co.uk/news/5067407/the-alcoholic-elephant-dumbo-film/

146 Pietras and Williamson, "Tortured Giant." Available online: https://www.thesun.co.uk/news/5067407/the-alcoholic-elephant-dumbo-film/

147 Betsy Golden Kellem, "How P.T. Barnum Helped the Early Days of Animal Rights, *The Atlantic* (May 10, 2017). Available online: https://www.theatlantic.com/entertainment/archive/2017/05/how-pt-barnum-helped-the-early-days-of-animal-rights/525489/

148 Cox, "100 years ago Houdini vanished an elephant." Available online: https://www.wildabouthoudini.com/2018/01/100-years-ago-houdini-vanished-elephant.html

The vanishing elephant act was wildly popular and his performances at the Hippodrome became the longest engagement of Houdini's career. While the feat itself is undoubtedly amazing (to this day, no one is certain how he accomplished it), what's interesting for us is the intentional connection that Houdini made between Jennie and Jumbo. What's more, Houdini was just as careful to *break* the connection between himself and Barnum, noting several times that unlike Barnum's treatment of Jumbo, Houdini and his team treated Jennie well. "I never allowed a hook to be used, relying on block sugar to make her go through her stunt," Houdini said, adding that, "She certainly is very fond of me."[149]

As we established in Chapter One, Houdini was a masterful storyteller, consistently leveraging the unknown and using ambiguity to his persuasive advantage. He leveraged the connections to Jumbo and to Barnum's circus in his story about Jennie in order to add awe and mystery to his act, which in turn helped him sell the audience on the idea that he used magic to make Jennie disappear.

Of course, we know that Jennie's disappearance was merely part of the illusion, and the question remains to this day as to whether Jennie was even Jumbo's daughter. Let us put the details of the act aside, though, and focus on what was most relevant to Houdini's spectators: how the story made them feel as it captivated their imaginations. Houdini took his audiences on a journey that triggered wonder, amazement, and awe, emotions that kept them coming back time after time.

In his book *Fooling Houdini*, Alex Stone recounts a conversation between famous magician Di Vernon and comedian and amateur magician Dick Cavett. "Just before Vernon died," Stone writes, "Cavett asked him if there was anything he wished for. Vernon's answer, like his magic, was simple. 'I wish somebody could fool me one more time.'"[150]

Magicians, like their audiences, love the feeling of wonder, amazement, and awe that's associated with being fooled. Stone writes of himself, "There's nothing I enjoy more than seeing a trick and having no clue how it's done, because it means there's some new principle at work that I have yet to learn,

---

149 Cox, "100 years ago Houdini vanished an elephant." Available online: https://www.wildabouthoudini.com/2018/01/100-years-ago-houdini-vanished-elephant.html

150 Alex Stone, ***Fooling Houdini: Magicians, Mentalists, Math Geeks and the Hidden Powers of the Mind*** (Bond Street Books, 2012), p. 291.

and behind that, a creative mind at play. This is the feeling of communing with genius—not unlike learning a new concept in physics or listening to a beautiful piece of music."[151]

Rationally, Houdini's audience knew that the elephant's disappearance was beyond the realm of possibility and that really didn't matter; the show was popular because people loved the way the illusion and story made them *feel*. Houdini used storytelling as he masterfully managed the perceptions of his audience in order to evoke their emotions, leading them to the Desired State of awe, curiosity, and intrigue.

Consider that today, more than a hundred years later, magicians still debate *how* Houdini created the illusion of Jennie's disappearance. What we do know for certain is that Houdini was extremely successful because he knew his audience and understood what was most relevant to them. Houdini engaged his spectators in the story line, and this allowed him to shift them toward his Desired State.

A WORD ON MAGIC

Houdini knew that in order to create the illusion of magic, which is often presented as either a dark art or a superpower, the real secret lies in a deep understanding of human psychology and the realization that what we believe to be reality is, in fact, based on our perceptions. In making Jennie the elephant seem to disappear, psychology rather than magic was at play. Always remember, our thinking impacts our emotions, which in turn drive our behavior. What appears to be *magic* is, in truth, a skillful play on human psychology—Houdini knew better than most how to intentionally manage perceptions and trigger emotions.

> Magic is hidden in the language we speak. The webs that you can tie and untie are at your command...
>
> –RICHARD BANDLER AND JOHN GRINDER, **THE STRUCTURE OF MAGIC**

151 Stone, *Fooling Houdini*, p. 291.

Our journey to persuasion is different than magic in the true sense of the word although, as Bandler and Grinder suggest, there is a hint of magic to the untrained eye in the results we're able to achieve. What seems magical to others is merely the result of paying close attention to our environment and to the dynamics of how those around us interact.

Results seem magical when you master the science and art of persuasion and influence, and as we well know, there is usually more at play than meets the eye. As with most worthwhile endeavors, it takes diligent practice to become an expert. In your journey to mastering the arts of persuasion, influence, and effective communication, strive to always remain curious, authentic, and sincere as you engage and guide others toward a Desired State.

CHANGING THE CIRCUS

P.T. Barnum used subjective validation (which you'll recall is a process in which our mind regularly deletes, distorts, and generalizes incoming information to make it match our unique perception of reality) to increase circus attendance and, in doing so, he leveraged ambiguity to shift society's views about the circus. Fast-forward to today's modern "circus," Cirque du Soleil, and we see so many of the principles we've discussed play out before our very eyes.

Have you seen a Cirque du Soleil performance? Several years ago, Natalie and I had family visiting from Ireland and we wanted to surprise them with a special treat. One of our friends suggested taking them to a Cirque du Soleil show. Instantly, my mind imagined clowns on unicycles, cotton candy, and tightrope walkers. "I was thinking of something a little nicer than a circus," I told him.

My friend insisted that Cirque du Soleil was an experience like no other, one that was so powerful it brought him to tears. A spectacle so unique, it was difficult to describe. Skeptical and also intrigued, I booked tickets, thinking, "How can a circus make someone tear up?"

After seeing the show for myself, I finally understood.

The musical and visual storytelling techniques were surprising and riveting, fraught with ambiguity of the unsaid, evoking a flurry of emotions leading to an experience that was simultaneously relevant to each individual person in the audience. Our entire party, and indeed the whole audience, was captivated.

The athletic abilities of the trapeze artists evoked Houdini-like amazement, leaving us wondering how such feats were humanly possible. The light and temperature changed with the storyline and the entire experience created a sensory overload that, as my friend promised, was truly indescribable.

Since then, I've been fortunate enough to see several other Cirque du Soleil performances and have thoroughly enjoyed each one. Upon reflection, I realize that each offered a brilliant compilation of storytelling at its finest. Cirque du Soleil is influence in action!

Like Barnum, Cirque du Soleil has evolved the idea of a circus, shifted expectations and established a new understanding about what a circus can be. The entire sensory-rich experience is Houdini-esque in that it engages audiences and guides them on an adventure that captures their imaginations, triggers their emotions and results in them returning year after year, show after show. The circus has been transformed.

Like so many businesses when the COVID-19 pandemic spread around the world in the winter of 2020, Cirque du Soleil underwent another kind of change. With performances brought to a halt because of the virus, how would the beloved Cirque transform again to survive?

> Between stimulus and response, there is a space. In that space is our power to choose our response. In our response lies our growth and our freedom.
>
> –VIKTOR FRANKL

On July 17, 2020 the Canadian Press reported that the company, which had laid off 95% of its staff during the initial months of the pandemic, was undergoing a court-supervised auction.[152] As this book is going to print, Cirque du Soleil is in the middle of a "stalking horse bid," in which a creditor proposal led by the Toronto-based Catalyst Capital Group, valued at approximately $1.2 billion US, would ensure that "up to $375 million US will be made available to

152 The Canadian Press, "Quebec court gives OK to Cirque du Soleil's 'stalking horse' deal to sell itself," *CBC News* (July 17, 2020). Available online: https://www.cbc.ca/news/business/cirque-du-soleil-sale-1.5653656

the Cirque... while two funds totaling $20 million US will be set up to pay money owed to former employees and artisans."[153] The agreement would also ensure Cirque du Soleil's head office remains in Montreal for at least five years.

While the future of the travel and entertainment industries remain uncertain, Cirque du Soleil has found a creative solution to ensure its people are cared for and its base remains rooted in its hometown of Montreal, Quebec, for the foreseeable future. All in all, many people view the takeover as a successful negotiation undertaken by the company's leadership team.

AS THE WORLD CLOSED

Early in January, 2020, Natalie and I embarked on a world cruise aboard the *Seabourn Sojourn*. During this research trip, we were focused on studying beliefs and values in different cultures around the globe. A few weeks into the trip we started to hear reports of a virus in China, and we soon realized that in all likelihood our plans to go to Hong Kong would be cancelled. We continued on with our tour of the west coast of Africa including Senegal, The Gambia, Ivory Coast, Ghana, and Angola, where we were privileged to see ways of life unlike anything we had experienced before.

We continued on to Namibia and South Africa, and it was in Cape Town that we were told that our entire fifty-one-day Asian itinerary had been cancelled. In place of Asia, the cruise line offered us the opportunity to see more of Australia and to visit New Zealand, which had originally been excluded from our itinerary. We were happy with this new plan and both Natalie and I decided to take things as they came, day by day. Considering that we were there for research purposes, we had been given a fantastic opportunity to study how different people reacted to rapid change and to examine the different tolerances for risk that were revealed!

As you can imagine, some people took the changes in stride as part of the adventure, and others were very upset, angry, or even fearful. We watched as many people (ourselves included) took the time to make new plans, and then just as the plans were completed, everything changed once again.

---

153 "Quebec court gives OK to Cirque du Soleil's 'stalking horse' deal to sell itself." Available online: https://www.cbc.ca/news/business/cirque-du-soleil-sale-1.5653656

Many people on board still wanted to go to Asia, feeling that their risk of contracting the virus was quite low, while other people were very relieved that part of the itinerary had been dropped completely. Disappointment started to creep in as our plans constantly changed.

Like anxiety, disappointment is an emotion of the future. For it to occur, we must anticipate something positive in the future that we're looking forward to and, when that plan is changed, it creates the state of disappointment.

For Natalie and me, rather than dwelling on the things that we had been looking forward to that we would now miss, we chose instead to focus on remaining in the moment and enjoying the now by making new plans. We made each plan tentatively, full of hope that it would materialize. One of these plans was to book a dinner reservation at a restaurant in Colombo, Sri Lanka, with a lovely couple we met onboard. We all looked forward to enjoying the restaurant's world-famous Sri Lankan mud crab.

The day we arrived in Colombo—which was our only stop in South Asia before heading directly to Australia—we were told that the country had closed its borders the night before. While the ship was able to fuel up and reprovision, no one was permitted to disembark, not even Sri Lankan crew members whose contracts had ended and who had been planning to get off the ship and go home to their families.

Remember the Stress Management Equation? There are times in life when things are literally outside of our control. The more we attempt to control those things that are outside of our control, the more demands we place on ourselves and the more stress we experience.

Once I heard the news that we had to stay onboard the ship in Colombo, I went and made a request of our head chef. I said, "What are the chances of you getting some of these Sri Lankan mud crabs included with your provisioning order and preparing a special meal for us and a few of our friends? I know it's a big ask and I'm confident that if anyone could pull it off, it would be you." He graciously said he would do his best while stopping short of making any promises.

Later that evening, when Natalie and I sat down to have dinner in the dining room, the head chef came to our table to let us know that he had received the mud crabs! He explained that they had been delivered too late for him to prepare them for dinner that night and we would be able to have them for lunch the next day, assuming the crabs survived the night (since they could only be cooked if they were still alive). Another tentative plan and yet we allowed ourselves to get excited about the possibility! We invited the Cruise Director and the Destinations Manager to join us for lunch the next day, as well as the couple who had been planning to dine at the restaurant with us. We hoped and prayed that the mud crabs would live, and indeed they did! Our head chef had carefully and beautifully prepared the crabs for us, and we enjoyed a spectacular lunch with newfound friends for which we were extremely grateful.

> Travel is fatal to prejudice, bigotry, and narrow-mindedness, and many of our people need it sorely on these accounts. Broad, wholesome, charitable views of men and things cannot be acquired by vegetating in one little corner of the earth all one's lifetime.
>
> –MARK TWAIN

If we assume things are impossible or if we fail to ask for them, then they'll never happen. If we believe there's always a way, and we're committed to figuring it out and putting the effort and energy into making it happen, then we can very often accomplish a lot more than we think.

During our trip, Natalie and I experienced more change, more rapidly than at any other time in our lives. We witnessed the pandemic unfold from an individual perspective, in observing how other passengers reacted to such rapid change and uncertainty and, indeed, how we ourselves reacted. We also watched the pandemic unfold from a corporate perspective, in how the crew of the *Sojourn* reacted with resilience and resourcefulness to the changing circumstances.

By early March, the talk onboard had changed from cancelled excursions to the cancellation of the remainder of the voyage itself. Inevitably, the Captain announced that our world tour would end in Perth, Australia, on March 21, 2020.

We were so thankful that there were no cases of the coronavirus on the ship. Given that at this point we had been at sea for more than two weeks, we knew that none of the passengers or crew had had any interaction with anyone outside of the ship, so we were able to gather onboard in groups as one extended social bubble. In fact, we all agreed that the ship was truly the safest place for us to be at that time. The first feelings of anxiety we experienced were when our Captain told us that we had to disembark sooner than planned, on March 18th, for fear that Australia would close its borders before we arrived there.

Our trip of a lifetime was over! We faced a long and arduous journey home, bouncing around on available flights from Perth to Sydney to Abu Dhabi to Toronto—a total of thirty-six hours in the air. Natalie summed up our experience perfectly when she said, "We went to see the world to research beliefs, values, and culture and the world was closed."

> When we are no longer able to change a situation, we are challenged to change ourselves.
>
> —VIKTOR FRANKL

Although the world was closed, Natalie and I met so many wonderful people who opened their hearts to us. We expanded our understanding of other cultures and had amazing experiences that taught us valuable lessons and changed us forever. We witnessed, experienced, and learned so much that we decided to document our journey in podcast form (you can find "The Stephen McGarvey Podcast" on Apple Podcasts, Spotify, Stitcher, and other popular podcast directories). The silver lining of our cancelled trip and time in isolation on the *Sojourn* was that we were able to listen to and learn from the amazing life stories of those we met on board, people like the extremely talented artist and Royal portrait painter, Richard Stone who, along with his lovely wife Rhonda, was only able to sit down with us because of the time COVID had granted us. Richard generously shared stories of his childhood and his journey to becoming an artist, the bond that he developed with Koko the gorilla as he painted her, and highlights of his career, which included painting many royals, dignitaries, and celebrities including Nelson Mandela and Elizabeth II.

Throughout all these experiences, Natalie and I endeavored to focus on the positives and, in doing so, we found many uplifting truths. Toward the end of the cruise, in the last eighteen days isolating at sea in order to be able to enter Australia, we both decided to take the time given to us to challenge ourselves and do something completely outside of our comfort zones. Our discussions and interactions with other passengers and staff on board inspired us to the point that we each decided to learn a new skill. I took dance lessons and Natalie, who has always counted her singing voice as a detriment, decided to join the ship's choir—completely unaware that the group would end up performing on stage as background singers for the professional entertainers! Although others dropped out when they realized the choir would be performing for the entire ship, Natalie stuck with it—and she is so glad she did. Challenging herself in this way afforded her a once-in-a-lifetime opportunity and a sense of accomplishment that she would have otherwise missed out on completely. It's worth repeating again what Alice said when she came to the fork in the road: "Which road do I take?" she asked the Cheshire cat, who replied, "Where do you want to go?" "I don't know," Alice answered. "Then," said the cat, "It doesn't matter."

Natalie and I cultivated a sense of adaptability as our cruise came to an end, which is one of the qualities that has led many people and organizations to thrive during the pandemic. On July 21, 2020, nine major companies around the world announced that they intended to build a more sustainable economy. Microsoft, Nike, and Starbucks are founding members of the initiative, which is called *Transform to Net Zero*. In the midst of the global coronavirus pandemic, these companies, rather than focusing inward, decided to look outward and work together to reduce the effects of climate change. Their goal is lofty: to eliminate CO2 emissions entirely over the next thirty years, reaching a carbon negative (which means they'll remove more carbon than they put into the atmosphere) by 2050.[154] As part of their commitment, these companies have agreed

154 Microsoft Corporation, "Nine Leading Businesses Launch New Initiative to Accelerate Progress to a Net Zero Future," *Cision* (July 21, 2020). Available online: https://www.newswire.ca/news-releases/nine-leading-businesses-launch-new-initiative-to-accelerate-progress-to-a-net-zero-future-851705148.html

to freely share their best practices, research, innovations, and technologies with the world in an effort to reduce carbon emissions globally.

While Fortune 500 companies like Microsoft and Nike have the wealth and resources to use the pandemic as a pivot point to tackle issues such as global warming, we're also seeing examples of companies of all sizes, all over the world, in all industries, shift as they manifest flexibility, adaptability, and resourcefulness in making the best of the hand that has been dealt to all of us.

Certainly, for some industries—travel and entertainment come to mind—the economic impact of the pandemic has been tremendous, and yet there are examples of those who have successfully pivoted while remaining true to the core elements of their brand.

Gibb's Farm, an organic farm and coffee-growing estate in Tanzania was forced to temporarily close its doors to tourists. During the height of the pandemic, they shifted their focus, committing to feeding their community and staff by providing a basket of food to each staff member to take home each week.[155]

Ecological and community responsibility are growing trends throughout the hospitality industry. Within the Wild, an ecolodge in Alaska, temporarily closed its doors as well. Staff took it as an opportunity to turn their energy to food production, learning new skills that can contribute to the local community on an ongoing basis. As Kirsten Dixon, co-owner of Within the Wild, told *Business Insider*, "We've got some time. Let's go do and learn these new things." She continues, "Let's learn new stuff while we have this free space, and not waste time worrying about what we can't control."[156]

Does Dixon's attitude remind you of the Law of Requisite Variety, where the person who is mentally, emotionally, and behaviorally most flexible will have the most control over a system or situation? Dixon's attitude is also fundamental to the Stress Management Equation we spoke about in the last chapter.

---

155 Molly O'Brien, "These 5 eco-friendly resorts around the world have survived the pandemic without guests by focusing on sustainability, caring for their orchards and farms, and delivering fresh food to locals," *Business Insider* (July 18, 2020). Available online: https://www.businessinsider.com/how-eco-friendly-resorts-around-world-survived-pandemic-without-guests-2020-7

156 O'Brien, "These 5 eco-friendly resorts." Available online: https://www.businessinsider.com/how-eco-friendly-resorts-around-world-survived-pandemic-without-guests-2020-7

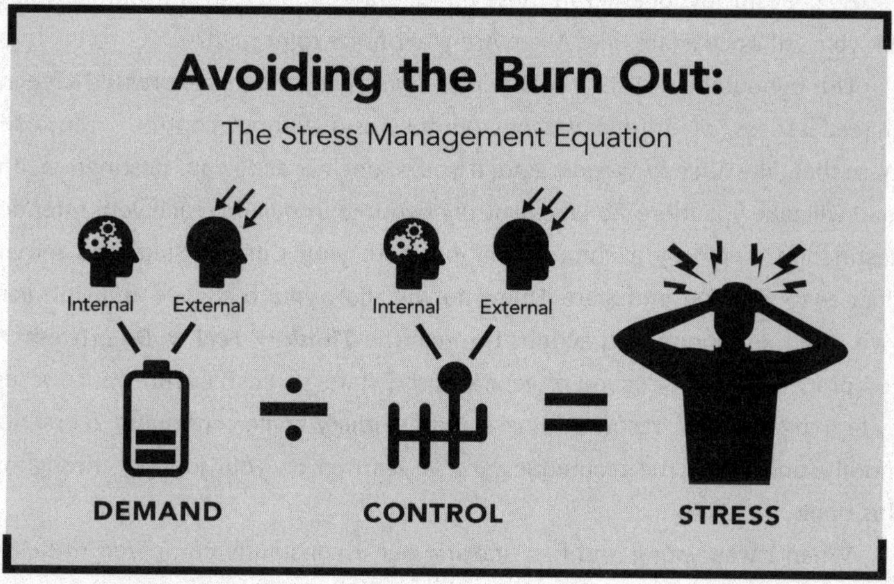

As most of us learned during the pandemic, uncertainty is part of our everyday lives. Now—more than ever—it's vital for us to use this equation to manage that uncertainty.

Like the rest of the world, Natalie and I experienced a tremendous shift in our business upon returning home from our truncated cruise. Although I am most comfortable presenting live, in front of an audience, as the world closed its doors, I shifted my offerings from in-person to virtual events.

In addition to my podcast, Natalie and I updated and re-launched our website, created complimentary webinars and video series for clients, and completely revamped our training delivery methods to ensure the safety of our team and our clients. And, of course, we finished this book! True to the Stress Management Equation, we focused on what we could control, and this led to exciting new opportunities.

What remained constant throughout all this uncertainty, though, are the techniques and principles that I've shared with you in this book. Whether virtually or in person, the ***Think → Feel → Do***, as well as the concepts and techniques discussed here, remain as—or even more—relevant than ever in what appears to be a new post-pandemic reality.

As our journey together in these pages draws to a close, I encourage you to ask yourself once again, like Alice: Are you on the right road?

Throughout the COVID-19 pandemic, many of our clients expressed a feeling of restlessness, of drifting without purpose and without control. I reminded them that, like Alice in Wonderland, if you're unclear as to your destination, any road will take you there. To take control of your journey and reach your intended destination, begin by accurately mapping out your Current State and remain clear as to your Desired State. Doing so will allow you to engage and shift your own mind, emotions, and actions through the ***Think → Feel → Do*** process. As you proceed in the direction of your Desired State, you can ensure your success by tapping into your resourcefulness and flexibility while continuing to practice, modify, and refine the techniques you've learned on your journey throughout this book.

When I was young and first starting out, I constantly compared myself to those who had already succeeded. I experienced Imposter Syndrome, measuring myself against the top people in the field and was left feeling that I wasn't good enough. A wise person once gave me the following sage advice: "If you're always comparing yourself to where you want to be, you'll feel discouraged. If you always compare yourself to where you began and consider how far you've come, you'll feel encouraged."

As the adage goes, "It's only when you get to as far as you can currently see that you're then able to see further." Mastering persuasion and influence is a lifelong journey and you've taken the first steps. Keep learning, continue studying, and constantly sharpen and refine your skills with ongoing practice. Moving forward, recognize your accomplishments, and celebrate how far you've come while keeping your eye on your destination. Like Alice, you'll get where you want to go, and your journey will be successful when you lead the way with intention and purpose.

Acknowledgments

I'd like to express my immense gratitude to those intellects and geniuses who modeled excellence and made their knowledge accessible to all who would seek it out. John Grinder, Richard Bandler, and Robert Dilts introduced me to a subject matter that changed my life and would become one of my passions and my vocation. Thank you for teaching me the magic!

Thanks to my early instructors, Deanna Sager, Chris Dunkley, Jan Inwood, Laird Brown, Topher Morrison, and Tad James: your patience and guidance was immeasurable as you taught me to think about thinking and to understand that the map is simply a representation of the territory. I'm still exploring and learning.

I would like to acknowledge all those clients whom I have learned so much from over the years both in private practice and as a consultant to global corporations. There are too many of you to mention and you know who you are. As I share my experience and learnings with you, I continue to be enriched with each interaction! Thank you all for your engagement, support, and willingness to join me on this journey.

A special thanks to my young friend Grace Russell for reading one of the earliest drafts of this book and for providing input and suggestions that represent the filters of a younger generation.

I'm extremely grateful to all the people who have graciously taken the time to review *Ignite a Shift* and who have provided their feedback and suggestions along the way. Your support and insights have been extremely valuable.

Thank you to my wonderful friends for your support and mentorship, including my late uncle Noel Wallace, Deborah and John May, Robert Clark, and Joe DeSousa.

Thanks to Cindi Ross who helps us keep all the balls in the air and whose support has contributed greatly to our success. You are an integral part of our team.

Thanks to my friend Ken Cadinouche for your ongoing dedication, loyalty, and support over the years and for helping make *Ignite a Shift* a reality.

Thanks to Kimberley Fowler and the team at Creative Campbellville for your skill, patience, and dedication as you captured my voice and brought this book to life.

Thank you to Rachel Freedman Stapleton, whose thoughtful and patient copyediting gave *Ignite a Shift* the polish it needed to shine.

A big thank you to the entire team at Morgan James Publishing for their guidance and support.

Most importantly, I'd like to thank my wife and partner Natalie. Thank you for spending countless hours perfecting the manuscript, for ensuring it is accurate and well-written, and above all for pushing me forward and challenging me onward. *Ignite a Shift* exists because of you and it as much your accomplishment as my own.

And thanks to you, the reader! I'd like to leave you with an old Irish blessing:

May love and laughter light your days and warm your heart and home.

May good and faithful friends be yours wherever you may roam.

May peace and plenty bless your world with joy that long endures.

May all life's passing seasons bring the best to you and yours!

This gift from God that we call life is full of learnings and opportunities. Embrace the journey and enjoy every moment!

About the Author

Stephen McGarvey is an international speaker, an expert on persuasion and influence, and the founder of a boutique consulting firm, Solutions In Mind. He lives in Oakville, Ontario, with his wife and business partner, Natalie Sarlo-McGarvey.

Stephen and Natalie are strong supporters of the charity Ratanak International, a Christian organization that works collaboratively to provide hope, freedom and dignity for trafficking survivors by empowering people experiencing exploitation and addressing the systems that exploit them. Visit Ratanak.org to learn more about Ratanak International.